DATE DUE

MR 2 '84			
MY 7 '93			
NO 28 '94			
AP 20 '99			
MR 20 '00			

The
Three
R's

The complete classroom-tested

instructional manual for teaching

reading, writing and arithmetic

in the classroom...or in the home

ACROPOLIS BOOKS LTD.
WASHINGTON, D.C. 20009

The Three R's

A Handbook for Teachers, Tutors and Parents

by Gary Don Hadley

Published by **ACROPOLIS BOOKS LTD.** • WASHINGTON, D.C. 20009

ACROPOLIS BOOKS LTD.
Colortone Building, 2400 17th St., N.W., Washington, D.C. 20009

Printed in the United States of America by
COLORTONE PRESS, Creative Graphics, Inc.
Washington, D.C. 20009

Library of Congress Cataloging in Publication Data

Hadley, Gary Don, 1945-
    The three R's.

    1. Language arts. 2. Arithmetic—Study and teaching,
I. Title.
Index
LB1576.H2   372.6   77-14052
ISBN 0-87491-187-7
ISBN 0-87491-186-9 pbk.

Dedicated to my beloved family

CONTENTS

FOREWORD

"**L**ET'S GET BACK TO THE THREE R'S!**"** is heard all over the country. Parents, teachers, and people in all segments of society express a growing concern over the decline in children's skills. This book is an answer to those disappointed parents and frustrated teachers who need a practical guide for teaching reading, writing and arithmetic. In simple, nontheoretical language, it gives complete explanations of the learning process and thorough descriptions of programs for beginning instruction or remedial help.

Other books have asked why Johnny can't read, write or figure. But this one goes beyond stating the problem. It is rather a "How To Do It" for understanding and solving children's learning problems regardless of their ages or grade levels. It serves both as a step-by-step teaching manual for parents to use in improving children's ability and as a fundamental text and resource handbook for teachers. Whether you are a parent or teacher, this book can help you participate to any desired degree in improving the education of a particular child or group of children. Remember, "the three R's" are the fundamentals which determine the limits or horizons of each child's future—and the future of our country as well.

This book is the kind of handbook which every parent needs at home and which every teacher needs in the classroom for any educational "emergency" that a child might have during the school years. Neither parents nor teachers will feel overwhelmed or unable to help if this book is on hand.

Due to the unique organization of this book and in order to avoid any unnecessary repetitions, parts of the introductory material prior to the actual lesson plans in the reading section also serve as a general guide for the book as a whole. This introductory material includes valuable information which is directly applicable to each area of the 3R's and covers such material as: the value of home instruction, the teaching process, scheduling and timing lessons, pupil involvement, the use of incentives, and accelerating learning with study techniques. In order to focus the reader's attention on each topic, both headings and subheads are given as guides for the reader's convenience. The aim of such a general introduction with a multiple purpose is to set the tone for the overall book. Thus the adult reader will benefit through understanding and then applying these data to any area of the 3R's—whether it is reading, writing or arithmetic. Furthermore, by reading the entire book parents and teachers will not only find ways to help a child in a specific problem area but can discover how to improve or upgrade a child's competency in all subjects related to the basics.

The teaching techniques and the process of diagnosing and remediating learning difficulties, as described in this book, can work not only for children in both self-contained and departmentalized classrooms and from elementary grades through high school but also for some adults.

This text can be used as the CORE OF INSTRUCTION ON THE BASICS FOR DEVELOPING PROGRAMS TO TEACH OLDER PUPILS AND ADULT STUDENTS (INCLUDING NON-ENGLISH SPEAKING STUDENTS), by avoiding the use of any educational games or activities which might be inappropriate as teaching aids for that particular age group.

For more mature students, both the level of difficulty and the complexity of instruction in reading, writing and arithmetic can be increased as explained in later pages within this handbook.

With respect to my experience, I have worked with children of various ages and abilities from first grade through junior high school. I was a paraprofessional with "teachable" mentally retarded children and a group counselor in Juvenile Hall where I helped children of ages up through high school grades with learning problems. In addition, I have been teaching in regular classrooms since 1969. At present I am a fourth grade teacher at Travis Air Force Base in California, where I frequently work with children who have learning or behavior problems and those who need remedial help.

The material in this book is the result of all my experiences with children, my reading and research, my college and university course work, my personal reflections on children's learning problems and experimentation with teaching methods and techniques. Discovering a need for a book like this and not finding one, I wrote what I felt parents and teachers need to know to improve children's skills and abilities in the three basic subjects. Throughout the book, the feelings of children as well as their abilities are given serious consideration.

Please note that the male pronouns *he, his* and *him* are used as general terms throughout this book as a means to refer to children and adults of either sex just as "man" in the generic sense is used to include both males and females. Much thought was given to the alternate use of both male and female pronouns, like *he* and *she,* but it was eventually decided that the continued switching of gender throughout the book might tend to disorient some readers. With this in mind, readers should remember that both the adults and children referred to in this handbook can be of either sex along with the fact that the material within this book is suitable for teaching both girls and boys.

Gary Hadley

Fairfield, California

The Three R's

SECTION I

Reading, the First R

1. INTRODUCTION

THIS SECTION WAS WRITTEN as a guide for persons who want to teach a particular child or group of children to read but who lack experience or instruction in the teaching of reading. Parents can use it to act as home tutors, improving their children's reading and forming closer relationships with them at the same time. Teachers of specific subjects in the higher grades will find it useful to help the poor readers in their classes who are handicapped in reading their textbooks. Even elementary teachers can find it of value as a refresher and a source for developing new reading programs, as well as a book to suggest to parents who wish to help their children by tutoring them at home.

The offered material is organized to be practical and clear, rather than theoretical and possibly confusing. Included is: (1) a basic discussion of reading; (2) explanations of the steps in diagnosing reading problems and improving performance; (3) a complete program for beginning and remedial reading instruction; (4) methods for making and obtaining economical teaching aids and reading materials; (5) descriptions of games and activities for teaching reading skills.

A vital factor in a successful reading program is the attitude of the parent or teacher who is administering it. This book can provide the information but you must supply the necessary enthusiasm and excitement about teaching a child to read.

Reading in our modern society

Mankind has always felt a need for a better and less limiting method of expressing, communicating and recording his ideas. In a

1

primitive state, man used sign language or body gestures. Finding this too limited, he invented the spoken word or oral language. Finally, seeking a form of language that would reach farther and last longer than his own voice, he developed written language and the recording of ideas and events we call history. The need for recording and transferring concepts has grown until society has become completely dependent upon written language. Without it, the modern world would collapse.

Yet illiteracy is not declining in America but growing. An increasingly common statistic is the number of children in schools who are below average in reading ability. Comparisons of state and nationwide testing reveal declining reading test scores. Colleges and universities are openly dismayed by the lack of acceptable reading and writing skills among incoming students.

A report issued by the U.S. Office of Education in 1973 discusses surveys which reveal that an estimated 20 million people in our country are "functional illiterates" and that this number is increasing. The report, titled *The Reading Crisis,* states, "Millions of Americans are handicapped economically and socially because they cannot read. Jobs are unobtainable, opportunities denied, and a large segment of the American people never achieve their potential."

Another report released by the U.S. Office of Education in 1975 on the *Four Year Adult Performance Level Study,* which redefined functional literacy as the ability to apply the basics to consumer skills, stated, "It is surprising, perhaps even shocking, to suggest that approximately one of five Americans is incompetent or functions with difficulty and that about half of the adult population is merely functional and not at all proficient in necessary skills and knowledge."

Poor readers are limited in their ability to benefit from written language, putting them at a great disadvantage in our word-filled world. Such persons are overwhelmed by an endless range of daily activities which involve reading. On any day they may be called upon to read warnings, directions, labels, operating instructions, regulations, manuals, sales slips, invoices, memos, contracts, insurance or banking forms, and newspapers. There certainly isn't much of a place in our literate society for someone who can't read a job application well enough to fill it out.

2

A nonreader's handicap even cripples the development of his other skills and abilities. This is because not being able to read is considered so negative that people overlook the possibility of other abilities, and because tests for intelligence and aptitudes so often involve reading skills. The poor reader, handicapped in both education and employment, is at a disadvantage in school and society.

And not only the personal future of the handicapped reader is at stake. History has shown that democracy requires a well-informed and literate citizenship to survive.

The value of home instruction

Many children need home instruction to achieve maximum educational development. Schools teach children in groups. Even if a child receives individual attention from a teacher, it can only be on a limited basis.

A parent acting as tutor will be better able to understand his child's growth, development, potential and limitations. He will gain insight into his child's problems, will be able to improve the child's school performance, and reduce or even eliminate emotional or mental problems related to his schooling. By making the home part of the educational experience, a parent can broaden and extend his child's learning as well as achieving a better understanding of his responsibilities as a parent. The child who benefits from home teaching academically also profits from the emotional satisfaction of individual attention. Family love grows stronger while the child's reading skills improve.

Parents involved in their children's learning find themselves in the position of being able to judge the effectiveness of school programs. More parent involvement in the affairs of the school and joint participation of parents and teachers in home tutoring can only result in better meeting the needs of individual children and of children in general. There is an increasing awareness of each child's mind as a valuable natural resource to be nurtured and developed.

The parent or teacher tutor should openly explain to the child that he is very much concerned about the child's learning problem and his attitude toward education. To be successful at the job of instructing, adults should honestly express their feelings and reasons for doing things instead of announcing to the child that he's a poor reader and that he has to start learning to read today! A tutor's approach might begin, "Reading has made such an important difference in my life that I'll feel better if we work together on improving your reading while we also share our learning experiences."

Both child and parent often experience greater success as the tutoring program develops. As a result of the joint effort of sharing a problem and seeking a solution, parents become more enthusiastic and more aware of the growing relationship with their children. Thus success becomes twofold, strengthening family bonds and improving school performance.

Children's hunger for knowledge increases with each successful new lesson. As their confidence grows, attitudes as well as educational skills improve. Further, a child's success at home tends to carry over into the classroom where he often takes pride in demonstrating his improved ability. Overall attitudes toward school improve. Even children with discipline problems sometimes change their behavior, generally when they realize that their improved learning ability allows them to win attention by studying rather than by misbehaving. When a child experiences the joy of improvement, he begins to feel like a success.

When tutor and child work together, a very special understanding can develop. Both individuals gain a deeper insight into each other's life and begin to make adjustments out of respect for each other. Personalities tend to become more clearly defined and accepted as each becomes more aware of the other's limits and abilities.

As skills improve, even the act of learning becomes more appreciated. Education turns into a process in which both instructor and child share the common goal of improvement. As understanding increases, it becomes clearer to both that learning is a tool which determines each person's future growth. Since education allows individuals to gain access to knowledge and thereby power, learning is necessary to grow and be successful in our complex technological society.

2. TEACHING READING

READING IS SIMPLY DECODING the meaning of written words, which are symbols for ideas and concepts. When the symbol is read the word communicates meaning. Yet reading demands participation. To learn the meanings of words, a reader must actively want to understand them.

When a child has "reading readiness," it means he has the capability and maturity to be able to learn to read. He is ready physically, mentally, and emotionally. While different children mature at different rates, most children who can perform the following tasks are ready for beginning instruction.

Reading Readiness Assessment

Can the child:
(1)   physically hold a book and turn its pages?
(2)   grasp a pencil and trace letters?
(3)   see letters and distinguish between them?
(4)   speak and pronounce the sounds of the letters of the alphabet?
(5)   hear pronunciations and repeat the sounds?
(6)   concentrate long enough to listen to and follow spoken directions?

Another signal of readiness is when the child exhibits a desire to read. Many children pretend to be able to read and ask, "When can I go to school?" They attempt to copy adults and older siblings as they read. This part of readiness can be encouraged by paying attention, helping the child hold and turn book pages and reading to him.

In general, children benefit from the earliest possible reading instruction. Even those who can't yet hold a pencil but can recognize, identify and reproduce the sounds of letters can profit from as much instruction as they are capable of absorbing. Children who read either before or better than other children will have a head start toward school success.

Remedial reading helps children already in school to overcome or remedy reading handicaps. A child can be considered handicapped when a reading problem interferes with either his normal functioning or his expected performance level. He may have either poor or satisfactory grades. The child with poor grades may lack maturity but have a reading problem as well. Even a child with satisfactory grades may not be reaching his full potential because of a reading problem.

Remedial help should be given as soon as a child appears to be having difficulty. Warning signals go up when a child avoids reading, is not reading as well as you think he should, is placed in a below-average reading group at school, gets poor marks or marks below his ability level, comes home from school emotionally upset, and/or has school discipline problems.

The longer you wait to give remedial help, the worse the problem becomes. Poor readers often become ashamed of their reading performance and, to cover up their pain and embarrassment, act as if they don't care. They easily fall victim to a continuing cycle of failure and unhappiness. If it appears to the poor reader that his problem can't be overcome, he's likely to quit trying and fall even further behind, making failure a self-fulfilling prophecy.

A parent or teacher who understands this failure cycle will realize that he needs to remedy feelings before he can remedy skills. He develops in the child positive attitudes toward reading by being encouraging and enthusiastic, pointing out that the child's reading can be improved by teamwork. No longer feeling alone and helpless, the child's self-confidence grows. Once the emotional scars are eradicated, the remediation of deficient skills can begin.

Diagnostic testing

Diagnostic tests are procedures for evaluating children's reading abilities and identifying specific reading problems. Formal testing consisting of standardized tests administered by trained personnel can usually be done in either the child's school or school district, or by an outside professional.

However, such formalized instruments as the commercial group intelligence and achievement tests have come under increasingly heavy criticism by both parents and teachers in regard to their high cost, validity and reliability. The question arises as to whether the tests accurately diagnose each child's disabilities or precisely measure each child's abilities. Many teachers have doubts or suspicions concerning the use of standardized group test results when evaluating either a child's problems or abilities. Parents frequently resent the labels or boxes which such tests place on their children in school. Both parents and teachers often realize that each child's attitude, mood or health on that particular day of testing can alter the results. Furthermore, commercial testing has also come under heavy fire by both newspapers and television. In general, the use of a single commercial formal test for an analysis of a child and the child's grouping in school classes has become questionable.

Yet informal testing can be as exact, more convenient, often more economical, and probably more valuable for our purposes. It can easily be done either at home or at school with available materials.

Because oral reading involves all the basic reading skills, it is an excellent basis for informal testing. School textbooks or newspapers can be used for reading material. Reading textbooks are generally chosen to fit the child's ability level. Comparisons can be made by using texts for other subjects, which are geared for the average child and vary in difficulty according to subject matter. Handwriting and spelling textbooks are as a rule less difficult with science and health texts the most difficult. Newspapers, because of their need to be readable to a wide range of people, are average to easy reading.

Have several selections available for testing.

Deficient reading skills can be identified by listening to a child read aloud and noting the areas of difficulty. In general, good readers read aloud well, average readers stumble occasionally, and poor readers have a great deal of trouble. To isolate specific problems, it's best to use a check list like the sample on page 12. The list is broken down into the areas which affect reading performance and thus designate the areas in which remedial help is needed.

After you have read the following explanations of the items on the check list, you will be ready to give the test. Note what time the child starts his oral reading, listen and check the given items, and note the time he finishes. For purposes to be explained, have him reread the same material to himself as you time him again. If you don't feel able to check all the items in one session, just take one section at a time.

The problem areas are as follows:

Mispronunciations—These include beginning consonant sounds, ending consonant sounds, simple (short) vowel sounds, and complex (long) vowel sounds. They occur when the child fails to associate the correct sounds with the letters. If he does not know the sounds of consonants, consonant blends and vowels, the student will probably experience difficulty in sounding out words. The skills used in decoding words in order to pronounce them correctly are called word attack or *"phonic skills."*

Omissions—The reader leaves out or omits words in a sentence. This may be due to carelessness or too fast reading, and may be easily corrected by cautioning the child. Or he may be deliberately skipping the word because he can't pronounce it.

Additions—This refers to words being added to those printed. As with omissions, this error may be due to carelessness or overly rapid reading. It may also be due to the child's not understanding the sentence and feeling that the added word makes it clearer.

Substitutions—A word is substituted orally for the word that is printed. This error isn't too serious if the substitution is reasonable and doesn't happen too frequently. It is more serious if substitutions occur frequently and distort the meaning of the sentence. It can indicate carelessness, reading too fast, or that the material is too difficult for the child to understand.

Reversals—These are errors in which individual letters are confused with similar ones, the order of the letters is confused to form another word, or the order of the words in the sentence is rearranged. Faulty letter recognition or faulty left-to-right eye movement is generally the cause.

Repetitions—This refers to a habit of repeating words or phrases that have already been read, giving the reading a halting or jerky sound. It is often caused by poor word recognition or too difficult material. Trying to understand what he's reading, the child stops and repeats.

Sight vocabulary—These are words that a child can read without sounding them out. A child who consistently fails to recognize familiar words needs to practice with flash cards to develop his sight vocabulary. He also needs to learn the meaning and correct usage of missed words.

Comprehension—This term refers to how well a child understands what he reads. Comprehension may be low because of lack of concentration, poor word recognition, lack of word attack or pronunciation skills, and poor vocabulary. To evaluate a child's ability to comprehend and recall a story, it's best to use material which is well within his ability level. If he has difficulty decoding the words, he'll find it hard to grasp the meaning of the sentence. If he has to struggle with a sentence, he'll probably lose sight of the main point of the paragraph.

Comprehension requires three levels of mind functioning and test questions should reflect these levels. Recall is the simplest level, comparing and contrasting more difficult, and developing and applying the most difficult.

Recall

1. What was the name of the cat in the story?
2. Who fell off the bicycle?
3. When did the train stop?
4. Where was the wagon heading?

Comparing and contrasting

1. Who was the strongest football player?
2. Which person was the "bad guy"?
3. How was the hero different from the other workers?
4. Tell how the main character was like or unlike you.

Developing and applying

1. What other ending could have been used in the story?
2. Where could this knowledge be used today?
3. How did you feel about the hero or heroine?
4. Explain why you think the main characters behaved the way they did in the story.

It's best to ask comprehension questions immediately after the oral reading. Studies on learning suggest that more material is remembered immediately after reading or studying. Asking the recall questions first reminds the child of story details and helps make them stick in his memory. If necessary, allow him to glance back through the material to find the answers.

Some children may have trouble with the second-level questions but improve with practice. Only a few third-level questions will be necessary for testing purposes because of their greater difficulty.

Punctuation usage—A child who doesn't understand the use of punctuation will not understand what he has read. Sentences will be run-on and meaningless, voice flat and dull. Be sure that the child understands the use of commas, periods, question marks, exclamation points and quotation marks. A comma is a signal to pause; a period indicates a complete thought; a question mark shows a question was asked; an exclamation point shows high emotion; quotation marks indicate exactly what a character is saying.

Skimming—This refers to the ability to pick out the main points of reading material by reading it rapidly. Skimming requires good comprehension, so reading material which the child has little difficulty in handling should be used to test it. A competent skimmer must ignore unimportant words and even sentences, concentrate on sorting through a maze of information to quickly classify and utilize facts. Skim reading is a valuable tool when time is an important factor. Tutors may wish to have the child practice skimming exercises.

Body language—This is the name for the visible bodily movements and positions which express an individual's feelings. Children's body language can be read by the tester to evaluate children's moods and attitude toward reading. Sitting attentively and even leaning slightly forward can be interpreted as a high level of interest and involvement. Restlessness, slouching and leaning back demonstrate disinterest and uninvolvement.

When a child's body language reveals disinterest, the reading session may have gone on too long, the material may be boring or too difficult, the child may be tired, emotionally upset or sick. Change the material, change the activity, take a break or halt the session.

Timing—Problems may exist when the child makes little or no improvement in the time period required to read a paragraph after several attempts, or when there's a considerable difference in his oral and silent reading rate. In the first case, the material may be too advanced for the child's ability level or he may have poor concentration. When a timed paragraph is new to him, the child's trouble is more likely to be phonics and vocabulary.

It is to be expected that silent reading will be faster than oral because of the additional effort of speech. A huge difference, however, may indicate that the child is only partially reading the paragraph to himself. In this case, the timed oral reading rate is more reliable as a measure of the child's reading ability.

Voice—A child's voice often points to problems which can interfere with reading. A strained or quivering voice may be a sign that the child is tense and nervous. Parents and teachers should try to relieve the child's anxiety by reassuring him.

A flat monotone can mean that the child is saying the words without understanding them. Slower reading, more vocabulary work, or less difficult material can help remedy this problem. Lack of expression, directly related to lack of comprehension, needs to be corrected as soon as possible to insure that children will receive the most pleasure and benefit from their reading.

Physical health—The tester should be alert for any signs of physical problems. Note the child's general state of health and any signs of poor coordination or abnormal body movement. Watch carefully to spot any vision difficulties. Are the child's eyes moving from left to right as he reads? Does he squint, blink or stare at the print? Does he have any physical difficulties in speaking or pronouncing words? This may also be a factor in reading problems. If a physical problem is suspected, take the child for a medical checkup and advice.

Following is the sample evaluation sheet for use as an informal reading diagnosis. The mistakes a child makes while reading can be recorded simply by checking the appropriate blanks and the number of errors by ticking them off as they occur.

READING EVALUATION SHEET

Child's name _____

Date _____

Mispronunciations (Total of a, b, c, d) _____

_____ a. Beginning consonant sounds
_____ b. Ending consonant sounds
_____ c. Simple (short) vowel sounds
_____ d. Complex (long) vowel sounds

_____ Omissions
_____ Additions
_____ Substitutions
_____ Reversals
_____ Repetitions
_____ Sight vocabulary (words missed)

Comprehension	Good _____	Average_____	Poor _____
Punctuation usage	Good _____	Average_____	Poor _____
Skimming	Good _____	Average_____	Poor _____
Body language	Good _____	Average_____	Poor _____
Timing	Good _____	Average_____	Poor _____
Voice	Good _____	Average_____	Poor _____
Physical health	Good _____	Average_____	Poor _____

_____ minutes for timed oral reading

_____ minutes for timed silent reading

12

Planning the program

The evaluation of the child's reading ability is likely to show that his reading is being hindered by several weaknesses rather than just one. To help develop his weak areas while improving his strengths, a tutoring program should involve a child in as many aspects of reading as possible. It should also develop his self-confidence and enthusiasm for reading. The detailed reading program outlined later has been designed with this in mind.

By following the suggested lessons, tutors can gain confidence while children improve. But in order to structure personalized reading lessons, the tutor must weigh and compensate for both the personality of the child and the degree of reading handicap. The program is flexible and versatile. For example, to help avoid initial discouragement for either child or tutor, the program starts at a pace that is comfortable and with material that is not too advanced. There need not be a different lesson every day, especially if a child demonstrates a great deal of difficulty with particular sounds or vocabulary words. After the tutor becomes more comfortable in the role of instructor, he'll be able to adjust the lesson length to fit the child's needs. He'll also be able to make use of the flexibility in lesson content, as in substituting games that are better liked.

Teaching process

The process of teaching involves three parts—human relationships, techniques or methods and materials. Since each child is a unique individual with needs different from other children's, tutors should adjust the teacher-student relationship, their methods and their materials to best serve the child's special needs. By doing this, parents will also gain a greater understanding of their child as a very special human being.

The suggested reading program includes activities that will (1) strengthen phonic skills, (2) develop vocabulary, (3) improve oral reading, and (4) reinforce learning.

Phonics instruction to learn the letter/sounds is vitally important since it is the tool that readers use to decode words. The benefits of knowing how to decode unfamiliar words extend all through a person's life. Since a child's speaking and hearing vocabulary is generally larger than his reading or sight vocabulary, encourage the child to experiment with all the possible letter/ sounds until he recognizes the printed word as a familiar word that he's heard before. This is a good approach for identifying printed words due to some differences in sounds for the same vowel letter and due to the larger number of sounds in words with many letters.

To be able to read smoothly and easily, a child must build a sight vocabulary, that is, he must memorize the commonly used words to the point where he instantly recognizes them. (See Table 7 in Appendix A.) These common words serve as the foundation for constructing meaning out of the sentences a child encounters as he reads. Only when he can sight-read these words is it time to introduce longer and more difficult ones.

Learning the common words is more useful than having children memorize rules for pronouncing and spelling words. There are so many rules with exceptions that children can become confused trying to remember which rule to use and how or where to use it for decoding. Such confusion can cause reading to remain slow and jerky.

It must be emphasized to the child that he must learn to remember letter/sounds and vocabulary words, especially the sight words. In fact, he needs to memorize rather than just try to remember them.

Lessons that begin with phonics, proceed to vocabulary, oral reading, and written exercises follow a natural progression from simple to more complex. Phonics helps children to decode the meaning of words, sentences, and paragraphs, which in turn are used in oral and silent reading.

Making reading lessons into games, as this program does, arouses children's interest, helps them concentrate, and encourages good attitudes toward reading. Games can be invented to both strengthen phonic skills and build vocabulary, like those described later. Any of the child's favorite games can be adapted to reading practice after you become familiar with those suggested here. Another value of the games approach is that sharing the fun strengthens the emotional bond between parent and child, encouraging more personal contact and greater communication. Finally, playing games helps the tutor as well as the child look forward to the learning sessions.

Scheduling and timing lessons

Lessons should be regularly scheduled for at least three days a week, since studies indicate that learning occurs more rapidly and is retained longer when it is regularly reinforced. The program charts cover 48 lessons, three a week for 16 weeks. Parents may find it best to schedule them every other day. Teachers may wish to do the same, or schedule daily reading instruction.

Although lessons should be held regularly and frequently, it should not be at a time resented by either the adult or the child. To avoid conflicts that might interfere with the program's effectiveness as with treasured TV programs or after-school sports, allow the child if possible to share in deciding on what days and times to schedule reading lessons. This also helps the child feel more involved.

A conference to share evaluations is recommended at the end of every week's lesson series. A child will be more willing to repeat a lesson, for example, if he helps make the decision. Conferences also help him focus on what he needs to do to improve his reading performance. Being consulted by an adult reinforces his feelings of self-worth. A child being consulted may at first respond "I don't know" or "I'm not sure," but with time he can learn to respond effectively. Self-awareness and the ability to communicate thoughts and feelings are learned.

Total lesson time should be 45 minutes to an hour. To a home tutor, this may seem an alarmingly long time. In practice, it won't seem nearly enough! The three individual instructional areas should be covered for about 15 minutes each, since keeping the activity level high maintains the child's interest and concentrates learning. The 15 minutes is only a guide, but try to keep the three areas in balance. It's a good idea to keep a clock in view so you can pace yourself.

It is often best to present the lesson objective, review it, and then include it in a phonic or vocabulary game. It's also helpful in both phonic and vocabulary games to include some review words. Thus previously learned material is reinforced as the new lesson is mastered. Because the child is already familiar with some of the lesson, his feelings of success will help with the new and more difficult part.

Since phonics deals with the sounds of the letters in vocabulary words, many of the reading games can be used for either purpose by simply changing the emphasis to meet the needs or preferences of the tutor or the student.

To help keep children's interest and attention, lessons should be given in a room with good light, comfortable temperature, adequate fresh air, and suitable seating.

Pupil involvement

The emotional atmosphere is important, too, for getting children involved in their education. A warm, friendly, relaxed and enthusiastic air will do much to make a child responsive, cooperative, and receptive to learning. Since children are so sensitive to emotions and moods, they'll know if you are feeling tense, anxious, bored or cross. A child can be made to sit, even hold the book and look at the words, but it is difficult or impossible to "make" him learn. Reassuring the child of your love and respect while reinforcing his self-image modifies a negative attitude toward learning, breaks down resistance and encourages him to work at his reading.

Allowing the student to help plan lessons, choose games and develop comprehension questions also encourages him to become more involved in the reading program. In essence, a partnership is formed between adult and child to reach a common goal. In addition, the child who helps with the planning improves his level of understanding, which in turn improves his reading ability.

Especially during the first lessons, remember to reinforce strongly any and all of the student's successes. This is another way to help change negative attitudes and encourage work toward further success.

Incentives

Incentives for satisfactory performance in learning fall into three categories: (1) affection, like smiles or kind words, which show the tutor's pleasure; (2) tokens, which have no value except as part of a game or as assigned by the tutor; and (3) sweets, like candy or soft drinks.

There's no disagreement about using affection as an encouragement for children to learn and little on the subject of tokens, except the charge that they constitute bribery. Such bribery, it is argued, won't be carried on in school or society and so give children poor training for later life. Advocates point out that all rewards to get children to perform are basically bribes. A greater controversy exists over sweet rewards, which are said to be not only bribes but bad nutritionally. Arguments in favor state that such small amounts of sweets are not harmful, and that they are effective with some children that can't be motivated in any other way.

Parents and teachers must weigh both sides and reach their own decisions. Each instructor has to consider the unique behavior of each child when seeking to motivate him to learn.

Progress charts on which children can keep a record of their performance and visibly show their improvement can help motivate learning, especially if the charts are unusual and imaginative. Some children enjoy keeping a record of their progress so much that they are eager to help design new charts of their own.

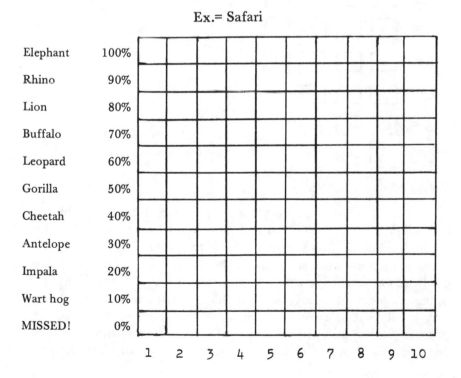

Ex.= Safari

		1	2	3	4	5	6	7	8	9	10
Elephant	100%										
Rhino	90%										
Lion	80%										
Buffalo	70%										
Leopard	60%										
Gorilla	50%										
Cheetah	40%										
Antelope	30%										
Impala	20%										
Wart hog	10%										
MISSED!	0%										

The big game that children "bag" depends upon the percentage points they have earned (ex.= 7 finished out of 10 = 70% = buffalo). A small drawing of a camera or the animal is placed in the correct space for record keeping.

Another way to motivate children to study is to occasionally offer them a surprise reward. These can be given outright when a particularly difficult lesson has been learned, or the awarding of the prize can be made into a game.

Ex.= Trick or Treat

100%	☐ ☐ ☐ ☐ ☐ ☐ ☐ ☐ ☐ ☐
90%	☐ ☐ ☐ ☐ ☐ ☐ ☐ ☐ ☐
80%	☐ ☐ ☐ ☐ ☐ ☐ ☐ ☐
70%	☐ ☐ ☐ ☐ ☐ ☐ ☐
60%	☐ ☐ ☐ ☐ ☐ ☐
50%	☐ ☐ ☐ ☐ ☐
40%	☐ ☐ ☐ ☐
30%	☐ ☐ ☐
20%	☐ ☐
10%	☐
0%	

Each space contains a piece of paper or a card on which a "trick" or "treat" is written and placed face down so it can't be read. A child chooses any card in the row across from the percentage score that he makes. The higher the score, the more cards he has to choose from. A treat can be things like a penny, an orange, a piece of candy, or a privilege. A trick might be either a very small treat or possibly a bonus point with a certain number of points winning an optional small prize. A good mixture of treats and tricks is about 75 to 25 per cent, or 45 treats to 15 tricks. Put

18

a special treat in the 100% row, and let the child know it's there!

Accelerating learning

It is valuable for both tutor and child to know that studies suggest learning occurs most rapidly and is retained longer when the child: (1) finds the reading material understandable; (2) finds the material interesting; (3) concentrates on the task; (4) uses and thereby reinforces what he reads; (5) uses the information immediately; and (6) associates the ideas with previously learned material, thus making them familiar and meaningful.

Tutors can help children to memorize letters and sounds, word spellings and word meanings by teaching them a few techniques. For a start, tell children that learning does not just happen when they stare at a letter or word! They have to try actively to learn by printing in their mind as clear a picture as possible, and by using repetition and reinforcement. Here are some suggestions—not all of them will be needed every time, of course.

(1) Look at a word, close your eyes, and see a picture of it in your mind.
(2) Copy a word over and over until you can write it without seeing it.
(3) Pronounce or spell a word over and over again.
(4) Look the word up in a dictionary and read or write its definition.
(5) Associate the word with something else that you already know or understand.
(6) Think of different ways to use the word in a sentence.
(7) Use the word in a poem or song.
(8) Make up a story using the word as many times as you can.
(9) Use the word a different way each day.
(10) Draw a picture which represents or somehow involves the word.
(11) Ask someone to give you the word to pronounce, spell or define as in an informal quiz.
(12) Review the word regularly.

Lesson plans

Parents and teachers should encourage daily reading habits outside of lessons. The more a child enjoys reading, the more he reads, and the better reader he tends to become. Parents who take children to the library, subscribe to newspapers and magazines and join in a reading time every day show children that adults value and enjoy reading. A pleasant and useful activity at mealtimes or before bed is for family members to share what they like or have learned from their current reading. Teachers who allow free reading time, read in class out loud or to themselves and encourage sharing of ideas and pleasures accomplish similar goals.

When this set of lessons is finished, the instructor who pretested the child using the suggested check list may use the same list as a posttest. Although the child's improvement may seem very noticeable, comparison of the two tests will be more specific and will give you a permanent record.

The child who completes the lessons will have a strong foundation for improved reading ability. It is likely that it will be of even more value to the child to keep up the reading lessons as a long-term project, if both the child and the tutor elect to do so. In that case, the instructor need only to continue to (1) review word attack skills with phonics, (2) expand children's vocabulary, (3) introduce more difficult reading material as the student's reading ability develops, and (4) increase the complexity of the enrichment exercises and activities.

This same procedure for the organization of the lesson plans works for any child regardless of age and grade level from nursery school through high school. Only the reading material itself must be adjusted or suited to each individual's reading level. Thus you would not necessarily choose a picture book, generally suited for very young children, as a book for high school students to read orally since it might embarrass them.

NOTE: However, one way to get around this if picture books are deemed suitable, is to tell the high school students that they are going to do a survey of children's literature on a particular subject or topic and then have the students do such projects as reviews which can be given to local school libraries for use in their card catalogues.

Pages 22-52 outline the objectives, methods and materials for 48 lessons to be completed over a 16-week period. If it suits his or her individual style of planning, the parent or teacher may wish to prepare weekly outlines for quick reference. Preparing such outlines helps the tutor organize the material in his own mind and provides a natural format for inserting personal or original ideas to be used in teaching. Suggested format for such outline appears below.

FORMAT FOR 1ST TO 15TH WEEK

		LESSON 1	LESSON 2	LESSON 3
45 MINUTES TO 1 HOUR	PHONICS (15-20 mins.)	Objective - - - - - - Method - - - - - - Materials - - - - - -	Objective - - - - - - etc.	Objective - - - - - - etc.
	VOCABULARY (15-20 mins.)	Objective - - - - - - Method - - - - - - Materials - - - - - -		
	ORAL READING (15-20 mins.)	Weekly Objective - Weekly Methods - Materials - - - - - - - - - - - - - -		
	OPTIONAL EXERCISES AND ACTIVITIES	- - - - - -		

21

The inexpensive materials and sources of reading matter you'll need for the lessons are described in unit 3, with further directions about the many ways they can be used. The games, activities and exercises referred to in the lessons make up unit 4.

1st WEEK OF TEACHING
45 minutes to 1 hour
Phonics (15-20 mins.)
Vocabulary (15-20 mins.)
Oral Reading (15-20 mins.)
Optional Activities and Exercises

Lesson 1
PHONICS
Objective: To pretest the child's word attack skills.
Method: Phonic Buzz game (p. 64), using a random sample of phonic flash cards.
Materials: Phonic flash cards (p. 53), including *all* letters.
VOCABULARY
Objective: To pretest the child's functional vocabulary.
Method: Vocabulary Tic-Tac-Toe (p. 72).
Materials: Vocabulary flash cards (p. 58), using random sample including high frequency words.
ORAL READING
Weekly Objective: To develop oral reading performance while checking comprehension and recall.
Weekly Method: Oral reading session in which: (1) child reads with adult help in sounding out problem words; (2) child and adult read aloud together; or (3) child reads each word aloud immediately after it is spoken by adult. Following oral reading, tutor discusses reading material with the child to assess recall and comprehension.
Materials: Selected high-interest reading material.
OPTIONAL ACTIVITIES AND EXERCISES
Listing Words exercise (p. 81).

Lesson 2
PHONICS
Objective: To study simple vowel sounds ă, ĕ, ĭ, ŏ, ŭ (p. 208-210).
Method: Sound Doctor game (p. 65).
Materials: Phonic flash cards using the above letters.

22

VOCABULARY
Objective: To strengthen word association.
Method: Secret Word game (p. 72), with emphasis on word clue relationships.
Materials: Vocabulary flash cards.
ORAL READING
Weekly Objective: To develop oral reading performance while checking comprehension and recall.
Weekly Method: Oral reading session in which: (1) child reads with adult help in sounding out problem words; (2) child and adult read aloud together; or (3) child reads each word aloud immediately after it is spoken by adult. Following oral reading, tutor discusses reading material with the child to assess recall and comprehension.
OPTIONAL ACTIVITIES AND EXERCISES
Crossword Puzzle activity (p. 86).

Lesson 3
PHONICS
Objective: To study complex vowel sounds $\bar{a}$, $\bar{e}$, $\bar{i}$, $\bar{o}$, $\bar{u}$, (p. 208-210).
Method: Wise Old Owl game (p. 65).
Materials: Phonic flash cards using the above letters.
VOCABULARY
Objective: To develop word recognition of high frequency words.
Method: Connect-A-Word game (p. 73), with emphasis on vocabulary development.
Materials: Vocabulary flash cards.
ORAL READING
Weekly Objective: To develop oral reading performance while checking comprehension and recall.
Weekly Method: Oral reading session in which: (1) child reads with adult help in sounding out problem words; (2) child and adult read aloud together; or (3) child reads each word aloud immediately after it is spoken by adult. Following oral reading, tutor discusses reading material with the child to assess recall and comprehension.
OPTIONAL ACTIVITIES AND EXERCISES
Cartoons activity (p. 87).

2nd WEEK OF TEACHING
45 minutes to 1 hour
Phonics (15-20 mins.)
Vocabulary (15-20 mins.)
Oral Reading (15-20 mins.)
Optional Activities and Exercises

Lesson 4
PHONICS
Objective: To review both simple and complex vowel sounds (p. 208-210).
Method: Phonic Baseball game (p. 65),
Materials: Phonic flash cards, materials to draw baseball diamond.
VOCABULARY
Objective: To speed word recognition.
Method: Vocabulary Football game (p. 73).
Materials: Vocabulary flash cards, materials to draw football field.
ORAL READING
Weekly Objective: To develop oral reading performance while checking comprehension and recall.
Weekly Method: Oral reading session in which: (1) child reads with adult help in sounding out problem words; (2) child and adult read aloud together; or (3) child reads each word aloud immediately after it is spoken by adult. Following oral reading, tutor discusses reading material with the child to assess recall and comprehension.
Materials: Selected high-interest reading material.
OPTIONAL ACTIVITIES AND EXERCISES
Vocabulary Word Puzzle activity (p. 88).

Lesson 5
PHONICS
Objective: To study the sounds of the consonant letters b, c, d, f, g (p. 211).
Method: Phonic Match-up game (p. 66), with emphasis on phonics and word attack skills.

Materials: Phonic flash cards.

VOCABULARY

Objective: To expand word meanings.

Method: Build-A-Word game (p. 74).

Materials: Phonic flash cards of alphabet letters and vocabulary flash cards.

ORAL READING

Weekly Objective: To develop oral reading performance while checking comprehension and recall.

Weekly Method: Oral reading session in which: (1) child reads with adult help in sounding out problem words; (2) child and adult read aloud together; or (3) child reads each word aloud immediately after it is spoken by adult. Following oral reading, tutor discusses reading material with the child to assess recall and comprehension.

OPTIONAL ACTIVITIES AND EXERCISES

Rhyming exercise (p. 82).

Lesson 6

PHONICS

Objective: To study the sounds of the consonant letters h, j, k, l, m (p. 211-212).

Method: Train game (p. 66).

Materials: Phonic flash cards.

VOCABULARY

Objective: To extend word families.

Method: Identification game (p. 75).

Materials: Vocabulary flash cards.

ORAL READING

Weekly Objective: To develop oral reading performance while checking comprehension and recall.

Weekly Method: Oral reading session in which: (1) child reads with adult help in sounding out problem words; (2) child and adult read aloud together; or (3) child reads each word aloud immediately after it is spoken by adult. Following oral reading, tutor discusses reading material with the child to assess recall and comprehension.

OPTIONAL ACTIVITIES AND EXERCISES

Multiple Choice exercise (p. 82).

3rd WEEK OF TEACHING
45 minutes to 1 hour
Phonics (15-20 mins.)
Vocabulary (15-20 mins.)
Oral Reading (15-20 mins.)
Optional Activities and Exercises

Lesson 7
PHONICS
Objective: To study the sounds of the consonant letters n, p, q, r, s (p. 212-213).
Method: Phonic Relay game (p. 67).
Materials: Phonic flash cards.
VOCABULARY
Objective: To develop and speed recognition of high-frequency words.
Method: Secret Agent game (p. 76).
Materials: Vocabulary flash cards, pencils, paper, and secret agent badge.
ORAL READING
Weekly Objective: To develop oral reading performance while checking comprehension and recall.
Weekly Method: Oral reading session in which: (1) child reads with adult help in sounding out problem words; (2) child and adult read aloud together; or (3) child reads each word aloud immediately after it is spoken by adult. Following oral reading, tutor discusses reading material with the child to assess recall and comprehension.
Materials: Selected high-interest reading material.
OPTIONAL ACTIVITIES AND EXERCISES
Listing Words exercise (p. 81).

Lesson 8
PHONICS
Objective: To study the sounds of the consonant letters t, v, w, x, z (p. 213-214).
Method: Banker game (p. 67).
Materials: Phonic flash cards and vocabulary flash cards.
VOCABULARY
Objective: To strengthen sight vocabulary.

26

Method: Connect-A-Word game (p. 73), with emphasis on vocabulary development.

Materials: Alphabet flash cards, checkerboard.

ORAL READING

Weekly Objective: To develop oral reading performance while checking comprehension and recall.

Weekly Method: Oral reading session in which: (1) child reads with adult help in sounding out problem words; (2) child and adult read aloud together; or (3) child reads each word aloud immediately after it is spoken by adult. Following oral reading, tutor discusses reading material with the child to assess recall and comprehension.

OPTIONAL ACTIVITIES AND EXERCISES

Paragraph Jigsaw Puzzle activity (p. 88).

Lesson 9

PHONICS

Objective: To review the sounds of the consonant letters (p. 211-214).

Method: Phonic Tic-Tac-Toe (p. 68), with emphasis on phonics and word attack skills.

Materials: Phonic flash cards.

VOCABULARY

Objective: To expand and apply vocabulary usage to sentences.

Method: Card Conversation game (p. 77), with emphasis on sentence structure and the proper use of words.

Materials: Vocabulary flash cards.

ORAL READING

Weekly Objective: To develop oral reading performance while checking comprehension and recall.

Weekly Method: Oral reading session in which: (1) child reads with adult help in sounding out problem words; (2) child and adult read aloud together; or (3) child reads each word aloud immediately after it is spoken by adult. Following oral reading, tutor discusses reading material with the child to assess recall and comprehension.

OPTIONAL ACTIVITIES AND EXERCISES

Multiple Choice exercise (p. 82).

4th WEEK OF TEACHING
45 minutes to 1 hour
Phonics (15-20 mins.)
Vocabulary (15-20 mins.)
Oral Reading (15-20 mins.)
Optional Activities and Exercises

Lesson 10
PHONICS
Objective: To study the sounds of the consonant blends **bl, br, ch, ck** (p. 215).
Method: Horse Race game (p. 68).
Materials: Phonic flash cards and blank cards for making the race track.
VOCABULARY
Objective: To develop an understanding of word meanings.
Method: Vocabulary Match-up game (p. 77).
Materials: Vocabulary flash cards using sample words given earlier and a dictionary.
ORAL READING
Weekly Objective: To develop oral reading performance while checking comprehension and recall.
Weekly Method: Oral reading session in which: (1) child reads with adult help in sounding out problem words; (2) child and adult read aloud together; or (3) child reads each word aloud immediately after it is spoken by adult. Following oral reading, tutor discusses reading material with the child to assess recall and comprehension.
Materials: Selected high-interest reading material.
OPTIONAL ACTIVITIES AND EXERCISES
Write-In-Answer exercise (p. 85).

Lesson 11
PHONICS
Objective: To study the sounds of the consonant blends **cl, cr, dl, dr** (p. 215-216).
Method: Phonic 8-Card game (p. 69).
Materials: Phonic flash cards for use as playing cards.
VOCABULARY
Objective: To improve word recognition.

28

Method: Vocabulary Football game (p. 73).
Materials: Vocabulary flash cards, materials to draw football field.
ORAL READING
Weekly Objective: To develop oral reading performance while checking comprehension and recall.
Weekly Method: Oral reading session in which: (1) child reads with adult help in sounding out problem words; (2) child and adult read aloud together; or (3) child reads each word aloud immediately after it is spoken by adult. Following oral reading, tutor discusses reading material with the child to assess recall and comprehension.
OPTIONAL ACTIVITIES AND EXERCISES
True & False exercise (p. 83).

Lesson 12
PHONICS
Objective: To study the sounds of the consonant blends **fl**, **fr**, **gl**, **gr** (p. 216).
Method: Phonic Home-Run Derby (p. 65), with emphasis on phonics and word attack skills.
Materials: Phonic flash cards and materials to make a baseball diamond.
VOCABULARY
Objective: To extend word families.
Method: Secret Word game (p. 72), to review root words with a variety of endings and changes in meaning.
Materials: Vocabulary flash cards.
ORAL READING
Weekly Objective: To develop oral reading performance while checking comprehension and recall.
Weekly Method: Oral reading session in which: (1) child reads with adult help in sounding out problem words; (2) child and adult read aloud together; or (3) child reads each word aloud immediately after it is spoken by adult. Following oral reading, tutor discusses reading material with the child to assess recall and comprehension.
OPTIONAL ACTIVITIES AND EXERCISES
Matching exercise (p. 84).

5th WEEK OF TEACHING
45 minutes to 1 hour
Phonics (15-20 mins.)
Vocabulary (15-20 mins.)
Oral Reading (15-20 mins.)
Optional Activities and Exercises

Lesson 13
PHONICS
Objective: To study the sounds of the consonant blends **pl, pr, sc, sh** (p. 217).
Method: Wise Old Owl game (p. 65).
Materials: Phonic flash cards, a picture of the owl and his house.
VOCABULARY
Objective: To increase vocabulary.
Method: Identification game (p. 75).
Materials: Vocabulary flash cards with emphasis on sight recognition and meaning.
ORAL READING
Weekly Objective: To develop oral reading performance while checking comprehension and recall.
Weekly Method: Oral reading session in which: (1) child reads with adult help in sounding out problem words; (2) child and adult read aloud together; or (3) child reads each word aloud immediately after it is spoken by adult. Following oral reading, tutor discusses reading material with the child to assess recall and comprehension.
Materials: Selected high-interest reading material.
OPTIONAL ACTIVITIES AND EXERCISES
Crossword Puzzle activity (p. 86).

Lesson 14
PHONICS
Objective: To study the sounds of the consonant blends **sk, sl, sm, sn** (p. 217-218).
Method: Phonic Buzz game (p. 64).
Materials: Phonic flash cards, to include the consonant blends.
VOCABULARY
Objective: To expand word meanings.
Method: Secret Word game (p. 72).

Materials: Vocabulary flash cards.

ORAL READING

Weekly Objective: To develop oral reading performance while checking comprehension and recall.

Weekly Method: Oral reading session in which: (1) child reads with adult help in sounding out problem words; (2) child and adult read aloud together; or (3) child reads each word aloud immediately after it is spoken by adult. Following oral reading, tutor discusses reading material with the child to assess recall and comprehension.

OPTIONAL ACTIVITIES AND EXERCISES

Rhyming exercise (p. 82).

Lesson 15

PHONICS

Objective: To study the sounds of the consonant blends sp, st, sw, th (p. 218).

Method: Phonic Relay game (p. 67).

Materials: Phonic flash cards to show alone and in combinations to make words.

VOCABULARY

Objective: To improve and speed word recognition.

Method: Big Word—Little Word game (p. 77).

Materials: Vocabulary flash cards.

ORAL READING

Weekly Objective: To develop oral reading performance while checking comprehension and recall.

Weekly Method: Oral reading session in which: (1) child reads with adult help in sounding out problem words; (2) child and adult read aloud together; or (3) child reads each word aloud immediately after it is spoken by adult. Following oral reading, tutor discusses reading material with the child to assess recall and comprehension.

OPTIONAL ACTIVITIES AND EXERCISES

Play activity (p. 89).

6th WEEK OF TEACHING
45 minutes to 1 hour
Phonics (15-20 mins.)

Vocabulary (15-20 mins.)
Oral Reading (15-20 mins.)
Optional Activities and Exercises

Lesson 16
PHONICS
Objective: To study the sounds of the consonant blends **tl, tr, tw, wh** (p. 219).
Method: Phonic Question-Answer game (p. 69).
Materials: Phonic flash cards.
VOCABULARY
Objective: To learn about compound words and their meanings.
Method: Identification game (p. 75).
Materials: Vocabulary flash cards using sample words given earlier, dictionary.
ORAL READING
Weekly Objective: To develop oral reading performance while checking comprehension and recall.
Weekly Method: Oral reading session in which: (1) child reads with adult help in sounding out problem words; (2) child and adult read aloud together; or (3) child reads each word aloud immediately after it is spoken by adult. Following oral reading, tutor discusses reading material with the child to assess recall and comprehension.
Materials: Selected high-interest reading material.
OPTIONAL ACTIVITIES AND EXERCISES
Puppet Show activity (p. 89).

Lesson 17
PHONICS
Objective: To review the sounds of the consonant blends (p. 215-219).
Method: Train game (p. 66).
Materials: Phonic flash cards arranged in mixed order.
VOCABULARY
Objective: To extend vocabulary.
Method: Build-A-Word game (p. 74).
Materials: Vocabulary flash cards, to include new and review words.

32

ORAL READING

Weekly Objective: To develop oral reading performance while checking comprehension and recall.

Weekly Method: Oral reading session in which: (1) child reads with adult help in sounding out problem words; (2) child and adult read aloud together; or (3) child reads each word aloud immediately after it is spoken by adult. Following oral reading, tutor discusses reading material with the child to assess recall and comprehension.

OPTIONAL ACTIVITIES AND EXERCISES

Listing Words exercise (p. 81).

Lesson 18

PHONICS

Objective: To study the common letter families **ab, ace, ack, ad** combined with beginning consonants and blends (p. 220).

Method: Sound Doctor game (p. 65).

Materials: Phonic flash cards and a homemade "hospital."

VOCABULARY

Objective: To practice using words in the context of a sentence.

Method: Card Conversation game (p. 77).

Materials: Vocabulary flash cards with emphasis on usage and meaning of words.

ORAL READING

Weekly Objective: To develop oral reading performance while checking comprehension and recall.

Weekly Method: Oral reading session in which: (1) child reads with adult help in sounding out problem words; (2) child and adult read aloud together; or (3) child reads each word aloud immediately after it is spoken by adult. Following oral reading, tutor discusses reading material with the child to assess recall and comprehension.

OPTIONAL ACTIVITIES AND EXERCISES

Comprehension Questions exercise (p. 85).

7th WEEK OF TEACHING
45 minutes to 1 hour
Phonics (15-20 mins.)
Vocabulary (15-20 mins.)

Lesson 19
PHONICS
Objective: To study common letter families **ade, ag, age, ain** with beginning consonants and blends (p. 220).
Method: Sound-A-Word game (p. 69), with emphasis on word attack skills.
Materials: Phonic flash cards.
VOCABULARY
Objective: To expand word family recognition and definitions and encourage dictionary use.
Method: Letter-Word game (p. 78).
Materials: Blank flash cards, pencils, dictionary.
ORAL READING
Weekly Objective: To develop oral reading performance while checking comprehension and recall.
Weekly Method: Oral reading session in which: (1) child reads with adult help in sounding out problem words; (2) child and adult read aloud together; or (3) child reads each word aloud immediately after it is spoken by adult. Following oral reading, tutor discusses reading material with the child to assess recall and comprehension.
Materials: Selected high-interest reading material.
OPTIONAL ACTIVITIES AND EXERCISES
Fill-In-Blanks exercise (p. 83).

Lesson 20
PHONICS
Objective: To study common letter families **ake, all, am, ame** with beginning consonants and blends (p. 221).
Method: Four Across game (p. 70).
Materials: Alphabet flash cards, homemade game cards, markers.
VOCABULARY
Objective: To encourage use and development of vocabulary.
Method: Big Word—Little Word game (p. 77).
Materials: Selected long words, paper, pencils, dictionary.

ORAL READING

Weekly Objective: To develop oral reading performance while checking comprehension and recall.

Weekly Method: Oral reading session in which: (1) child reads with adult help in sounding out problem words; (2) child and adult read aloud together; or (3) child reads each word aloud immediately after it is spoken by adult. Following oral reading, tutor discusses reading material with the child to assess recall and comprehension.

OPTIONAL ACTIVITIES AND EXERCISES

Newspaper activity (p. 60).

Lesson 21

PHONICS

Objective: To study common letter families **an, and, ane, ank** with beginning consonants and blends (p. 221).

Method: Banker game (p. 67).

Materials: Phonic and vocabulary flash cards.

VOCABULARY

Objective: To work on the context meaning of words.

Method: Spin-A-Word game (p. 79).

Materials: Vocabulary flash cards, homemade spin chart, paper, pencils.

ORAL READING

Weekly Objective: To develop oral reading performance while checking comprehension and recall.

Weekly Method: Oral reading session in which: (1) child reads with adult help in sounding out problem words; (2) child and adult read aloud together; or (3) child reads each word aloud immediately after it is spoken by adult. Following oral reading, tutor discusses reading material with the child to assess recall and comprehension.

OPTIONAL ACTIVITIES AND EXERCISES

True & False exercise (p. 83).

8th WEEK OF TEACHING
45 minutes to 1 hour
Phonics (15-20 mins.)
Vocabulary (15-20 mins.)

35

Lesson 22
PHONICS
Objective: To study common letter families **ap, ar, are, ash** with beginning consonants and blends (p. 221-222).
Method: Phonic 8-Card game (p. 69).
Materials: Phonic flash cards to use as playing cards.
VOCABULARY
Objective: To help recognition of words and their meanings.
Method: Vocabulary Match-up game (p. 77).
Materials: Vocabulary flash cards.
ORAL READING
Weekly Objective: To develop oral reading performance while checking comprehension and recall.
Weekly Method: Oral reading session in which: (1) child reads with adult help in sounding out problem words; (2) child and adult read aloud together; or (3) child reads each word aloud immediately after it is spoken by adult. Following oral reading, tutor discusses reading material with the child to assess recall and comprehension.
Materials: Selected high-interest reading material.
OPTIONAL ACTIVITIES AND EXERCISES
Multiple Choice exercise (p. 82).

Lesson 23
PHONICS
Objective: To study common letter families **ast, at, ate, ave** with beginning consonants and blends (p. 222).
Method: Spin-A-Letter/Sound game (p. 71).
Materials: Paper, pencils, a homemade spin chart.
VOCABULARY
Objective: To practice organizing letters into words and words into sentences.
Method: Secret Agent game (p. 76).
Materials: Several sets of numbered alphabet flash cards, paper, pencils, homemade secret agent's badge.

ORAL READING

Weekly Objective: To develop oral reading performance while checking comprehension and recall.

Weekly Method: Oral reading session in which: (1) child reads with adult help in sounding out problem words; (2) child and adult read aloud together; or (3) child reads each word aloud immediately after it is spoken by adult. Following oral reading, tutor discusses reading material with the child to assess recall and comprehension.

OPTIONAL ACTIVITIES AND EXERCISES

Comprehension Questions exercise (p. 85).

Lesson 24

PHONICS

Objective: To study common letter families aw, ed, eat, ead with beginning consonants and blends (p. 222-223).

Method: Horse Race game (p. 68).

Materials: Phonic flash cards and blank cards to form race track.

VOCABULARY

Objective: To give concrete experiences to word definitions, following directions, and the activity of reading.

Method: Read-See-Do game (p. 80).

Materials: Vocabulary flash cards and instruction cards.

ORAL READING

Weekly Objective: To develop oral reading performance while checking comprehension and recall.

Weekly Method: Oral reading session in which: (1) child reads with adult help in sounding out problem words; (2) child and adult read aloud together; or (3) child reads each word aloud immediately after it is spoken by adult. Following oral reading, tutor discusses reading material with the child to assess recall and comprehension.

OPTIONAL ACTIVITIES AND EXERCISES

Fill-In-Blanks exercise (p. 83).

9th WEEK OF TEACHING
45 minutes to 1 hour
Phonics (15-20 mins.)

37

Vocabulary (15-20 mins.)
Oral Reading (15-20 mins.)
Optional Activities and Exercises

Lesson 25
PHONICS
Objective: To study common letter families **eed, eek, eep, en** with beginning consonants and blends (p. 223).
Method: Phonic Baseball Game (p. 65).
Materials: Phonic flash cards, paper, pencils, materials to draw baseball diamond.
VOCABULARY
Objective: To encourage use and development of vocabulary.
Method: Big Word—Little Word game (p. 77).
Materials: Selected big words, paper, pencils, dictionary.
ORAL READING
Weekly Objective: To develop oral reading performance while checking comprehension and recall.
Weekly Method: Oral reading session in which: (1) child reads with adult help in sounding out problem words; (2) child and adult read aloud together; or (3) child reads each word aloud immediately after it is spoken by adult. Following oral reading, tutor discusses reading material with the child to assess recall and comprehension.
Materials: Selected high-interest reading material.
OPTIONAL ACTIVITIES AND EXERCISES
Rhyming exercise (p. 82).

Lesson 26
PHONICS
Objective: To study common letter families **end, ent, et, ick** with beginning consonants and blends (p. 223-224).
Method: Phonic Play-A-Card game (p. 72).
Materials: Several sets of alphabet flash cards, a score card.
VOCABULARY
Objective: To give concrete experiences to word definitions, following directions and the activity of reading.
Method: Read-See-Do game (p. 80).
Materials: Vocabulary flash cards, instruction cards.

38

ORAL READING

Weekly Objective: To develop oral reading performance while checking comprehension and recall.

Weekly Method: Oral reading session in which: (1) child reads with adult help in sounding out problem words; (2) child and adult read aloud together; or (3) child reads each word aloud immediately after it is spoken by adult. Following oral reading, tutor discusses reading material with the child to assess recall and comprehension.

OPTIONAL ACTIVITIES AND EXERCISES

Fill-In-Blanks exercise (p. 83).

Lesson 27

PHONICS

Objective: To study common letter families **id, ide, ig, ight** with beginning consonants and blends (p. 224).

Method: Phonic Match-up game (p. 66).

Materials: Sets of alphabet flash cards, paper, pencils, dictionary.

VOCABULARY

Objective: To stimulate the recall of words and their meanings.

Method: Vocabulary Challenge game (p. 80).

Materials: Sets of vocabulary flash cards, dictionary.

ORAL READING

Weekly Objective: To develop oral reading performance while checking comprehension and recall.

Weekly Method: Oral reading session in which: (1) child reads with adult help in sounding out problem words; (2) child and adult read aloud together; or (3) child reads each word aloud immediately after it is spoken by adult. Following oral reading, tutor discusses reading material with the child to assess recall and comprehension.

OPTIONAL ACTIVITIES AND EXERCISES

Matching exercise (p. 84).

10th WEEK OF TEACHING
45 minutes to 1 hour
Phonics (15-20 mins.)
Vocabulary (15-20 mins.)
Oral Reading (15-20 mins.)
Optional Activities and Exercises

Lesson 28

PHONICS

Objective: To study common letter families **ill, im, ime, in** with beginning consonants and blends (p. 224).

Method: Phonic Tic-Tac-Toe game (p. 68).

Materials: Phonic flash cards, paper, pencils.

VOCABULARY

Objective: To work on the context meanings of words.

Method: Spin-A-Word game (p. 79).

Materials: Vocabulary flash cards, paper, pencils, homemade spin chart.

ORAL READING:

Weekly Objective: To develop oral reading performance while checking comprehension and recall.

Weekly Method: Oral reading session in which: (1) child reads with adult help in sounding out problem words; (2) child and adult read aloud together; or (3) child reads each word aloud immediately after it is spoken by adult. Following oral reading, tutor discusses reading material with the child to assess recall and comprehension.

Materials: Selected high-interest reading material.

OPTIONAL ACTIVITIES AND EXERCISES

Crossword Puzzle activity (p. 86).

Lesson 29

PHONICS

Objective: To study common letter families **ine, ing, ink, ip, iss** with beginning consonants and blends (p. 225).

Method: Spin-A-Letter/Sound game (p. 71).

Materials: Paper, pencils, homemade spin chart, dictionary.

VOCABULARY

Objective: To help develop recall of newly introduced vocabulary words.

Method: Identification game (p. 75).

Materials: Vocabulary flash cards, paper, pencils.

ORAL READING

Weekly Objective: To develop oral reading performance while checking comprehension and recall.

Weekly Method: Oral reading session in which: (1) child reads with adult help in sounding out problem words; (2) child and adult read aloud together; or (3) child reads each word aloud immediately after it is spoken by adult. Following oral reading, tutor discusses reading material with the child to assess recall and comprehension.

OPTIONAL ACTIVITIES AND EXERCISES
Paragraph Jigsaw Puzzle activity (p. 88).

Lesson 30
PHONICS
Objective: To study common letter families it, **ob, ock, od, one** with beginning consonants and blends (p. 225-226).
Method: Horse Race game (p. 68).
Material: Phonic flash cards, blank cards for race track.

VOCABULARY
Objective: To practice spelling words and reinforce their meanings.
Method: Connect-A-Word game (p. 73).
Materials: Alphabet flash cards, homemade board or checkerboard.

ORAL READING
Weekly Objective: To develop oral reading performance while checking comprehension and recall.
Weekly Method: Oral reading session in which: (1) child reads with adult help in sounding out problem words; (2) child and adult read aloud together; or (3) child reads each word aloud immediately after it is spoken by adult. Following oral reading, tutor discusses reading material with the child to assess recall and comprehension.

OPTIONAL ACTIVITIES AND EXERCISES
True & False exercise (p. 83).

11th WEEK OF TEACHING
45 minutes to 1 hour
Phonics (15-20 mins.)
Vocabulary (15-20 mins.)
Oral Reading (15-20 mins.)
Optional Activities and Exercises

Lesson 31
PHONICS
Objective: To study common letter families **ong, ook, op, ope, ore**
    with beginning consonants and blends (p. 226).
Method: Banker game (p. 67).
Materials: Phonic flash cards.
VOCABULARY
Objective: To practice organizing letters into words and words
    into sentences.
Method: Secret Agent game (p. 76).
Materials: Numbered alphabet flash cards, paper, pencils, a secret
    agent badge.
ORAL READING
Weekly Objective: To develop oral reading performance while
    checking comprehension and recall.
Weekly Method: Oral reading session in which: (1) child reads
    with adult help in sounding out problem words; (2) child and
    adult read aloud together; or (3) child reads each word aloud
    immediately after it is spoken by adult. Following oral
    reading, tutor discusses reading material with the child to
    assess recall and comprehension.
Materials: Selected high-interest reading material.
OPTIONAL ACTIVITIES AND EXERCISES
Write-In-Answers exercise (p. 85).

Lesson 32
PHONICS
Objective: To study common letter families **ot, ound, ow, own, ub**
    with beginning consonants and blends (p. 226-227).
Method: Phonic Question-Answer game (p. 69).
Materials: Phonic flash cards.
VOCABULARY
Objective: To work on the context meanings of words.
Method: Spin-A-Word game (p. 79).
Materials: Vocabulary flash cards, paper, pencils, homemade spin
    chart.
ORAL READING
Weekly Objective: To develop oral reading performance while
    checking comprehension and recall.

Weekly Method: Oral reading session in which: (1) child reads with adult help in sounding out problem words; (2) child and adult read aloud together; or (3) child reads each word aloud immediately after it is spoken by adult. Following oral reading, tutor discusses reading material with the child to assess recall and comprehension.

OPTIONAL ACTIVITIES AND EXERCISES
Vocabulary Word Puzzle activity (p. 88).

Lesson 33
PHONICS
Objective: To study common letter families ug, um, un, ung, ur with beginning consonants and blends (p. 227).
Method: Sound-A-Word game (p. 69).
Materials: Phonic flash cards.

VOCABULARY
Objective: To stimulate vocabulary development.
Method: Vocabulary Football game (p. 73).
Materials: Vocabulary flash cards, materials to draw a football field.

ORAL READING
Weekly Objective: To develop oral reading performance while checking comprehension and recall.
Weekly Method: Oral reading session in which: (1) child reads with adult help in sounding out problem words; (2) child and adult read aloud together; or (3) child reads each word aloud immediately after it is spoken by adult. Following oral reading, tutor discusses reading material with the child to assess recall and comprehension.

OPTIONAL ACTIVITIES AND EXERCISES
Multiple Choice exercise (p. 82).

12th WEEK OF TEACHING
45 minutes to 1 hour
Phonics (15-20 mins.)
Vocabulary (15-20 mins.)
Oral Reading (15-20 mins.)
Optional Activities and Exercises

Lesson 34
PHONICS
Objective: To review both multiple and double letters and their word families (p. 220-227).
Method: Phonic Play-A-Card game (p. 72), with emphasis on word attack skills.
Materials: Phonic flash cards.
VOCABULARY
Objective: To expand word families and their meanings and to encourage dictionary use.
Method: Letter-Word game (p. 78).
Materials: Blank cards, pencils, dictionary.
ORAL READING
Weekly Objective: To develop oral reading performance while checking comprehension and recall.
Weekly Method: Oral reading session in which: (1) child reads with adult help in sounding out problem words; (2) child and adult read aloud together; or (3) child reads each word aloud immediately after it is spoken by adult. Following oral reading, tutor discusses reading material with the child to assess recall and comprehension.
Materials: Selected high-interest reading material.
OPTIONAL ACTIVITIES AND EXERCISES
Matching exercise (p. 84).

Lesson 35
PHONICS
Objective: To practice pronouncing the sounds of contractions (p. 230).
Method: Spin-A-Letter/Sound game (p. 71).
Materials: Paper, pencils, homemade spin chart, dictionary.
VOCABULARY
Objective: To stimulate learning which words are used to form contractions and their spellings.
Method: Card Conversation game (p. 77).
Materials: Vocabulary flash cards with emphasis on usage and meaning of contractions.
ORAL READING
Weekly Objective: To develop oral reading performance while checking comprehension and recall.

Weekly Method: Oral reading session in which: (1) child reads with adult help in sounding out problem words; (2) child and adult read aloud together; or (3) child reads each word aloud immediately after it is spoken by adult. Following oral reading, tutor discusses reading material with the child to assess recall and comprehension.

OPTIONAL ACTIVITIES AND EXERCISES

Paragraph Jigsaw Puzzle activity (p. 88).

Lesson 36

PHONICS

Objective: To study the vowel sounds of, o͞o, o͝o, ou, with each of their different spellings (p. 210).

Method: Phonic Buzz game (p. 64).

Materials: Phonic flash cards to include words as above with both spellings.

VOCABULARY

Objective: To practice using words and reinforce their meanings.

Method: Vocabulary Tic-Tac-Toe game (p. 72).

Materials: Vocabulary flash cards, paper, pencils.

ORAL READING

Weekly Objective: To develop oral reading performance while checking comprehension and recall.

Weekly Method: Oral reading session in which: (1) child reads with adult help in sounding out problem words; (2) child and adult read aloud together; or (3) child reads each word aloud immediately after it is spoken by adult. Following oral reading, tutor discusses reading material with the child to assess recall and comprehension.

OPTIONAL ACTIVITIES AND EXERCISES

Cartoons activity (p. 87).

13th WEEK OF TEACHING
45 minutes to 1 hour
Phonics (15-20 mins.)
Vocabulary (15-20 mins.)
Oral Reading (15-20 mins.)
Optional Activities and Exercises

Lesson 37

PHONICS

Objective: To study the vowel sounds of oi and au with each of their different spellings (p. 210).

Method: Phonic Match-Up game (p. 66), with emphasis on phonic word attack skills.

Materials: Phonic flash cards using varied spellings.

VOCABULARY

Objective: To associate relationships between words and their meanings.

Method: Secret Word game (p. 72).

Materials: Vocabulary flash cards.

ORAL READING

Weekly Objective: To develop oral reading performance while checking comprehension and recall.

Weekly Method: Oral reading session in which: (1) child reads with adult help in sounding out problem words; (2) child and adult read aloud together; or (3) child reads each word aloud immediately after it is spoken by adult. Following oral reading, tutor discusses reading material with the child to assess recall and comprehension.

Materials: Selected high-interest reading material.

OPTIONAL ACTIVITIES AND EXERCISES

Vocabulary Word Puzzle activity (p. 88).

Lesson 38

PHONICS

Objective: To review the vowel sounds of $\bar{oo}$, $\breve{oo}$, ou, oi, au, and their varied spellings (p. 210).

Method: Phonic 8-Card game (p. 69).

Materials: Phonic flash cards using these letters with different word examples.

VOCABULARY

Objective: To stimulate the recall of words and their meanings.

Method: Vocabulary Challenge game (p. 80).

Materials: Vocabulary flash cards.

ORAL READING

Weekly Objective: To develop oral reading performance while checking comprehension and recall.

Weekly Method: Oral reading session in which: (1) child reads with adult help in sounding out problem words; (2) child and adult read aloud together; or (3) child reads each word aloud immediatcly after it is spoken by adult. Following oral reading, tutor discusses reading material with the child to assess recall and comprehension.
OPTIONAL ACTIVITIES AND EXERCISES
Play activity (p. 89).

Lesson 39
PHONICS
Objective: To study prefixes or word beginnings like **re, non, un, dis, pre, de, anti, mid, in, be** (p. 228).
Method: Four Across game (p. 70).
Materials: Phonic flash cards, homemade game cards, markers.
VOCABULARY
Objective: To develop sight vocabulary.
Method: Vocabulary Tic-Tac-Toe game (p. 72).
Materials: Vocabulary flash cards, paper, pencils.
ORAL READING
Weekly Objective: To develop oral reading performance while checking comprehension and recall.
Weekly Method: Oral reading session in which: (1) child reads with adult help in sounding out problem words; (2) child and adult read aloud together; or (3) child reads each word aloud immediately after it is spoken by adult. Following oral reading, tutor discusses reading material with the child to assess recall and comprehension.
OPTIONAL ACTIVITIES AND EXERCISES
Write-In-Answer exercise (p. 85).

14th WEEK OF TEACHING
45 minutes to 1 hour
Phonics (15-20 mins.)
Vocabulary (15-20 mins.)
Oral Reading (15-20 mins.)
Optional Activities and Exercises

Lesson 40

PHONICS

Objective: To study suffixes or word endings like ed, s or es, er or or, ing, able, less, like, y, ous, ly, ful, ish, est (p. 228-229).

Method: Phonic Question-Answer game (p. 69).

Materials: Phonic flash cards using suffixes alone and with complete words.

VOCABULARY

Objective: To extend vocabulary.

Method: Build-A-Word game (p. 74).

Materials: Vocabulary flash cards including new and review words.

ORAL READING

Weekly Objective: To develop oral reading performance while checking comprehension and recall.

Weekly Method: Oral reading session in which: (1) child reads with adult help in sounding out problem words; (2) child and adult read aloud together; or (3) child reads each word aloud immediately after it is spoken by adult. Following oral reading, tutor discusses reading material with the child to assess recall and comprehension.

Materials: Selected high-interest reading material.

OPTIONAL ACTIVITIES AND EXERCISES

Crossword Puzzle activity (p. 86).

Lesson 41

PHONICS

Objective: To provide a combined study of the affixes, both prefixes and suffixes (p. 228-229).

Method: Sound Doctor game (p. 65).

Materials: Phonic flash cards with examples of both prefixes and suffixes.

VOCABULARY

Objective: To practice using words in the context of a sentence.

Method: Card Conversation game (p. 77).

Materials: Vocabulary flash cards with emphasis on usage and meaning of words.

ORAL READING

Weekly Objective: To develop oral reading performance while checking comprehension and recall.

Weekly Method: Oral reading session in which: (1) child reads with adult help in sounding out problem words; (2) child and adult read aloud together; or (3) child reads each word aloud immediately after it is spoken by adult. Following oral reading, tutor discusses reading material with the child to assess recall and comprehension.

OPTIONAL ACTIVITIES AND EXERCISES
Puppet Show activity (p. 89).

Lesson 42
PHONICS
Objective: To provide a basic review of the vowel letters and their sounds (p. 208-210).
Method: Sound-A-Word game (p. 69), with emphasis on word attack skills.
Materials: Phonic flash cards.
VOCABULARY
Objective: To give concrete experiences to word definitions and the activity of reading.
Method: Read-See-Do game (p. 80).
Materials: Vocabulary flash cards, instruction cards.
ORAL READING
Weekly Objective: To develop oral reading performance while checking comprehension and recall.
Weekly Method: Oral reading session in which: (1) child reads with adult help in sounding out problem words; (2) child and adult read aloud together; or (3) child reads each word aloud immediately after it is spoken by adult. Following oral reading, tutor discusses reading material with the child to assess recall and comprehension.
OPTIONAL ACTIVITIES AND EXERCISES
Comprehension Questions exercise (p. 85).

15th WEEK OF TEACHING
45 minutes to 1 hour
Phonics (15-20 mins.)
Vocabulary (15-20 mins.)
Oral Reading (15-20 mins.)
Optional Activities and Exercises

Lesson 43

PHONICS

Objective: To provide a basic review of the consonant letters and their sounds (p. 211-214).

Method: Phonic Relay game (p. 67).

Materials: Phonic flash cards including examples of consonants alone and in words.

VOCABULARY

Objective: To review vocabulary with emphasis on recognizing common or high-frequency words.

Method: Connect-A-Word game (p. 73).

Materials: Alphabet flash cards, homemade board or checkerboard.

ORAL READING

Weekly Objective: To develop oral reading performance while checking comprehension and recall.

Weekly Method: Oral reading session in which: (1) child reads with adult help in sounding out problem words; (2) child and adult read aloud together; or (3) child reads each word aloud immediately after it is spoken by adult. Following oral reading, tutor discusses reading material with the child to assess recall and comprehension.

Materials: Selected high-interest reading material.

OPTIONAL ACTIVITIES AND EXERCISES

Rhyming exercise (p. 82).

Lesson 44

PHONICS

Objective: To provide a basic review of the consonant blends and their sounds (p. 215-219).

Method: Wise Old Owl game (p. 65).

Materials: Phonic flash cards to include blends, a picture of the owl and his house.

VOCABULARY

Objective: To continue reviewing vocabulary with emphasis on sight vocabulary.

Method: Vocabulary Challenge game (p. 80).

Materials: Vocabulary flash cards.

ORAL READING

Weekly Objective: To develop oral reading performance while checking comprehension and recall.

Weekly Method: Oral reading session in which: (1) child reads
with adult help in sounding out problem words; (2) child and
adult read aloud together; or (3) child reads each word aloud
immediately after it is spoken by adult. Following oral
reading, tutor discusses reading material with the child to
assess recall and comprehension.
OPTIONAL ACTIVITIES AND EXERCISES
Listing Words exercise (p. 81).

Lesson 45
PHONICS
Objective: To provide a basic review of letter families and affixes
(p. 220-229).
Method: Phonic Tic-Tac-Toe game (p. 68).
Materials: Phonic flash cards including letter families and affixes,
paper, pencils.
VOCABULARY
Objective: To review vocabulary with emphasis on word meanings.
Method: Letter-Word game (p. 78).
Materials: Vocabulary flash cards
ORAL READING
Weekly Objective: To develop oral reading performance while
checking comprehension and recall.
Weekly Method: Oral reading session in which: (1) child reads
with adult help in sounding out problem words; (2) child and
adult read aloud together; or (3) child reads each word aloud
immediately after it is spoken by adult. Following oral
reading, tutor discusses reading material with the child to
assess recall and comprehension.
OPTIONAL ACTIVITIES AND EXERCISES
Cartoons activity (p. 87).

16th WEEK OF TEACHING
45 minutes to 1 hour
Phonics (15-20 mins.)
Vocabulary (15-20 mins.)
Oral Reading (15-20 mins.)
Optional Activities and Exercises

Lesson 46
PHONICS
Objective: To give a comprehensive review of phonic instruction.

Method: Phonic Baseball game (p. 65).

Materials: Phonic flash cards, materials to draw baseball diamond.

VOCABULARY

Objective: To give a comprehensive review of vocabulary instruction.

Method: Vocabulary Football game (p. 73).

Materials: Vocabulary flash cards, materials to draw football field.

ORAL READING

Weekly Objective: To develop oral reading performance while checking comprehension and recall.

Weekly Method: Oral reading session in which: (1) child reads with adult help in sounding out problem words; (2) child and adult read aloud together; or (3) child reads each word aloud immediately after it is spoken by adult. Following oral reading, tutor discusses reading material with the child to assess recall and comprehension.

Materials: Selected high-interest reading material.

Lesson 47

PHONICS

Optional Posttest

If you choose to do a posttest, use the same materials and check list as you used for the diagnostic pretest. Any game can be chosen for administering the test.

VOCABULARY

Optional Posttest

If you choose to do a posttest, use the same materials and check list as you used for the diagnostic pretest. Any game can be chosen for administering the test.

ORAL READING

Optional Posttest

If you choose to do a posttest, use the same materials and check list as you used for the diagnostic pretest.

Lesson 48

Conferences between tutor and child to discuss reading progress. Both plans for continuing the reading program and curing areas of weakness need to be included.

3. Materials for Teaching Reading

THE MOST OBVIOUS ADVANTAGE OF making your own teaching materials is economy. Professional educational supplies are expensive, yet it is doubtful if they are any better than materials carefully made by hand. Further, because schools often use commercial supplies, they become overfamiliar and boring to children.

Handmade materials are also more motivating than commercial products. If the child is involved in making them, it's only natural for him to want to use them correctly. The mutual enthusiasm and pride generated in the making of learning materials will in addition carry over into the learning of reading skills.

Making Phonic Flash Cards

Flash cards for phonics are among the most easily made and valuable supplies for teaching reading. Their main function is to focus children's attention upon the sounds of specific letters. When letters and their sounds are isolated, children find them easier to concentrate on and learn. It takes very little time to mark cards with crayon or felt tip pens. In addition, such an activity helps children visually recognize the letters or words.

Phonic flash cards should cover all the letters of the alphabet plus certain blends of letters. Both vowel and consonant letters and their sounds need to be learned. Practice on vowels must include both simple or soft sounds (ex.= măd) and complex or hard sounds (ex.= māde).

Practice on consonant sounds should include both the individual letters (ex.= the m sound in might) and certain blends of letters (ex.= the bl sound in blue). A full explanation of how to use the flash cards will be given later.

When making flash cards, you may wish to set off the vowel or consonant you are focusing on from the rest of the word rather than just pointing to the letter. A good way to do this is to underscore the specific letter (ex.- l i t, b i t, s ale, t ale, m ale).

The cards should be large enough to be easily read but not so large as to be hard to handle. In regard to the size of the letters and words, there is no specific size, but the letters should be large enough to be easily read by the child or children receiving instruction. In general, very young children need larger letters than older children and it may be wise to experiment with various letter sizes until you find one with which the child is comfortable. Remember though, that the end goal is to have the child eventually be able to read the smaller standard print. For individual letters, 2-inch or 3-inch squares are fine. Use stiff light-colored or white construction paper and cut it into equal-sized pieces. Using a ruler makes it easier to measure the size and draw the lines. For more adult-child involvement, let one measure and draw the lines and the other cut. Printing can begin when the cards have been cut.

It is often best to make only those flash cards needed for each lesson, and then put a tie or rubber band around them when finished. This prevents the possibility of mixing them up and having to sort them all out later. In addition, having the child help make the new cards serves as an introduction to new words and sounds, thereby reinforcing the lesson.

Several sets of flash cards can be made so each set can be used for a different purpose. The following sets need to be included in a complete reading program.

Set 1—Vowels Your first set of flash cards can include the vowel letters a, e, i, o, u with an example of simple and complex sounds. These cards show children the different names for sound of the same letter.

Ex.=	c a p	m a de	p e t	P e te
	t i e	k i ck	t o p	h o pe
		m u d f u se		

54

Examples of words that can be used for teaching vowel letter/sounds can be found in Table 1 of Appendix A (p. 208).

The word examples for sounds should be selected by the instructor but should not usually exceed 6 letters per word. The smaller the number of letters, the easier it is for the child to recognize and remember. When many different words are used to show the same sound, children benefit from both improved vowel recognition and an increased visual vocabulary. This is important because these words form part of his first lessons in sight vocabulary—words which are recognized on sight.

During teaching and while using word examples, however, a subtle learning occurs because all of the letter/sounds in the pronunciation of a word are imprinted on a child's mind even when the emphasis is on vowels so that even the rather static consonant sounds are also gradually becoming absorbed. This is because most all words are spoken as a combination of letter/sounds rather than just a single reproduced letter/sound.

The reading program is started by introducing the vowel letters since the vowel sounds are reinforced during practice with the more numerous and easier to learn consonants. The vowels are more difficult to learn because each vowel has more than one sound (ex.= bat, bar, bake).

The sounds of complex or long vowels can be easy for children to remember if you explain that the sounds name the alphabet letter (ex.= $\bar{a}$ as in bay, $\bar{i}$ as in bite, $\bar{e}$ as in eat, $\bar{o}$ as in toe, u as in use).

The sounds of simple or short vowels are usually harder for students to remember. It is often helpful to suggest that they memorize certain word examples for each vowel sound. Children can then distinguish the various vowel sounds of other words by comparison with their memorized word examples. Tutor and child should decide together whether it is easier to remember vowel sound key words that start with the same consonant or different consonants. Once a child has memorized a set of key words for vowel sounds he will always have a reference when identifying vowel sounds in new words.

Exs.= Vowel Sound Key Words with same beginning consonant:

b <u>a</u> t, b <u>e</u> t, b <u>i</u> t, b <u>o</u> ttom, b <u>u</u> g

Vowel Sound Key Words with different beginning consonants:

r a̱ t, n e̱ t, s i̱ t, l o̱ t, d u̱ g

Many language experts consider the vowel sounds of o͞o, o͝o, ou, oi, and au to be different from the simple or complex vowel sounds. Tutors may wish to show children these vowel combinations and their sounds as the words are encountered or as a separate lesson at the end of the program. These vowel sounds have different spellings.

Exs. = Vowel sound	o͞o	s oo n, n ew
	o͝o	b oo k, p u sh
	ou	p ou t, p ow
	oi	b oi l, t oy
	au	h au l, cl aw, f a ll, s o ng, b ough t, t augh t

Examples of words to be used for teaching all of these vowel letter/sounds can be found in Table 1 of Appendix A (p. 208). Other examples for combinations of vowels and consonants, including the "vowel-r" sounds, can be found in Table 4 of Appendix A (p. 220).

Set 2—Consonants The second set of phonic flash cards can include all the consonant letters of the alphabet. These cards will help the child recognize the names of consonant letters. It's a good idea to make several copies of each letter for later use in phonic games. Individual letters lend themselves to more complex word-making games as well.

Consonant flash cards can be made either by combining capital and lower case letters on one card or by putting them on separate cards. It is sometimes a good idea to have cards made both ways to encourage children to identify and match them up.

Exs.= | B b | | B | | b | | C c | | C | | c |

To obtain word examples for teaching consonant letter/ sounds, see Table 2 in Appendix A (p. 211).

Set 3—Consonant Blends A third set of flash cards should be printed with the consonant blends. Consonant blends are combinations of consonants that produce specific sounds. Such blends often occur at the beginning of words. The consonant blends that commonly occur in words and need to be included in a reading program are bl, br, ch, ck, cl, cr, dl, dr, fl, fr, gl, gr, pl, pr, sc, sh, sk, sl, sm, sn, sp, st, sw, th, tl, tr, tw, wh.

The flash cards can be printed either with the consonant blend by itself or with an example of a word containing that sound. However, it is often an advantage to have both types of cards.

Exs.=

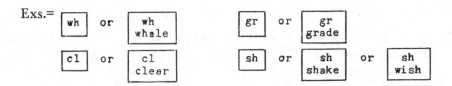

For word examples for teaching the sounds of consonant blends, refer to Table 3 in Appendix A (p. 215).

Set 4—Letter Families and Word Groups This fourth set of flash cards is used with the other three sets. These letter families are frequently combined with initial consonants to make a complete group of words. An example is using the **and** letters to make such groups of words as b **and**, s **and**, l **and**, bl **and**. Such letter families as **and**, **ent**, **ake**, **ain**, **ine**, and **ore** should be included because of their common occurrence in words.

Using this set of cards, complete words can be made through combinations with consonants and consonant blends. This changing of first consonant letters or blends helps children practice their word attack skills and increase their sight vocabulary.

Other letter families and word groups may be found in Table 4 of Appendix A (p. 220).

Set 5—Affixes The fifth set of flash cards consists of common word beginnings or prefixes and word endings or suffixes, which together are called affixes. These flash cards are used to attach to other words. Since affixes occur frequently, it's a good idea for children to become familiar with both their spellings and sounds. Examples of prefixes are re-, non-, un-, dis-, pre-, de-, anti-, mid-, in-, be-, ex-. Examples of suffixes are -ed, -s or -es, -er or -or, -ing,

-able, -less, -like, -y, -ous, -ly, -ful, -ish, -est. Explain how affixes affect word meanings, as re- in replay means to play again, non- in nonsense means no sense, un- as in unhappy means not happy; -ed added to walk makes walked, meaning did walk; er added to walk makes walker, meaning a person who walks. One way to both teach and reinforce the spelling or use of affixes is to make families of root words with either prefixes (ex.= retie, untie, pretie) or suffixes (ex.= worked, working, worker). Other examples of affixes may be added as they are encountered in reading.

For a discussion of studying affixes and a list of the most common ones, see Table 5 in Appendix A (p. 228).

Set 6—Contractions Since contractions do occur in reading material, tutors may wish to include a set of flash cards featuring them. Most contractions are formed from small words which occur frequently so learning contractions and their meanings helps to reinforce children's sight vocabulary of basic words. Examples of the words used in contractions are I, are, am, they, we, have, had, not, could, will, do, can, is, has, you, were, would, he, she, it.

When studying contractions, the child practices sounding out the letters in both of the two words (ex.= we are) and the contraction (ex.= we're), improving his phonic skills and his vocabulary at the same time.

Refer to Appendix A, Table 6 (p. 230) for more material on teaching and making flash cards for contractions.

Making vocabulary flash cards

Flash cards for developing vocabulary have two functions: (1) to familiarize children with words which are commonly used in reading material; and (2) to help children learn words which give them a particularly difficult time during reading.

To make flash cards for the commonly occurring words, use those small words which tend to reappear throughout reading material. Examples of such words are a, the, and, for, is, are, you, am, was, were, be, to, if, by, also, we, they, I, me, an. A list of such words will be found in Table 7, Appendix A (p. 231). Children must make these words part of their sight vocabulary, which means they should be able to recognize them immediately when they see them without sounding them out.

An informal survey of common words can be turned into a game involving both instructor and child. Each takes one sheet of newspaper and circles words which are printed more than once. Write the circled words in a list and count the times each word appears. The child can then transfer words from the list to flash cards, reinforcing both the shape of the word and its spelling in his mind.

Words which a child has difficulty in remembering or pronouncing can be written on flash cards for later use. By pronouncing these words as he writes them, the tutor can help the child become familiar with them and reinforce both his memory and self-confidence.

The making of vocabulary flash cards is a continuous process, since new words need to be constantly introduced to expand children's vocabulary.

Tachistoscopes and reading rate guides

A tachistoscope is a device which allows only one word or a few words to be seen by the reader by covering the words around it. If children become confused by all the words on a page, this tool will help focus their attention on a few words at a time.

Informal tachistoscopes are easily made from index cards or pieces of construction paper from 3 by 5 inches to 5 by 7 inches. Cut a small rectangular window in the card which will reveal the word or words while hiding the rest of the sentence. Decide the size of the window by estimating the size of the wording that is to be read.

Exs.=   Single Word

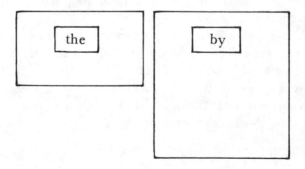

Multiple words

Reading rate guides are devices to control and help increase the speed at which a child reads. A tachistoscope can be moved along the line of type, a ruler or sheet of paper can be laid under the lines and moved downward, or a pointer can indicate words as fast as the child can read without stress. It is best to start slowly and increase the speed of exposure gradually. Remember that good readers read phrases rather than single words.

Inexpensive textbook, the newspaper

Newspapers are an excellent but often overlooked source of reading material. Since they are oriented to a mass readership, their vocabulary must be readable by most people. Newspapers generally contain a wide variety of subjects and interest levels. For a small price, tutors have a form of reading material which changes daily and is cheap enough to cut up for games.

Newspaper cartoons and comic strips are a main attraction for children. First the artwork catches their attention and then they wonder what the characters are saying. They are entertained while they practice their word attack skills.

A good reading exercise is prepared by taking a group of cartoon strips, cutting out each frame separately, and mixing them up. The child sorts the frames into matching cartoon strips and arranges them in the appropriate order. He not only follows the picture clues but must also read in order to put the strips back together so they make sense.

Another good reading activity with cartoons is to have children write their own dialogue or captions for the pictures in the cartoon strip and read them aloud. This activity requires them to recognize a sequence of events and then express themselves by writing an appropriate dialogue. This exercise reinforces the importance of both the child's choice of words and their meanings.

This can be revised to make still another reading exercise. Have children read the dialogue in a cartoon strip and then draw a different set of pictures to accompany it. To make sense, children must read the dialogue carefully and think about how they can relate it to a set of illustrations.

Newspaper want ad sections lend themselves to a variety of reading games. For example, in a game called Fox Hunt, the child is to find a "fox" such as a horse or a guitar. He must skim-read the ads until he finds the horse under "Livestock" and the guitar under "Musical Merchandise."

Advice columns such as Ann Landers are very interesting to older children, since they deal with real-life problems. By reading the questions and answers, children practice and improve their reading skills. Children can be impressed by the value of reading by submitting a letter to such a column and receiving a reply.

Sports sections of the newspaper interest both boys and girls who enjoy the active life. With increasing coverage begin given to women athletes, they can find interesting articles on sportswomen as well as sportsmen. If you can find what sports the child enjoys, you can focus his reading activity in that direction. Reading can be reinforced by adult and child practicing together those skills involved in the sport, like playing catch for baseball or practicing casting for fishing. Children can also be encouraged to check out library books on their favorite sports.

Finally, single words or whole sentences can be cut out of the paper for use in a variety of reading activities. The variations in type size allow children to use large letters for alphabetical arrangements. Words in smaller type can be used in exercises like these:

1. Circle words starting with the letter ___ (any letter or combination of letters).
2. Draw a box around words ending in ___ (any letter or combination of letters).
3. Make ___ sentences (any number) with words that are cut out of the paper.
4. List ___ words (any number) that you don't know and use a dictionary to define them.
5. See if you can find ___ (a certain word) in ___ minutes.
6. Write a new headline for a newspaper story.

7. Make a list of ___ (certain types of words) by pasting letters and words cut from the newspaper.
8. Fill in sentences (given) with words from the newspaper.
9. Find words in the paper that rhyme with ___ .

These activities are only samples of reading tasks that can be supplied by newspapers or any other inexpensive reading material. The limit of activities depends only upon the tutor's imagination and desire to use them.

The public library

As an additional resource for reading material, the public library is available to all. Libraries offer a broad range of reading material to help meet the needs and abilities of most children.

Instructors can utilize the library by having children regularly check out books on their favorite subjects. Generally, libraries have a special section for children's books. If you give the librarians the age and grade level of the child, then they will often be able to recommend a certain group of books. These can form the starting point to find other books geared to the child's particular reading level or ability.

The strength of the public library lies in the large number of books on a variety of subjects. For teaching reading, however, its value lies mainly in offering stories on topics in which children have an interest. Unlike homemade or throw-away publications, books from the library cannot be cut up, drawn on, or written in. While the act of checking out books can help instill the habit of reading in children, the library generally offers recreational reading and not instructional material for reading development.

4. Reading Games and Activities

INCLUDING A WIDE VARIETY OF GAMES and activities in the reading program aids concentration, strengthens interest, reinforces skills, and motivates learning. The reasons for using games for teaching have been discussed, but basically they make it fun (for both instructor and child) to do the work necessary to make the reading program a success.

In the following pages, the purpose, materials and procedure are given for each game along with descriptions of those suggested activities named in the weekly reading program plans in unit 2. These categories are included:

(1) Games to strengthen phonic skills
(2) Games to develop vocabulary
(3) Written exercises and additional activities to reinforce basics and check comprehension and recall

Some of the games may be played by a child alone, many with the tutor and many with other children, as indicated at the end of each description. The instructor may participate as a player or as an observer or umpire, depending upon the situation and number of children involved.

Although the games are designed to implement either phonics or vocabulary work, many of them can be used for either purpose by substituting types of flash cards and changing the game emphasis. In fact, some of the games can be used to teach arithmetic facts as well, as described in Section 3.

By following a similar pattern, you will be able to adapt other games the children already know and enjoy for similar teaching purposes.

While individual interests and preferences vary, the games described in the following pages are suitable for use with children of elementary, junior high and high school grades (except such a game as "Train" for young children). Suitability of the games for children of different ages doesn't constitute a problem simply because it is a relatively easy matter to read the games or even try them out to see if both the tutor and children enjoy them as learning aids. Furthermore, the level of difficulty involved in the games can be easily increased by simply challenging the students with longer and harder vocabulary words.

Phonic Games

GAME—Phonic Buzz

PURPOSE—To practice rapid discrimination between letter/sounds.

MATERIALS—Vocabulary or phonic flash cards.

PLAYERS—Tutor and child, two children, or group of children.

PROCEDURE—Explain to the player or players that different word flash cards will be shown at a rapid pace. They are to pronounce the word unless they see a "Buzz," which is a word that includes any letter that the tutor or player who is "It" designates. When a child identifies a buzz word, he says "Buzz!" instead of pronouncing the word. Played in a group, children identify the flash cards in rotation, and the player who misses drops out. With two players, one shows the cards until the other misses, then they change roles. The tutor can flash cards to the child until he goes through the pack with no misses. Try to speed up the flash time because as the pace quickens the game becomes more fun and educationally more valuable.

A simpler version is to use letter flash cards rather than words. Players are to name the letter except when it is a "Buzz."

Exs.= Buzz is ā   Buzz is ā

bell Player says "bell"   t   Player says "t"

sit   Player says "sit"   ā   Player says "buzz"

ate   Player says "buzz"   k   Player says "k"

too   Player says "too"   ă   Player says "ă"
                                     (using correct sound)

64

GAME—Sound Doctor

PURPOSE—To help with the remediation of deficient phonic skills.

MATERIALS—Flash cards, a box labeled "Hospital" and possibly a badge for each doctor.

PLAYERS—Tutor and child, or group of children.

PROCEDURE—Start with a set of flash cards. Show each card to the child for him to pronounce one at a time. When the player makes a mistake, tell him this card is "sick" and needs to go to the hospital to get well. Upon finishing the stack of cards, it's time to go to the hospital to treat the sick cards. Cards are cured when the child doctor can answer phonic questions about the card correctly. Depending on your feelings toward rewards, you can give the doctor candy or some other reward as medicine to help get that card off the sick list.

GAME—Wise Old Owl

PURPOSE—To help children recognize and work on specific phonic disabilities.

MATERIALS—Sets of phonic flash cards, a magazine picture or handmade drawing of an owl wearing glasses and his house covered with letters.

PLAYERS—Tutor and child, or group of children.

PROCEDURE—Run through the various sets of flash cards, displaying one card at a time to the player. Each time a child makes a mistake in identification, tell him that this card is in trouble and should go to the Wise Old Owl's house for help. After the troublesome cards have been isolated, tell the child the owl has been working with the words and now it's time for the team to work with them. Many younger children enjoy this game of pretend.

GAME—Phonic Home-Run Derby and Phonic Baseball

PURPOSE—To increase the speed of phonic recognition.

MATERIALS—Flash cards, materials to draw a baseball diamond.

PLAYERS—Tutor and child, or group of children.

PROCEDURE—Draw a baseball diamond on paper or on a chalkboard, marking each base inside the field and 16 steps on the outside, 4 to a base.

Each player draws a cartoon baseball player and names him. The game begins with one player as the pitcher who shows the flash cards. The other player is the hitter who must answer the phonic question. The batter must answer correctly and promptly to move one step. When he has answered 16 questions correctly, he crosses home plate for a home run. When a player misses, he is thrown out and becomes the pitcher.

The Phonic Baseball variation of this game is played using the regular rules of baseball with two teams, three outs to an inning, and so on. Correct answers to 4 questions can be one base hit.

GAME—Phonic Match-up

PURPOSE—To identify letters and their sounds in words.

MATERIALS—Vocabulary flash cards.

PLAYERS—Tutor with child, child alone, or group of children.

PROCEDURE—Each game can vary with an emphasis on different phonic skills. Make or choose cards with words that can be paired with another having the same beginning, ending, or vowel letters and sounds, 16 to 20 of them. Turn the cards over, shuffle them, and lay out in rows with backs up. Each player in turn flips over 2 cards. If they are not a match, he turns them down and loses his turn. If the two cards are a match and he can identify the required letters and sounds, he keeps the cards and takes another turn. The player with the most cards wins.

GAME—Train

PURPOSE—To improve the speed of recognition.

MATERIALS—Phonic flash cards.

PLAYERS—Tutor and child, or group of children.

PROCEDURE—Review the letters and sounds on the flash cards with the child or children until they are familiar with them. Then explain how a train begins slowly chugging and gradually picks up speed. Proceed to show the cards one at a time, gradually speeding up the exposure time to imitate the train increasing its speed. Continue until the speed is too fast and then pretend to pull the cord and let the child mimic the sound of the train whistle.

GAME—Phonic Relay

PURPOSE—To speed recognition of various combinations of initial consonants.

MATERIALS—Phonic flash cards of initial consonants and letter families.

PLAYERS—Tutor and child, or group of children.

PROCEDURE—Players line up facing the flash-card holder 10 to 15 feet away. One card at a time is shown. The first player who answers the phonic question correctly—or players, if they answer the question at the same time—takes one step forward. The first player to reach the leader wins.

GAME—Banker

PURPOSE—To associate phonic pronunciation with specific words.

MATERIALS—Phonic and vocabulary flash cards.

PLAYERS—Tutor and child, or group of children.

PROCEDURE—The bank is a pile of vocabulary flash cards placed face down and a large group of alphabet cards placed face up. The first player picks up a card from the vocabulary cards. He takes out a loan from the bank of alphabet letters and uses the letters to sound out and spell the word he drew. Each player who successfully sounds out and spells a word keeps it and his loan is cancelled. The winner is the player with the most cards or assets at the end of the game.

67

GAME—Phonic Tic-Tac-Toe

PURPOSE—To practice distinguishing between letters and their sounds.

MATERIALS—Phonic flash cards, paper and pencils.

PLAYERS—Tutor and child, or two children.

PROCEDURE—The two players draw the tic-tac-toe grid

and choose any letter or symbol for marking the spaces. Each player has a set of phonic flash cards. The first player asks the other a question about the beginning consonant sound, vowel sound or ending consonant sound. If the opponent answers correctly, he marks his symbol in any of the spaces. If the opponent misses, the player asking the question makes his mark. The first player whose symbols form a straight line of three horizontally, vertically or diagonally wins.

GAME—Horse Race

PURPOSE—To study and review word attack skills.

MATERIALS—Vocabulary flash cards, a small bell or equivalent.

PLAYERS—Tutor and child, or two children.

PROCEDURE—Players form a race track by lining up blank cards end to end, with a "Start" card and a "Finish" card. Then they each draw a horse, color him if they want, and name him. The flash cards are placed in a stack face down, and horses are placed on Start. At the starting signal (a bell or pencil tapped on a glass), one player takes a card and asks his opponent to identify the beginning consonant, vowel sound, or ending consonant sound. If the other player answers correctly, he moves his horse one card toward the finish. If he misses, his horse cannot move. It is then the second player's turn to take a card and proceed to ask a question and so on. The winner, the owner of the first horse to reach the finish line, gets to ring the "winner's bell."

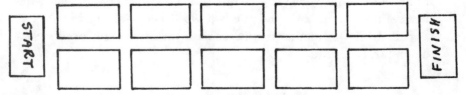

GAME—Phonic 8-Card

PURPOSE—To reinforce visual recognition of vowels.

MATERIALS—Phonic and vocabulary cards.

PLAYERS—Tutor and child, or group of children.

PROCEDURE—Shuffle the cards and deal out 8 cards to each player. Set the rest of the deck of flash cards face down, turn the top card up and lay it to one side. The turned-up card serves to start the game, the object of which is for each player to try to discard all his cards before the other players do. To discard, players must hold a card which contains one of the vowels on the turned-up card. If the player does not have such a card, he must draw one from the deck. Discards are placed face up on the pile started by the first turned-up card, so the next player must lay down a card containing one of the vowels of the latest discard. The vowels required for playing frequently change with each turn.

A variation is that a player can play a card if it contains any of the consonant letters on the turned-up card.

GAME—Phonic Question-Answer

PURPOSE—To increase phonic recognition.

MATERIALS—Phonic and vocabulary flash cards.

PLAYERS—Tutor and child, or two children.

PROCEDURE—Each player takes an equal number of flash cards and turns them face down. One player takes a card and asks his opponent a phonic question about the beginning consonant, vowel sounds, or ending consonant. If the opponent answers correctly, he takes the card. If the opponent answers incorrectly, the player keeps his card. When each player has gone through his stack of cards, he counts his total cards. The player with the largest number if the winner.

GAME—Sound-A-Word

PURPOSE—To strengthen phonic skills.

MATERIALS—Large quantity of alphabet flash cards.

PLAYERS—Tutor and child, or group of children.

PROCEDURE—The alphabet cards are placed face up on the table. The first player spells a word with them, which can be a word he knows or one he copies from a newspaper or other printed material. To keep his word on the table, he must defend it by correctly answering a question from his opponent about the word's beginning consonant sound, vowel sound, or ending consonant sound. The next player now spells a word, building on one of the letters of the first word, and answers a phonic question about it. The winner is the player who has the most words on the table at the end of the game.

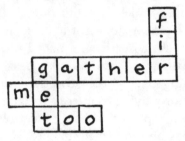

GAME—Four Across

PURPOSE—To practice auditory and visual letter/sound associations.

MATERIALS—Phonic flash cards of vowels, consonants, and blends; game cards and objects to use as markers.

PLAYERS—Tutor and child, or group of children.

PROCEDURE—Make game cards by dividing a 4" by 4", 6" by 6" or 8" by 8" sheet of paper into 16 squares and marking the squares with vowels, consonants, and consonant blends at random. Each player takes a card and place markers such as pennies, buttons, or anything suitable, even pieces of paper cut to the correct size. Explain that when players hear and see a phonic flash card, they are to check their game card and if they find the letter or blend there, place a marker on that square. The first player to get four markers in a row horizontally, vertically, or diagonally calls our "Four Across!" The caller turns up the phonic flash cards one at a time, pronounces it with a word example (ex.= p as in pet), and puts it down face up where it can be seen by all the players. After a player calls "Four Across," his markers are

70

checked with the turned-up flash cards. When his game card is validated, the winning player becomes the caller for the next game.

a	ch	e	h
bl	p	dr	K
n	g	y	X
z	m	c	o

GAME—Spin-A-Letter/Sound

PURPOSE—To practice combining the letter/sounds of consonants with vowels and reinforce dictionary usage.

MATERIALS—Dictionary, paper and pencils, homemade spin chart.

PLAYERS—Child alone, tutor and child or group of children.

PROCEDURE—Make a spin chart as shown below, with a paper spinner fastened at the circles' center with a pin, thumbtack, or paper fastener. Each player spins the arrow and makes a word with the consonant blend and vowel on which it stops (ex.= arrow stops on **pl** and **a**, word can be **play**). If the player can write and pronounce his word correctly, he receives one point. If he can't spell the word, he has two to four minutes to look up its spelling in the dictionary. If he still can't spell it, he gets no point. Each word can be used only once by any player. The game ends when the players can no longer think of examples. The winner has the most words on his list and therefore the most points.

Be sure children know how to use a dictionary before you start, and give several examples of small words to look up.

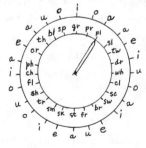

GAME—Phonic Play-A-Card

PURPOSE—To strengthen and reinforce basic phonic skills.

MATERIALS—Phonic flash cards of alphabet letters.

PLAYERS—Tutor and child, or group of children.

PROCEDURE—The deck of flash cards are shuffled and dealt out 7 cards to a player, the remaining cards placed in a stack face down. The object is to lay down all your cards before the other players do. To lay down cards, they must be (1) in sets of 3 (ex.= a, a, a) or 4 (ex.= b, b, b, b), (2) in words of 3 or 4 letters (ex.= sit or bake), or (3) both. The first player takes a card from the face-down stack of cards. If he has any sets or words, he puts the cards down face up in front of him. Whether he can lay down cards or not, he must now discard a card from his hand, putting it face up beside the stack. The next player can pick up the discard or choose to take the top card from the deck. He then in turn lays cards down if he can, and discards. Only the top card in the discard pile can ever be played. The winner is the player who first lays down all his cards.

Vocabulary Games

GAME—Vocabulary Tic-Tac-Toe

PURPOSE—To reinforce word meaning.

MATERIALS—Vocabulary flash cards, paper and pencils.

PLAYERS—Tutor and child, or two children.

PROCEDURE—Flash cards are divided into two piles and a Tic-Tac-Toe grid is drawn. The game starts by one player showing the other a flash card. The opponent must correctly identify the word and its meaning to have the opportunity to mark his symbol in one of the nine spaces. If he can't identify the word and its meaning, he loses his turn. The second player now shows a card, and his opponent must correctly identify and define the word to make his mark in one of the remaining spaces. The winner is the first player to put three of his marks in a straight line vertically, horizontally, or diagonally.

GAME—Secret Word

PURPOSE—To associate relationships between words and meanings.

MATERIAL—Vocabulary flash cards.

PLAYERS—Tutor and child, or two children.

PROCEDURE—The vocabulary cards are shuffled and placed face down in a pile. The first player picks up the top card, which gives him the secret word. He then gives another word as a clue to enable the other player to guess the word. If he cannot guess, another clue is given. (Ex.= Secret word is **puppy**, first clue **dog**, second clue **little**.) Up to 7 clues are given, until the other player guesses correctly or the secret is revealed. Keep score by giving 7 points for a word guessed correctly on the first clue, 6 for the second clue, and so on. When the word has been revealed, it is often helpful to explain to the child the relationship between the secret word and the clue words, this helps to develop both his vocabulary and reasoning ability.

GAME—Connect-A-Word

PURPOSE—To practice spelling words and reinforce their meanings.

MATERIALS—Alphabet flash cards (several sets), checkerboard.

PLAYERS—Tutor and child, or group of children.

PROCEDURE—Spread out the alphabet letters and explain that they are used to make or connect words on the board. The game can have 2 variations: (1) all words must connect with starters which have been placed on the board or other words already on it, or (2) a word can be placed anywhere but cannot touch another word or go outside the board boundaries. The object in both variations is to use up as many letters as possible and fill up most of the space on the board. As the children become more familiar with the game, the rules can gradually be made more complex. Starting simple keeps the children's interest and makes them feel successful.

GAME—Vocabulary Football

PURPOSE—To stimulate vocabulary development.

MATERIALS—Vocabulary flash cards, materials to draw football field and players.

PLAYERS—Tutor and child, or two children.

PROCEDURE—The football field is drawn and each player draws a football player to represent a team. A coin is flipped to see which player will be on defense or offense, and which side of the field each will take. The game begins with the offensive player on his 20-yard line. The defensive player now shows him a card from a large stack of face-down vocabulary flash cards. The offensive player must choose to call either a run or a pass. A run means he will correctly identify and pronounce the word for an advance of 3 yards; a pass means he will correctly identify and define the word for a gain of 6 yards. If the offensive player's "run" or "pass" answer is incorrect, he is thrown for a loss and moves back 3 or 6 yards. When he has made his fourth mistake, he becomes the defensive player and the other player the offense. He starts on his 20-yard line and plays as above. A touchdown is scored when the offensive player crosses his opponent's goal line. The winner is the team with either the first touchdown or the highest number of touchdowns.

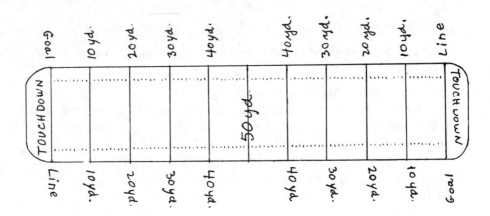

GAME—Build-A-Word

PURPOSE—To improve sight vocabulary and the recall of word meanings.

MATERIALS—Alphabet letter phonic flash cards.

PLAYERS—Tutor and child, or group of children.

PROCEDURE—Spread the alphabet letters out on the table face up. The first player chooses a single letter. His opponent adds letters to spell a word and gives the correct definition. Each letter in the correctly spelled word counts 1 point, and if the definition is correct the score is doubled. The score is recorded and the turn passes to the next player.

GAME—Identification

PURPOSE—To help develop recall of newly introduced vocabulary words.

MATERIALS—Vocabulary flash cards, paper and pencils.

PLAYERS—Tutor and child, or group of children.

PROCEDURE—Review the flash cards (and the word meanings). Shuffle the pack and place it face down. The game begins by one player taking the top card, looking at it so no one else can see it, then drawing a number of small rectangles or boxes to represent the number of letters in the word (ex.- **read** would be represented by ☐ ☐ ☐ ☐). He flashes the card to the next player for a given number of seconds (depending upon the age or ability of the child), who remembers all the letters he can, writing them in the correct boxes. Track is kept of the number of flashes he needs to identify the word. He now takes the next flash card, draws the correct number of boxes, and flashes the card to the next player. The player with the least total number of flashes is the winner.

A variation is called Stickman, where a part of a body is drawn for each flash card needed before the word is correctly identified. The object is to identify the word before the body is fully drawn. The drawing proceeds in the following manner to allow for 6 attempts.

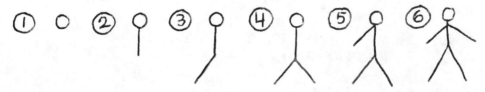

75

Note: Such things as hands, feet and hair can be added to the stickman for extra attempts.

GAME—Secret Agent

PURPOSE—To practice organizing letters into words and words into sentences.

MATERIALS—Several sets of alphabet flash cards with each letter numbered as shown, paper, pencils, a homemade secret agent badge.

Ex.=

Aa	Bb	Cc	Dd
1	2	3	4

PLAYERS—Tutor and child, or group of children.

PROCEDURE—The cards are laid out in rows face up and in a sequential order of numbers. Each player writes a secret message by using the numbers instead of the letters to spell out words. Spaces between the numbers indicate the end of a code word and the beginning of the next. Messages are exchanged and deciphered, then read out loud.

Many variations of this code can be formed by changing the number for each letter.

Example of a number-alphabet code

Aa	Bb	Cc	Dd	Ee	Ff	Gg	Hh	Ii	Jj	Kk	Ll	Mm
1	2	3	4	5	6	7	8	9	10	11	12	13

Nn	Oo	Pp	Qq	Rr	Ss	Tt	Uu	Vv	Ww	Xx	Yy	Zz
14	15	16	17	18	19	20	21	22	23	24	25	26

Example of a coded message

3, 1, 14   25, 15, 21
  CAN   YOU

21, 14, 4, 5, 18, 19, 20, 1, 14, 4
        UNDERSTAND

20, 8, 9, 19, ?
  THIS?

GAME—Card Conversation

PURPOSE—To practice using words in the context of a sentence.

MATERIALS—Vocabulary flash cards.

PLAYERS—Tutor and child, or group of children.

PROCEDURE—The object of the game is to talk to each other using the flash cards. Spread the cards out so they're easy to see. The first person chooses cards that ask a question and places them in a row. The next player answers with his selection of cards. (Ex.= How are you ? Player 2 answers, I am fine .) Continue the question-answer pattern as long as there are words, then switch roles of questioner and answerer. Children often enjoy silly questions like, "Have you ever had a cat for lunch?" and funny answers.

A variation of this game that is easier for some children consists of simply taking turns to make a sentence using the flash cards. Keep on making sentences as long as you can.

GAME—Vocabulary Match-up

PURPOSE—To improve visual recognition of words.

MATERIALS—Vocabulary flash cards.

PLAYERS—Child alone, tutor and child, or two children.

PROCEDURE—Choose 10 to 16 words and make two cards for each word. Shuffle the pack and spread them out in rows face down. The first player turns up two cards, leaving them in place. If the words don't match, both cards are turned back over and it is the other player's turn. If a player does get a match, he keeps those cards and turns up two more, one at a time. If he turns up a card and remembers where he has seen its matching card, he can then turn it up. The winner is the player with the most cards when all have been matched. Change the flash cards to expose the players to more vocabulary words.

GAME—Big Word—Little Word

PURPOSE—To encourage children to use and develop their vocabulary.

MATERIALS—Paper, pencils, dictionary.

PLAYERS—Child alone, tutor and child, group of children.

PROCEDURE—The object of this game is for the players to make as many short words as they can from the letters of a long word. Each child takes a pencil and piece of paper, a word is given and a time limit from 5 to 15 minutes is set, depending upon the ability of the child or children. A player may use the dictionary to check his words. Any player may challenge another player's words and look them up in the dictionary. If a word is misspelled, it is disqualified and does not count. The winner is the player with the most words on his list when the time is up. The tutor may wish to discuss the meanings of words from each child's list.

Ex.=

Given word: PROBABLE

rob	able	ape	bop	a	bale
ale	babe	pale	lap	bar	lab
rap	pole	lop	are	Bob	bore
lore	ear	pare	bare	boar	bole
leap	lope	reap	pal	rope	bear

GAME—Letter-Word

PURPOSE—To expand word families sharing similar letter/sounds and encourage dictionary use.

MATERIALS—Blank flash cards, pencils, dictionary.

PLAYERS—Tutor and child, or pair of children.

PROCEDURE—One player begins by designating a beginning letter, vowel, or ending letter for the words to be used in the game (ex.= "We're going to make words starting with s"). The second player writes down an example (ex.= sand). Then the first player also gives a word example (ex.= sale). The players alternate until one can't think of another example. The winner is the one who gave the last example, receiving one point for each of his words. The loser chooses a new rule for making words. A dictionary can be used to challenge the spelling of a word. If it is misspelled, the player must give another example or lose the game. Five games are played to make a series. The series winner is the player with the highest total score.

GAME—Spin-A-Word

PURPOSE—To work on the context meaning of words.

MATERIALS—Paper, pencils, homemade spin chart.

PLAYERS—Tutor and child, or group of children.

PROCEDURE—Make a spin chart as shown below, using stiff paper and a spinner tacked to the circle center. The letters on the outside of the circle can be any that you are studying—vowels, consonants, consonant blends, consonant and vowel combinations, word families, or any combination of these. To play, each player in turn spins the arrow with his finger. When the arrow stops, he gives a word example using the letter or letters pointed to and uses it correctly in a sentence. For each correct answer, the player writes his word on his score sheet. Each word counts one point. The winner is the player with the most points after 20 spins apiece.

A variation of this game has the player giving a definition of the word rather than using it in a sentence.

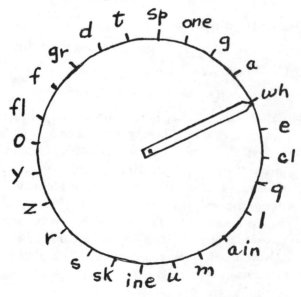

GAME—Read-See-Do

PURPOSE—To give concrete experiences to word definitions, following directions and the activity of reading.

MATERIALS—Vocabulary flash cards (nouns) and instruction cards (see examples).

PLAYERS—Tutor and child, or group of children.

PROCEDURE—Make two sets of flash cards, one with nouns (ex.= fish, bell, tree, dog) and the other with instructions for some sort of action (ex.= Act like a _____, Sound like a _____, Look like a _____, Move like a _____). The game begins with both stacks shuffled and set face down. The first player draws an instruction card, reads the directions aloud and shows it to the other players. He draws a noun card from the second stack and reads that aloud. He then follows the directions (ex.= acts like a frog). The next player draws his two cards and so on. Children enjoy this game and love to help look up strange nouns to be acted out.

A variation can be played with only one stack of cards that contain only action verbs (ex.= wiggle, move, smile, lift, bow, kneel, lay, bend, trot, run, scratch, jump, hug, shake, crawl, squeeze). Players take turns picking up a card, reading it silently, and acting it out for the others to guess.

GAME—Vocabulary Challenge

PURPOSE—To stimulate the recall of words and their meanings.

MATERIALS—Vocabulary flash cards.

PLAYERS—Tutor and child, or pair of children.

PROCEDURE—Prior to the game, tutors may introduce new words and their meanings. Two players divide the flash cards equally. The first player picks a card from his stack and shows it to the opponent. If the opponent correctly identifies the word and its meaning, he takes the card. If he does not identify it correctly, the player who showed the card keeps it. Players alternate in showing cards to each other. The winner is determined in one of two ways: (1) a player wins if he has more cards in his stack after all the cards have been displayed once; or (2) a player wins when he has all the cards.

Written Exercises and Additional Activities

These exercises and activities will be most useful when they are coordinated with the phonic or vocabulary lessons. The tutor who follows the sample lessons in this book can reinforce the skills which are taught that day with a related exercise or activity. After any written exercise, it is a good idea for the tutor to go over the paper with the child. Errors should be carefully explained so that the child will better understand his mistakes. The activities are designed to combine fun with a learning experience.

WRITTEN EXERCISE—Listing Words

DESCRIPTION—Write at the top of a sheet of paper some beginning consonants, beginning consonant blends, simple or soft vowels, complex or long vowels, ending consonant sounds, or ending consonant blends. Ask children to list underneath the letter or letters words he finds in a book or newspaper that are examples of their letter/sounds. This exercise improves recognition of the consonant and vowel sounds and helps increase phonic skills.

Ex.= Beginning consonants

b	l	s
bat	like	sat
below	love	seek

Beginning consonant blends

bl	sh	gr
blast	show	grow
blow	shave	grass

Simple or soft vowel sounds

a	e	i	o	u
bat	bell	sit	hot	hut
fat	met	sizzle	lot	but

Complex or long vowel sounds

a	e	i	o	u
bake	keep	bite	go	mule
cave	Peter	sight	blow	fuse

81

Ending consonant sounds

<u>r</u>	<u>n</u>	<u>s</u>
bea<u>r</u>	Be<u>n</u>	ba<u>ss</u>
si<u>r</u>	si<u>n</u>	me<u>ss</u>

Ending consonant blends

<u>sh</u>	t<u>ch</u>	<u>bl</u>
ca<u>sh</u>	cat<u>ch</u>	ab<u>le</u>
me<u>sh</u>	hat<u>ch</u>	tab<u>le</u>

WRITTEN EXERCISE—Rhyming

DESCRIPTION—Explain that words which rhyme always have similar sounds and give a few examples (cake, make, bake, take, lake). Start by writing some rhyming couplets while leaving off the rhyming word, then giving a list of the rhymes out of order. Have a child first read the sentences and then each of the possible answers in the boxes. When he listens to the sounds as he speaks the words, he will find it easier to find the rhyming word. After the children become more used to rhyming, omit the list of rhymes. These exercises will reinforce vocabulary meaning and word attack skills.

Ex.=   I had a flying **cat**
      That chased a flying _____.

tea

We caught a fish in a **lake**
      Which we were eager to _____.

bat

Once I saw a **bee**
      That fell into my _____.

pail

I carried a football on my **bike**
      While I practiced saying _____.

bake

When we tripped over the **nail**
      We spilled our _____.

hike

WRITTEN EXERCISE—Multiple Choice

DESCRIPTION—Make up some multiple choice questions that deal either with subjects familiar to the children or with material that has just been covered in reading. Explain to children that they are to read the question and circle the answer they choose. This exercise tests their degree of understanding and requires them to use their reasoning ability to differentiate between various possible answers. While children can guess the right answer, those who consistently do well generally are not guessing. To compensate for the possibility of guessing, tutors can ask children why they chose a particular answer.

Ex.= Which is a dog?

(a. collie)　　　b. hammer　　　c. can

Name a tool made out of metal.

a. balloon　　　b. cream　　　(c. saw)

A type of food often used for dessert is:

a. meat　　　(b. ice cream)　　　c. corn

WRITTEN EXERCISE—Fill In Blanks

DESCRIPTION—Write sentences that deal with subjects familiar to children or about details from a story they have read but leave a blank for one of the important words in the sentence. Furnish a list of the omitted words out of order. Explain to children that they are to choose the correct word and write it in the blank spot for each sentence. Emphasize that the sentences must make sense when the word is inserted. This exercise gives children practice in decoding words, understanding sentence meaning and using their reasoning. If the questions deal with a previously read story, the exercise helps develop children's recall and checks their comprehension.

Ex.= run　　　dog　　　Candy　　　rain

_____ tastes good.

Do you like to _____ in a race?

A lot of _____ fell from the clouds.

Is your _____ a good pet?

WRITTEN EXERCISE—True & False

DESCRIPTION—Write sentences about subjects that children

know about or use material from a story they have read, but deliberately making some of them wrong. Tell children that they must read the sentences, decide if they are true or false, then mark "T" for true and "F" for false in the blank place in front of the statements. Children thereby practice their reading while also exercising their memories and reasoning powers. With books closed, this is a simple and quick test for measuring comprehension but rather unreliable because children have a 50-50 chance of guessing the right answer and it may be testing general knowledge or reasoning ability rather than recall. Reliability can be improved by letting children look up the story and write down the page number where they find the answer.

Ex.= F   Tigers fly.   F   Tigers fly (p. 48)

       T   Tigers eat meat.   T   Tigers eat meat. (p. 61)

WRITTEN EXERCISE—Matching

DESCRIPTION—For this exercise, write questions and statements about vocabulary words or details of stories the child has read and then write short answers after them in the wrong order. Children are to draw a line from the question or statement to the word or phrase that gives the correct answer. The exercise requires children to discriminate between a number of words and their meanings, and to use logic and recall. It works well both as reinforcement of earlier learned vocabulary words and as a comprehension check of story details.

Ex.= Vocabulary

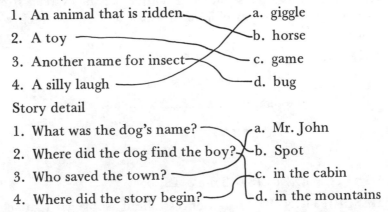

1. An animal that is ridden   a. giggle
2. A toy   b. horse
3. Another name for insect   c. game
4. A silly laugh   d. bug

Story detail

1. What was the dog's name?   a. Mr. John
2. Where did the dog find the boy? b. Spot
3. Who saved the town?   c. in the cabin
4. Where did the story begin?   d. in the mountains

WRITTEN EXERCISE—Write In Answers

DESCRIPTION—Questions that call for short, factual answers give children practice in reading, reasoning out what answers are wanted and recalling them or looking them up, and in writing answers. Asking questions about stories they have read will exercise their powers of recall, although if you are evaluating this remember that since there are no clues this is the most difficult way to test it. There's no harm in allowing children to check the printed material to answer questions because this gives them experience in skim reading and picking out relevant facts.

Ex.= 1. Who wrote the story?

2. How many people joined the actor's group?

3. Where was the opening scene located?

WRITTEN EXERCISE—Comprehension Questions

DESCRIPTION—Asking children questions about their reading will not only encourage them to pay more attention to details when they read but also helps them reflect on the story later. Furthermore, it helps children gain a deeper appreciation for reading. You may wish to review the discussion of the three levels of comprehension questions in the Diagnostic unit (p. 9), but remember that this is an *exercise,* not a test. Help children find the answers, discuss them, and when the answer is a matter of opinion, give the child's view every respect. Remember, the answer can also give you new insight into the thoughts and feelings of the child.

Ex.= 1. Who was the main character and what did he do in the story?
2. Tell what part of the story you liked best and why.
3. Give the order of events in the story.
4. Tell how you shared any feelings or thoughts with one of the characters.
5. How was this character like you or unlike you?
6. Write six questions (any number) about the story.
7. Have you read another story which this one reminds you of? Tell why.
8. Do you think this was a "true" or "make believe" story? Why?

9. If you had been one of the people in this story, would you have acted the same way?
10. Tell why you think the author chose this particular story title.
11. What do you think happened to one of the characters after the story ended?

ACTIVITY—Crossword Puzzle

DESCRIPTION—Construct a crossword puzzle by writing any word horizontally in squares, building vertically from it and so on, crossing between two verticals or two horizontal words when you can. Number the blocks and write brief definitions. Transfer the block patterns and clues to a clean sheet of paper for children to work. Point out that the number of blocks indicates how many letters are in the answer and that the first letter of the answer starts in the square which has the same number as the clue question. This activity serves to reinforce vocabulary development. It is also useful for children to help make crossword puzzles for someone else to do, which they often enjoy very much.

Ex.=

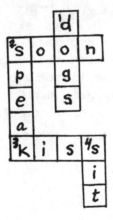

Clues

Across

2. A word meaning immediately
3. A sign of affection and love

Down

1. Plural of dog
2. To talk
4. What you do on a chair

86

ACTIVITY—Cartoons

DESCRIPTION—After reading a cartoon strip or a story, suggest that it would be fun to make a cartoon. Take a large piece of paper (about 18" by 12") and divide it into quarters with a ruler and pencil, making four frames. Number each frame and explain that the numbers will guide the readers.

Ex.=

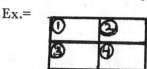

Show the child how to illustrate character's speaking by drawing an oval or balloon which points to the character's mouth and contains the spoken words. Next show how to illustrate character's thoughts instead of spoken words with separate ovals diminishing in size leading to the character's head.

Speech

Thought

Now have the child make up characters or choose his favorites and discuss what he will have happen in the frames. He may go ahead and draw and color if he chooses. How much direction you should give the child depends on his abilities and desires. Sometimes children will wish to use more pages to make the equivalent of a comic book.

ACTIVITY—Vocabulary Word Puzzles

DESCRIPTION—These are the puzzles that consist of a solid block of letters in which words reading horizontally, vertically and diagonally can be found and circled. They can be as large as desired and organized according to types of words you have been studying or subjects in which the child is particularly interested, such as animals, sports, names, colors, and so on.

Use graph paper or draw verticals on lined paper; select your words and write them in at different angles. (For children learning to read or with reading difficulties, don't have words read backwards since they must not be confused in learning to read left to right.) Fill in the rest of the squares with any combination of letters. You may at first wish to give the words in the puzzle, later just the category. If you have used one letter in two words, be sure to explain it. This activity reinforces the visual recognition of vocabulary words.

Ex.=

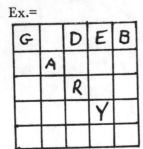
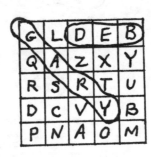

Find and circle these names:

Gary

Deb

ACTIVITY—Paragraph Jigsaw Puzzles

DESCRIPTION—Write or type on paper a paragraph which you may copy or make up, or even use a paragraph from a newspaper or magazine. Cut the paragraph out and glue it to heavy paper, tagboard or light cardboard. Cut the paragraph into irregular pieces, large ones for small children or smaller pieces for older children. Put the pieces in a container so they won't get lost.

Children are to put the puzzle together and then read it aloud for reading practice. Demonstrate that they can find where the pieces go not only by their size and shape but by whether the words make sense when read. This activity combines learning with practice in eye-to-hand coordination.

ACTIVITY—Plays and Puppet Shows

DESCRIPTION—Since plays involve large body movement, children can use up some of their energy and yet be involved in a reading-related activity. Explain that a plan or script has to be written so the actors will know what to do and say in the play. To start, take a scene in a story you've just read or that's an old favorite. Together write a brief description of the setting, the characters, and their starting position. Go on to write dialogue and stage directions. Proofread the script. From then on, it is up to both you and the children as to how elaborate to make the play, whether to have costumes, scenery, and so on.

A puppet show requires less large physical movement but is an activity that appeals to children and is also reading related. Some particularly shy children find it much easier to act as a puppeteer and the puppets appeal to their imaginations. Write the script as you would a play script. Then make your puppets. Hand puppets can be made very simply from paper sacks with crayoned or pasted-on features, and from plates (paper or aluminum) or fabric with button eyes, yarn hair, and glued or sewn-on scraps for clothing. Funny or monster puppets are especially attractive for children to make and use.

SECTION II

Writing, the second R

5. Introduction

THIS SECTION IS DESIGNED TO help parents and teachers improve the writing skills of children in order to increase their ability to communicate through written language. The three major contributing factors which cause poor writing ability are given individual consideration. There are detailed programs for teaching penmanship, both printing and cursive, spelling and expressive writing.

An adequate level of writing competency means that the writer is able to express his thoughts clearly in written language to the intended reader. This is the only way writing can perform its function as an effective communication medium.

Reading involves decoding written symbols to understand their meaning; writing involves manipulating written symbols to convey meaning. Both activities use the written language as a means of communication. The reader is seeking to understand what someone else has expressed in written form. The writer is seeking written symbols to express meaning to the reader.

To express himself in written form, a person must know how to read and must understand what he reads. Having learned to recognize written symbols and realizing their value for communicating ideas, the would-be writer then needs only to learn how to organize his thoughts and to choose the appropriate words.

The purpose of writing is communication, and this purpose is defeated if the writing is illegible. True, typewriters have replaced some of the functions of handwriting, but both children and adults must depend on handwriting for many tasks. Communication with the reader also breaks down when he encounters misspelled words, as he puzzles them out or misunderstands them completely. To insure proper understanding, the written message should also be well organized, clear and complete. Carefully chosen words and phrases can sharpen meaning and make sure of the correct transmission of the writer's thoughts.

The effect of poor writing skills

Not only teachers but parents and employers are becoming increasingly concerned about children's ability to express their thoughts adequately in written form. A continuing decline is being observed in the capacity of children to communicate effectively through their writing skills. This is of great concern to our society because a person who lacks basic competence in writing is not only a hindrance to himself in realizing his own full potential but also a liability to any group of which he is a member.

Poor writing ability extends through all of the grade levels up to and including college, which means that children in a wide range of ages are handicapped. Many children in elementary grades are unable to write a single complete sentence without errors. Older children are often unable to write a single paragraph which accurately expresses their thoughts legibly and without spelling mistakes. High school graduates are all too frequently unable to write clearly and without error in a concise and precise style. In fact, employers complain that high-school and even college graduates have not mastered the written language well enough to fill out job applications or write resumes, office memos, business letters and company reports—all of which are writing skills necessary in a business-oriented society. Without a doubt, writing skills can influence and even determine the advancement of individuals in a wide variety of careers.

Inadequate writing ability afflicts any child who has not had basic instruction in writing fundamentals and the discipline required by the act of writing reinforced through repeated practice. Children generally learn to write only as a direct result of the physical act of writing.

When the child needs help

When is a child really handicapped by his level of writing ability? When his writing skill hinders instead of accelerates his capacity to express his thoughts in writing. A person who is thus handicapped is also limited in his ability to communicate at a socially acceptable and desirable level.

Children need help when: (1) their writing is not readable or legible to others and thus the intended reader cannot decipher the written message; (2) their spelling distorts or changes the meaning of the message to the extent that the reader cannot understand it or breaks his concentration so he loses the train of thought; (3) their choice of words and sentence arrangements either misrepresents the intended message or makes it unintelligible. In each of these cases, the result of inadequate writing ability is the same—poor communication.

To decide between beginning instruction or remedial writing help, you must consider the individual needs and educational level of the child or children. If the child has not attended school, you will of course start at the beginning instructional level. Even if he is in the primary grades, it is wise to begin with the fundamentals and at least review the basic lessons. Children in the intermediate and upper grades, who have received some kind of formal education, benefit from remedial help to improve their writing skills.

Before starting lessons, a diagnosis should be made to determine the child's strengths and weaknesses. Whether the subject area is reading, writing or arithmetic, any diagnostic testing must take into account the general health of the child as well as physical and emotional factors that may hinder his receptiveness to learning. As suggested in the reading section, note the child's general state of health. Check for poor coordination, abnormal body movement or signs of vision difficulty and get medical advice if you suspect a problem.

Schedule lessons frequently and at times convenient to both tutor and child. A length of 45 minutes to 1 hour is suggested, but watch for restlessness and other signs of boredom and remain flexible as to length and content of lessons. Be sure the child understands that you are a team working together on what you have both agreed is a problem. Be calm and relaxed but businesslike. Have fun, but always with a purpose—to improve the child's skills in areas very necessary to his future.

Writing is both a physical art (as in penmanship) and an expressive art (as in creative writing). As with all art forms, diligent practice is required to develop and refine the skills needed for a high degree of mastery. Remembering this, be sure to encourage, praise and help children in each assigned writing task.

6. Teaching Penmanship

PENMANSHIP IS THE ART OF FORMING the standard symbols that we call letters in an easily recognized style. Learning handwriting differs from learning reading or arithmetic because of the need for drawing skill. Learning the art of drawing letters requires time, practice and attention to detail. It demands concentration and coordination between the mind, eyes and hands.

In essence, each child becomes an artist seeking to reproduce letters in an attractive but distinct style of his own. The goal is not to make a child a "mini-typewriter" but rather to allow for differences in individual style while encouraging readability. Unless a physical handicap is present, most children can learn to produce readable penmanship by overcoming the two most common agents of illegibility, carelessness and haste.

For these lessons, alphabet letter guides are very useful. Parents and teachers can use the guides starting on page 98, buy commercial alphabet strips, or even make their own. The guides should include both printing and cursive styles with capital letters (upper case) and small letters (lower case) for each. Pin them up in the study room, and if possible leave them there or some place else where the child can see them between lessons.

Ex.=

Printing *A a B b C c D d*

Cursive *A a B b C c D d*

Very young children need to learn the printed alphabet to help them become familiar with the printed letters that they are

95

learning to read. Also having them memorize and practice copying the printed letters helps reinforce their learning of the alphabet names. Older children who can already recognize and name printed letters need to focus their attention on writing cursive letters.

An easy way to analyze a child's penmanship is to have him write the letters of the alphabet, then copy a paragraph from a book or newspaper or even a handwritten letter. This way the instructor can evaluate the child's writing both of individual letters and of letters combined into words. For diagnostic purposes, writing should meet certain standards. Here is a brief check list.

Penmanship Evaluation List

Letters should be:

(1) correctly shaped

(2) uniformly sized

(3) of proper height

(4) positioned between the line margins

(5) slanted in one direction

(6) equally spaced

Each of these general categories is developed in the specific lessons.

Penmanship lessons

The first step in teaching penmanship is to have children learn how to manipulate the essential tools of pencil and paper. A child needs to know how to hold a pencil in a manner which will help rather than hinder the development of good writing skills. This basic hand position should be reversed for left-handed writers.

Basic hand position

This   Not this

Many minor variations of this basic position can be used successfully if they are more comfortable due to differences in hand sizes and shapes, curling the bottom fingers into the palm, for example. Without exception, though, the wrist and forearm should rest very close to the surface of the writing area and generally in contact with it.

If a very young child has trouble grasping a standard-size pencil, try one with a larger diameter, contrary as that may seem.

When children start to write, make sure they hold the paper with their free hand to prevent movement. Paper should slant to the left for right-handers, to the right for left-handers. The free hand should push paper up during writing so the body does not have to move out of position. Have children sit comfortably but erect. A comfortable position is more likely to result in good performance but a slouch can affect it detrimentally. Lighting should be arranged so that no shadows from either the hand itself or other objects will fall on the paper. Since the printed alphabet is the same as the one children are learning to read, printing is the first writing skill taught. Cursive writing, the longhand writing used in our adult society, should be taught for two reasons: (1) it is faster than printing, and (2) it is usually considered the more mature style of writing.

Begin instruction on either printing or cursive writing by showing children how to make each letter in the alphabet starting with **A**. Point out the details of each letter, showing that it is made up of straight lines, curves, loops, or a combination. Learning the letters in sequence reinforces the learning of alphabetical order. Later lessons cover practice in writing letters with similar shapes and combinations of letters used in words.

It may be best to demonstrate to children the order and direction of the strokes used in forming each letter as shown in the "Printing Guide" and "Cursive Guide" on pages 99-102. These guides are merely teaching aids, however, and if children find it easier to form the letters differently they may do so as long as the letters are made neatly and legibly. It is also generally more efficient to work from left to right even in writing individual letters. The goal is to teach children the correct shape of printing and cursive letters. Have children practice making left-to-right rows of each letter.

Printing Guide—See pages 99-100.

(Commas separate the strokes)

Cursive Guide—See pages 101-102.

(Commas separate the strokes)

If a child's lack of physical coordination causes him problems in forming small letters, have him use paper with large spaces. Then gradually get him used to reducing the size of his letters until they fit the standard spacing of regular binder paper.

After children have practiced making rows of each letter, have them practice rows of alternating letters. It is generally easier for children to draw straight lines rather than curved lines in printing, so now use those printing letters having only straight lines in various combinations (ex.= A E A E).

Printed letters with straight lines

Capital (upper case) letters: A , E , F , H , I , K , L , M , N , T , V , W , X , Y , Z

Small (lower case) letters: i , k , l , t , v , w , x , y , z

In cursive writing, it is easier for children to draw letters without loops (ex.= *l*) than with loops (ex.= *g*). So at first have children practice writing nonlooped letters in various combinations (ex.= *c i c i*).

Cursive letters without loops

Capital (upper case) letters: C , m , n , J , F , U , V , W , X

Small (lower case) letters: c , i , m , n , r , t , u , v , w , x

Next have children learning to print practice groups of letters that use curved lines in various combinations.

Printed letters with curved lines

Capital (upper case) letters: B , C , D , G , J , O , P , Q , R , S , U

PRINTING GUIDE
(Commas separate the strokes)

A = ↗, ⋀, A   a = ↻C, ↻a

B = ↓|, ↻, B)   b = ↓|, b

C = ↻C·   c = ↻c

D = ↓|, D)   d = ↻c, d↓

E = ↓|, →, →, E→   e = →, ↻e

F = ↓|, →, →   f = f, f→

G = ↻C, ↻G, ↻G   g = ↻c, g↓

H = ↓|, |, ↓, ↓H   h = ↓|, h↓

I = ↓|, →, I→   i = ↓|, i

J = J↓, J→   j = J↓, j

K = ↓|, ↗, K↓   k = ↓|, ↗, k↓

L = ↓|, L→   l = ↓|

$M = \nearrow/, \wedge\downarrow, \wedge\nearrow, M\downarrow$

$N = \nearrow/, \wedge\searrow, N\uparrow$

$O = \circlearrowleft O$

$P = \downarrow/, P\hookrightarrow$

$Q = Q, Q\searrow$

$R = \downarrow/, P\hookrightarrow R\searrow$

$S = S$

$T = \downarrow/, \overrightarrow{7}$

$U = U\uparrow$

$V = \downarrow/, V\uparrow$

$W = \downarrow/, V\searrow, \cup\downarrow, W\uparrow$

$X = \swarrow/, X\searrow$

$Y = \swarrow/, Y\downarrow$

$Z = \overrightarrow{z}, \nearrow\!\!\!\!\diagdown, Z\rightarrow$

$m = \downarrow/, \cap\nearrow, m\nearrow$

$n = \downarrow/, \cap\nearrow$

$o = Q$

$p = \downarrow/, P\hookrightarrow$

$q = C, q\downarrow$

$r = \downarrow/, r\rightarrow$

$s = S$

$t = \downarrow/, t\rightarrow$

$u = U\nearrow, u\downarrow$

$v = \downarrow/, v\nearrow$

$w = U, w\nearrow, w\rightarrow$

$x = \swarrow/, x\rightarrow$

$y = \swarrow/, y\downarrow$

$z = \overrightarrow{z}, \nearrow\!\!\!\!\diagdown, z\rightarrow$

CURSIVE GUIDE
(Commas separate the strokes)

a = ᶜC, aℓ   a = ᶜc, aℓ

B = ʾ, 1ʾ, Pʾ, Bʾ   b = ℓ), fℓ, ℓℓ, bℓ

C = ᶜC   c = ᶜℓ

D = ℓℓ, Dℓ, Dℓ   d = ᶜc, dℓ

E = ᶜC, ℰℓ   e = ℓℓ, ℓℓ

F = ᶜ, Jℓ, Fℓ   f = ℓℓ, fℓ, fℓ, fℓ

Gℓ, Gℓ, Gℓ   g = Gℓ, gℓ

Hℓ = ℓℓ, 1ℓℓ, ℋℓ   h = ℓℓ, fℓ, hℓ

dℓ = ℓ, dℓ, dℓ   i = ℓℓ, ℓℓ, i

Jℓ = ᶜℓ, ℋℓ, Jℓ   jℓ = ℓℓ, Jℓ, jℓ

Kℓ = ℓℓ, ℋℓ, Kℓ   k = ℓℓ, Jℓ, ℓℓ, kℓ

Lℓ = ℓℓ, Jℓ, Lℓ   lℓ = ℓℓ, Jℓ

101

M = , ,

N = ,

O = ,

P = , ,

Q = ,

R = , , ,

S = , ,

T = ,

U = , ,

V = ,

W = , , ,

X = ,

Y = , , ,

Z = , , ,

m = , ,

n = ,

o = ,

p = , , ,

q = , , ,

r = , ,

s = , ,

t = , ,

u = , ,

v = , ,

w = , , ,

x = , ,

y = , , ,

z = , ,

Small (lower case) letters: a , b , c , d , e , f , g , h , j , m , n , o , p , q , r , s , u , w .

For cursive writing, have children practice making the letters which contain loops in various combinations.

Cursive letters with loops

Capital (upper case) letters:

a , B , D , E , G , H , L , J , L , O , P , G , R , S , Y , Z

Small (lower case) letters:

a , b , d , e , f , g , h , j , k , l , o , p , q , s , y , z

Don't be overly concerned if children change their letters slightly by adding or subtracting lines and loops as their own personal style of writing develops. The point where you should be concerned is when the letters become less readable. Extend the same possibility for freedom of style which adults have. The criterion is legibility.

The next lesson for printing should combine straight and curved-line letters and for cursive writing looped and nonlooped letters. When a child is able to shift from writing one form of letter to another with little difficulty, have him start writing short common words. First the letters should be repeated separately, then the word repeated.

Ex.=   aaaaaaa ttttttt eeeeeee ate ate ate

or

bbbbbbb uuuuuuu yyyyyyy buy buy buy

If you use the vocabulary words listed in Appendix A for this writing practice, it will have the added effect of reinforcing the child's beginning reading vocabulary.

As the children's writing of short words improves, keep them practicing words while continuing to work on letters that are still

103

difficult. Include capitalized words since every sentence begins with a capital letter. Work up gradually to longer words which require more printing or cursive strokes. This also helps expand children's sight vocabulary.

The next step is practice writing complete sentences. You may wish to have children read orally a selection from a book and then write sentences from it in printing or cursive writing, or you may wish to give them sentences of your own choosing. While providing practice in writing mixed letters, this activity introduces children to reading and understanding complete thoughts as well.

After sentences comes the writing of complete paragraphs, which can be dictated or copied from books, magazines or newspapers. Writing letters is good penmanship practice, too. Many children become more enthused about writing practice when they correspond with relatives or pen pals.

Following is a discussion of the six criteria for writing that were given in the Writing Evaluation List.

Correctly shaped letters—Remind children that they are to try to make their letters look as much as possible like the alphabet guide so people will be able to recognize each letter easily. Letters should be shaped so they won't be confused with any other letter and should look the same every time they are written.

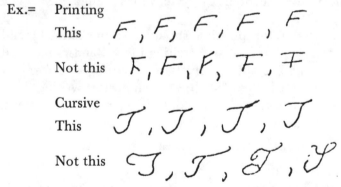

Ex.= Printing
This
Not this

Cursive
This
Not this

Uniformly sized letters—Only after children have learned to shape their letters correctly should emphasis be put on their proportionate size. Make sure children realize that the same letter should be the same size each time it is written. Uniformly sized letters give a smooth, flowing effect to both printing and cursive writing. If irregularly sized letters are a problem, have the child pay particular attention to making letters of uniform size when he is practicing.

Ex.= Printing
This

A A A A

Not this

A A A A A A

Cursive
This

a a a a

Not this

a a a a a a a

Proper height—To prevent children from writing too small or too large, emphasize the proper height of letters. Capital letters should touch the bottom line on at least one point and come close to the top line. Lower case letters also touch the bottom line. The short lower case letters rise to about half the distance to the top line, the tall ones almost to the top line or the same height as the capital letters. This is a practice norm. Letters can be slightly higher or lower without detracting from legibility as long as the height is consistent.

Ex.= Printing
This

B b C c D d E e

Not this

B b C c D d E e

Cursive
This

R r S s T t

Not this

R r S s T t

Letters positioned between the line margins—Explain that the lines printed across the page are there to guide the writing in a straight direction from left to right as well as to indicate the size limit of the letters. Each bottom line shows where letters should rest and each top line where the writing above will stop. Children should learn to avoid writing below the bottom line or too far above it.

Ex.=   Printing
        This   *about*

        Not this   *about*

        Cursive
        This   *about*

        Not this   *about*

The use of vertical margins is important for children to learn since the left margin provides a starting point for writing. Left margins are often indicated by a vertical red line. If there is no line, draw one until children can do without it. The margin makes the writing look neat, orderly and more legible as well.

Ex.=   Printing

        This | a a a a   Not this | a a a
                | b b b b | b b b b b
                | c c c c | c c

        Cursive

        This | a a a a   Not this | a a a a
                | b b b b | b b
                | c c c c | c c c c

Right-hand margins need not be as straight as left-hand ones and they are not usually indicated. They are still important for neat and legible writing, however, and children should practice stopping each line about an inch from the paper edge. If children encounter trouble with this, go ahead and draw this margin too until they get used to remembering to stop. The next step is to have children learn to judge where to stop without a drawn right hand margin.

Ex.=   Printing

        This | a a a a   Not this | a a a
                | b b b b | b b b b b b b
                | c c c c | c c c c c

106

Cursive _aaaa_   _aaaaaa_
                  bbbb   _bbb_
This   _cccc_   Not this   _ccccc_

Letters slanted in one direction—In printing, each letter is formed in as close to a vertical direction as possible. In cursive writing, the accepted form is a slight slant to the right of vertical. A normal range of slant is between 85 and 45 degrees with each individual's style tending to vary. Whatever the direction of the letters, both printing and cursive writing require consistency for a neater appearance and easy reading.

Ex.=   Printing

This   *About*   Not this   *A6ou t*

Cursive

This   *About*   Not this   *About*

Equal spacing—Consistent and equivalent spacing between letters and words is very important in producing attractive and easy to read writing. First, children need to be shown the effect of wrong spacing of letters in a word. A word becomes difficult to read if the letters are spaced too close together, too far apart, or irregularly.

Ex.=   Printing   Cursive

Proper spacing   *about*   *about*

Spaced too close   *abaut*   *abut*

Spaced too far apart   *a b o u t*   *a b o a t*

Irregular spacing   *ab o ut*   *ab at*

Children also need to become aware of the importance of spacing between words in sentences. If adequate and equal spacing is not left between words, they may appear to run together or the sentence can appear to fall apart, thereby making reading difficult.

Ex.=   Printing

Proper word spacing   *You are here now.*

Poor word spacing   *Youare   here   now.*

Cursive

Proper word spacing   *You are here now.*

Poor word spacing   *Youare   here   now.*

After children have learned to write with reasonable facility, they are likely to develop certain common errors that make handwriting hard to read, whether it is printing or cursive. These are usually caused by nothing more than carelessness and haste. This can be remedied by calling attention to each error and having children be more careful. The following examples of cursive writing show what errors to watch for and what to do about it.

	Lower case		Upper case	
	This	Not this	This	Not this
Close the letters	*a*	*a*	*a*	*a*
	d	*d*	*D*	*D*
	o	*o*	*O*	*o*
Maintain curved lines	*h*	*h*	*H*	*H*
	w	*w*	*W*	*W*
	u	*v*	*U*	*U*

108

	This	Not this	This	Not this

Avoid extra loops

Keep upper loops open

Keep lower loops open

Keep closed letters open

Stop trailing lines

This	Not this	This	Not this

110

7. Teaching Spelling

TO BE PROPERLY UNDERSTOOD, words need to be correctly spelled by the writer. It is often difficult for children to spell words correctly while they are writing because they are so intent on what they are trying to say.

Even when rereading their writing, children may not notice their spelling errors if the spelling seems close enough to express their thoughts. Explain that a misspelled word can confuse a reader or even actually change the meaning of a sentence (ex.= belev for **believe, sit** for **set, not** for **knot**).

Poor spellers are often poor readers, their errors reflecting the same mistakes in recognizing, pronouncing and writing words. Because of the close relationship between reading, writing and spelling, children should be brought to realize the need for spelling their words correctly. In addition, improving a child's spelling often improves his reading and pronunciation of troublesome words.

How to teach spelling

Teaching spelling will be simplified by remembering that a child who has a clear picture of a word in his mind will only need to think of it to be able to spell it automatically. The words a child learns to read, especially those in his sight vocabulary, often (though not always) have their letter shapes and sounds imprinted clearly enough so that he does not have to study them. A child with a firm grasp of the letter/sounds should easily be able to spell the words that are written in the same way that they sound. The other words, those that are not spelled the way they sound, are learned one at a time by memorization and practice. This is not as difficult as it sounds since about half of our written language is made up of a rather limited list of short, easily recognizable words. Many of the other words combine parts whose spelling is already known. Spelling rules are so numerous and have so many exceptions that, at this stage at least, effort is better spent learning the words directly.

The tutor should start the spelling lessons for both beginning and remedial work by explaining to children that just as they memorized words and their meanings in order to be able to read them, they must also remember their spellings. Also tell them that many words can be sounded out but others must be memorized. Remind children that memorization is active, not passive, that to memorize a word they must repeat it and use it in as many ways as they can. (See page 19 for suggestions.)

To find words that need to be studied, the tutor should first use the lists given in Appendix A. These tables provide lists of high-frequency and easy words which children must know how to spell. When you are giving spelling lists, pronounce each word and use it in a sentence (ex.= "Sat, Miss Muffet sat on a tuffet"), and have children write it down. Then either word for word or after a short list, have the child respond by pronouncing the word, spelling it aloud, telling what it means and using it in a sentence of his own. Any words that are missed should be written down by the child and studied until he knows them all.

After the commonly occurring words have been learned, children can be introduced to more difficult and less often used words. These can be taken from books, newspapers, magazines or even the dictionary. Often children are more enthusiastic about new spelling words that are taken from subjects that interest them. Children who like a particular topic are almost always eager to learn more.

Another method of selecting spelling words is to suggest that children sort out unfamiliar words from their readings. The tutor can ask them to try this test: (1) spell the word without looking at it; (2) give at least one meaning, more if they can; and (3) use the word properly in a sentence or sentences. If they can't do any one of the three, the word should be included in their list of study words. Involving children in choosing their own list of spelling words encourages them to become more aware of and question their current knowledge of word spellings and meanings.

Still another way to find words whose spelling should be learned is for the tutor to watch what the child writes. Some spelling errors are due to carelessness and this type needs only to be pointed out. Other errors need more serious study. If the child often misspells similar types of words, they can be grouped and studied together to reinforce learning (ex.= beet for beat, treet for treat, sheat for sheet).

The instructor can give an informal diagnostic test by dictating a paragraph or two to see which words the child misspells. When the child feels ready after studying these words, the same material can be dictated again. When he can write the same thing without errors, the student will see the progress he has made and be encouraged to continue to study.

Occasionally it is found that a child who spells dictated words incorrectly is not hearing them right. This, of course, calls for professional testing and advice.

Memorization and using vocabulary words as methods for improving spelling can be supplemented by playing games which involve spelling, as will be described.

The dictionary

A dictionary's value as a spelling aid and as a source of word pronunciations and meanings should be demonstrated by the tutor. Children can use the dictionary to: (1) pronounce and spell words they wish to use but are unsure of and (2) check the meaning of a word they wish to use to see if it expresses the desired thought. A third use is to discover how the word is divided into syllables.

Show children that the dictionary is in strict alphabetical order starting with the first letter, then the second, the third, and so on (ex.= a comes before able, able comes before about, about comes before above, above comes before act). Very young children may need to have an alphabet strip in view when looking up words to locate a letter's placement. Point out the guide words at the top of each dictionary page or column. Speed in locating words will develop with practice. A good way to develop dictionary skills is to hold "dictionary races" to see who can find words first. Make assignments of finding words, writing the meanings, using the words in a sentence to express one of the meanings and memorizing the spellings. The simplified definitions in children's dictionaries are probably best for that kind in children's dictionaries are probably best for that kind of task.

Be sure to introduce children to the pronunciation glossary located in front of the dictionary, explaining how the pronunciation marks indicate the sounds used to speak the words. This not only shows children another function of the dictionary but also helps reinforce phonic skills.

Children may have difficulty discriminating between very precise sounds. For this reason it is a good idea to have them memorize either the guide words in the pronunciation key with their markings or words of their choice containing the same letter sounds given in the samples. Once they learn the symbols and word examples, children always know what sound the symbol refers to by remembering their sample word. Then have children look up words in the dictionary for practice in using stress marks (indicating which syllable is emphasized or spoken loudest and sharpest) and the marks that indicate vowel sounds to pronounce the word correctly.

In using the dictionary to check the spelling of words, many people are puzzled about how to look up a word whose spelling they don't know. Tutors can explain that such a person must be a word detective. First he looks in the most likely place. Then he must remember different ways the same sound is spelled in other words and check under that spelling (ex.= **sugar** with its beginning sound **sh** can't be found between **shuffle** and **shun**; the word **sure**, which he knows how to spell, begins with the **sh** sound but is spelled **s-u**; look up **s-u-g** to find **sugar**). Lists of the various ways certain sounds can be spelled are found in some dictionaries and reference books.

A child who looks in the dictionary to check the meaning of a word he wants to use only to find it doesn't express his thought should be told that he has the choice of finding another word, rewriting the sentence or both. For alternative words, children can be directed to the synonyms in the dictionary or introduced to the thesaurus, inexpensive copies of which are available in paperback. Tutors should

114

point out, however, that few if any words have exactly the same meaning, and the search is not to find an unusual word but rather one that will express a thought precisely.

It is valuable for children to know how a word is divided into syllables to help with the pronunciation and spelling of long words along with knowing where to separate words at the end of writing lines.

Introduce a syllable as a unit of sound in the pronunciation of a word (ex.= **mad** is one syllable, **com/ing** is two). A syllable consists of a vowel alone or a vowel with one or more consonants ahead of or behind it. The number of syllables can usually be judged by sounding out a word. For dividing words in writing, two rules of thumb are useful: (1) words divide between an affix and the root word (ex.= **in/side, work/er** (2) words divide between two consonants with vowels on either side (ex.= **let/ter, con/fuse**) except when the two consonants form a blend. Only these two rules are included because of the large number of exceptions to the other rules. Words that are incorrectly divided are often confusing, as can be seen almost every day in computer type-set newspapers (ex.= **ahe/ad, acti/on, girlf/riend**).

A careful writer who is not sure of what a word means, how it is spelled or where it divides does not hesitate to look it up. Tutors should make sure that children are aware that a dictionary is as much of a tool for writing as a pencil or pen.

Spelling games

Once children recognize the importance of correct spelling, good spelling habits can be developed through practice and reinforced by playing games. Many of the games used for teaching reading either already include spelling or can easily be adapted. In games where players pronounce a word after seeing it on a flash card, for example, they can be required to spell the word after hearing it pronounced.

In addition to the appropriate games in the reading section, the following games which deal specifically with the sounds, meanings and spelling of words can be used by tutors to improve children's spelling skills.

GAME—Synonyms

PURPOSE—To learn about words that have similar meanings (ex.= **joyful, happy; sad, unhappy; jump, leap**).

115

MATERIALS—Vocabulary flash cards of synonyms (see "Materials for Teaching Reading").

PLAYERS—Tutor and child, or pair of children.

PROCEDURE—Make up a set of flash cards consisting of pairs of synonyms, using a dictionary or thesaurus as a source if necessary. Name the words on each pair of cards to the child, explain their meanings and have him repeat them. Shuffle the cards and place them in rows face up. The player chooses two cards that are synonyms and tells what the words mean. Each correct set of words counts 2 points. If either the words are not synonyms or the meaning is wrong, explain the error and begin again. Continue until all of the word pairs are correctly matched. Keep a record of point scores to demonstrate improvement.

GAME—Antonyms

PURPOSE—To learn about words that are the opposite of each other in meaning (ex.= **happy, sad; up, down; rich, poor**).

MATERIALS—Vocabulary flash cards of antonyms.

PLAYERS—Tutor and child, or pair of children.

PROCEDURE—Begin by identifying each word on the flash cards and explaining its meaning. Have the child repeat each one to reinforce its image in his memory. Shuffle the cards and lay them out face up in rows. The player picks out word pairs whose meanings are opposites of each other. Two points are given for each correct pair of antonyms. An error calls for an explanation and starting over. Maintain a scorecard to record the child's improvement.

GAME—Homonyms

PURPOSE—To learn about words that have similar sounds but different spellings and meanings.

MATERIALS—Vocabulary flash cards for homonyms (see examples below).

PLAYERS—Tutor and child, or pair of children.

PROCEDURE—Name each pair of words that sound alike but

distinguish between the meanings. Have the child repeat the words, their spellings and meanings. After going through the flash cards, mix them up and lay them down in rows face up. The player chooses a pair of homonyms. If he is correct, he receives 2 points. If he can correctly distinguish between the word meanings, he gets 2 more points. He continues until he makes a mistake. The tutor discusses the error with him and he starts over. Record his points on a card or chart as a record of his progress.

Ex. of homonyms: to, two; be, bee; see, sea; do, dew; pail, pale, beet, beat; sun, son; mussel, muscle; flea, flee; pane, pain; tail, tale; week, weak; steal, steel; peace, piece; hole, whole; sale, sail; threw, through; our, hour; or, oar; tear, tier; here, hear; hair, hare; their, there; bear, bare; fair, fare.

GAME—Find the Syllables

PURPOSE—To help recognition of the role of syllabication in pronunciation and to practice spelling.

MATERIALS—Vocabulary flash cards which vary in the number of syllables.

PLAYERS—Tutor and child, or pair of children.

PROCEDURE—Flash cards are placed on the table face up in rows. The game begins by one player choosing a word, pronouncing it, identifying the number of syllables, and then, putting it face down, spelling the word correctly. If his answers are correct, he keeps the card. If not, he places the flash card back down. Then it is the other player's turn. The winner is the player with the most cards at the game's end.

A variation can be played by having one pile of cards turned face down and another group spread out face up. A player turns one card up and pronounces it, then chooses a card with the same number of syllables from the face-up cards. If he makes a correct match, the player keeps his cards and so on.

GAME—Compound Words

PURPOSE—To provide instruction on the meaning, spelling and usage of compound words.

MATERIALS—Vocabulary flash cards containing the words that make up compound words.

Ex.= Compound word	Flash cards
everything	`every` `thing`
maybe	`may` `be`
anybody	`any` `body`
cowboy	`cow` `boy`

PLAYERS—Tutor and child, or group of children.

PROCEDURE—Before the game, introduce the correct pronunciation of each compound word and use it in a sentence. Repeat until the words are familiar. The object of the game is to put the broken compound words back together. Mix up the cards and lay them out in rows face up. The first player chooses two cards and puts them together to make a compound word, which he uses in a sentence. If he is correct, he keeps the cards. If the player can't make a compound word or makes a mistake, he returns the cards to their row. It is now the second player's turn. Repeat until all the flash cards have been picked up. The winner is the player holding the most cards.

Ex. of compound words: **maybe, without, myself, himself, anyway, anyone, anywhere, someone, everyone, everywhere, anything, whereby, cowboy, airport, railroad, snowman, bedroom, upstairs, afterward, backward, popcorn, bluebird, downhill, fireplace, flashlight, outdoors.**

GAME—Paragraph

PURPOSE—For practice in spelling and in using context meanings.

MATERIALS—A paragraph from a newspaper or book, paper, pencils.

PLAYERS—Tutor and child, or group of children.

PROCEDURE—Copy a paragraph, omitting a word from each sentence, and give it to the child to fill in the blanks with words of his own choice. The words must be spelled correctly and make sense in the context of the sentence. The paragraph can also be dictated with the child writing down a word to fill in the pauses. The resulting paragraphs are to be read aloud by the child or tutor, or tutor reading the sentences as the child furnishes the words he has chosen.

A variation is to take a story and omit the nouns and verbs in each sentence. Ask children to give you substitute nouns and verbs. Finally read the story with the replaced words. The result is often very funny. This activity helps children learn to listen better and develop a greater appreciation of the importance of word choice.

GAME—Scrambler

PURPOSE—To give practice in spelling tasks and reinforcing the correct spelling of words.

MATERIALS—Paper, pencils, dictionary to check spelling.

PLAYERS—Tutor and child, or group of children.

PROCEDURE—Choosing words which the children have already studied, change the order of the letters. Children are to unscramble the spelling.

Ex.=   Unscramble these words!

yabb   (baby)

tae   (eat, ate, or tea)

eeb   (bee)

ense   (seen)

An easier variation of this exercise is to have children match a list of scrambled words with a list of the correct spellings. This is useful when introducing new words from the children's reading material.

Ex.=   Matching

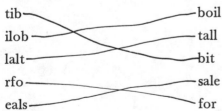

tib   boil
ilob   tall
lalt   bit
rfo   sale
eals   for

8. Teaching expressive and descriptive writing

EXPRESSIVE OR CREATIVE WRITING is not considered a usual adult activity in our society except for those who are particularly talented. Yet having children write stories and poems is important because: (1) it frees their imaginations, resulting in pleasure and creative problem-solving; (2) it helps them to better express and understand their own thoughts and emotions; and (3) it encourages the practice of writing skills which will be useful in later life. On the other hand, descriptive writing is an activity that will be of direct value in school and business or professional careers.

Here tutors will find directions for teaching the writing of stories, descriptive paragraphs, essays or reports and poems. There is also an explanation of how to teach children to edit and proofread their work, and suggestions for writing exercises that are for practice and fun.

Writing stories

Storytelling is one of the oldest art forms practiced by man. Before recorded history, stories passed culturally important information from one generation to the next. Mankind is still fascinated by stories, whether oral or recorded in writing or on film.

An interest in expressive writing can be developed in children through telling or reading stories to them. This exposes children to the use of words to express organized thoughts, and as a bonus gives them the attention they desire. The tutor can make up stories or take them from songs, books, movies and

121

folktales. The supply is endless and deals with all kinds of subjects. Children are even more attentive if the stories deal with subjects in which they are already interested.

After you have read or told some stories, point out that every story has: (1) a beginning, located some place and some time; (2) a main character doing things or having things done to him, speaking, thinking, and dealing with problems; and (3) a conclusion or an end. Have the children note, too, that a story deals with one subject or problem, and that the description alternates with direct speech or dialogue. Using this simple framework, instructors can help children develop their own stories in their minds before expressing them in words.

Children should be encouraged to let their imaginations soar freely, exploring the worlds of fantasy and reality before they communicate their experiences in writing. Creative writing requires a blend of imagination and detail. Be sure children understand they can "make believe."

If at first they seem at a loss, suggest that students tell something they dreamed about, saw, felt, or did recently. Stories can be about pets, vacations, holidays, friends, family or even school. Many times, story-telling sessions are all the encouragement they need.

The next step is to have children express each story in their own words. Very young children who can't yet read or write well can tell their stories while the tutor writes down each word, helping them choose their words and develop the sequence of action. This not only guides children in learning to write stories but also develops a closer relationship between adult and child.

If some children have difficulty in working out a whole story, tell one but stop at a high point of excitement and have them tell how they would like the story to end. Continue this activity until the child is ready to tell a whole story of his own.

Even in this free kind of writing, children often need help in beginning a story. Suggestive titles are useful to give children a subject and a direction or reason for writing. Story starters, an interesting first sentence or two, can also be used for this purpose. Tutors may wish to choose a title or story starter and show the different ways a story could be written.

Ex.= Story titles

How the Butterfly Won His Spots

How the Bird Learned to Sing Instead of Bark

Why Grasshoppers Hop

Why the Sky Is Blue

Where the Stars Came From

Where the Snow Goes Each Spring

What Happened When the Tiger Lost His Stripes

The Fish That Walked on Land

Ex.= Story starters

"Once in an apartment high above the city street lived a cat with a tail like a question mark."

"What was that? I suddenly sat up in bed and tried to see in the dark, my heart thumping."

"Susie's new blue dress hung carefully in the closet. But she was beginning to be afraid that she would never get a chance to wear it."

Only after children become comfortable in performing creative writing tasks should tutors gradually increase the emphasis on spelling, punctuation, complete sentences, capitalization and legible handwriting.

Writing paragraphs

The framework for organizing the ideas or facts of both creative and descriptive writing to make the material meaningful to the reader is the paragraph. Paragraphs are usually set off from each other by indenting the first word.

In imaginative writing, the material is broken into logical, inviting and easily readable parts. The only strict rule is that when direct quotation is written, a new paragraph is used for each change of speaker.

In descriptive writing, a paragraph generally begins with a topic sentence which states the subject of the rest of the paragraph. One or more sentences follow which deal with the subject, expressing feelings or adding details. The last statement either summarizes the other sentences or concludes with a specific point.

At first it is often best to have children look in books, magazines or newspapers for examples of paragraphs. Tutors can help identify the topic sentence, trace and number the related ideas and recognize the final statement.

After children learn to spot the parts of the paragraph, give them practice in organizing sentences and writing a paragraph. One easy way to do this is to give the steps of a cooking recipe or construction plan and have children write them in paragraph form.

Steps to be organized into a paragraph

a. Now you're going to learn to fry an egg.

b. First, select an egg, crack the shell and pour the egg into a bowl.

c. Second, remove any pieces of shell in the bowl and pour the egg into a frying pan.

d. Third, heat the pan with the egg in it over low heat until the egg white and yolk become as firm as you want them.

e. Fourth, take the egg out of the pan before it burns and place it on a plate.

f. Now that you've fried an egg, have a good meal!

In this example, there are numerical guide words—first, second, etc.—which indicate the placing of each sentence. Gradually eliminate the use of such words so children will look more at the contents of sentences to figure out in what order they should be arranged.

The next step is to have children write their own paragraphs on assigned topics or topics of their choice. At this time they may revert back to the numerical guide words until they feel more secure. Much practice may be required because organizing and writing a well stated, clear paragraph is difficult for many children. Even high school students often have trouble with it.

Composing essays

An essay is a written discussion or statement on a particular theme or subject. It should be divided into three parts: (1) the introduction, which presents the subject to be talked about; (2) the body of the discussion, which contains all the relevant details, facts and arguments; and (3) the conclusion, which may review what was talked about and does make a final statement based on the material given in the body.

Because of the large amount of material in even a short essay, problems in organizing the sentences can develop. An outline can be a useful tool in deciding where and in what order sentences should go. Instructors may wish to teach children how to make a simple outline by using the following model.

1. Introduction

    a.

    b.

    c.

    d.

2. Body

    a.

    b.

    c.

    d.

3. Conclusion

    a.

    b.

    c.

The outline may contain fewer or more letters depending upon the amount of material.

Explain to children that the outline can help them organize their thoughts. They should first decide what they want to say in the introduction. Then they decide in what order to put the points, statements or sentences and write each thought beside a letter. The same thing is done with the body and conclusion. After the sentences are arranged in outline form, children should proceed to write the sentences in paragraphs.

Until students become more accomplished in using the outline, they should write complete sentences beside the letters. Gradually urge them to write only the main points of each sentence beside the letters, changing the function of the outline to organizing main ideas rather than whole sentences. With this brief form of outline, children write complete sentences only when they are actually writing a paragraph.

Don't expect too much too soon in writing essays because they are not easy to learn. Even college freshmen have difficulty as shown by declining writing test scores and the increase in so-called "bonehead" English courses.

Writing poetry

Poetry or verse is a form of writing which differs greatly from stories, paragraphs or essays. Learning to write poetry does not seem as practical as learning to write prose. However, it serves as an exercise in vocabulary choice and developing expressiveness. Some children in particular benefit from writing poetry as a new and different means of self-expression, and to help make them more conscientious in the mechanics of spelling, punctuation, etc.

Tutors can first point out that poetry generally expresses mood and emotion, that it is written in rhythmic lines which usually rhyme, and that is has its own rules for capitalization, line length, and punctuation.

Start by writing down a verse that children have heard or already know.

Ex.=   Roses are red,

Violets are blue.

Sugar is sweet

And so are you!

Sound out the rhythm of the syllables. Then show that the last words in the second and fourth lines rhyme—that is, sound alike except for the beginning consonant (ex.= **ring, sing; see,**

126

tree; boat, float). Note that the lines are short, they are usually even in the number of syllables, and each line starts with a capital letter. The rules for punctuation in verse are: (1) the first word in each line is capitalized, as is the first word in any complete statement; (2) commas are used to indicate breathing pauses and sometimes to guide the rhythm; (3) periods, question marks and exclamation points indicate the end of complete thoughts, even in the middle of a line.

Go on to write new verses to the same pattern. First have children furnish one rhyming word, then the rhyming pair of words, then a whole rhyming line or couplet. Be sure the words you use in this exercise have a choice of rhymes.

Ex.= Dogs like to bark,   The sun shines by day,

   Cats like to mew.   The moon shines at _____ (night)

   Kids like to talk   Your teeth shine at all times

   And I do ____, (too)   If you keep them _____. (bright)

   I jump and I hop,   The car was old,

   I run like the breeze.   The brakes were bad.

   I chatter nonstop

   _____   _____

   Possibilities: Possibility:

   And sometimes I sneeze.   What happened then

   And eat lots of cheese.   Was very sad.

   And I love to tease.

Point out to children that what you'd like to say in verse often has to be modified in order to rhyme. When stuck for a rhyme, run through the alphabet for new beginning consonants or blends for a word you can use (ex.= rhyme for **king: bing, cling, ding, fling,** etc.) Some dictionaries or other reference books list rhyme vocabularies, though more learning occurs when a child looks for his own rhymes.

Examples of children's poems from schoolbooks or library books can be used to familiarize children with the many variations in rhyme schemes, numbers of lines, line lengths, rhythms, etc. Read the poem aloud or have a child read it. Analyze it as in our example, point out any new features, and again help children write one to a similar pattern. Be sure to include humor, limericks, sport subjects, dramatic poems and blank verse as well as the more usual lyrical forms. In doing these exercises, children will not only learn writing skills but develop an appreciation of poetry as well.

Remember, however, that appreciation and the ability to write poetry are developed by exposing children to it in ways that arouse their interest, not by trying to follow any rules or preconceptions of what a poem should be. See that children understand that to make sure meaning is communicated, the poet must be especially careful in his choice and spelling of words along with their arrangement.

Editing and proofreading

Children need to know that merely writing words on paper does not always mean that their thoughts have been expressed as they intended. Many children are surprised to find that what they wrote doesn't state what they originally wanted to say. For this reason, tutors need to show youngsters how to edit and proofread their writing.

After they finish a writing assignment, have children reread it to see if they have left out any words or put in any unnecessary words, and if they chose the words and word order which best express their intent. Have the children further check for capitalization, punctuation or spelling errors and handwriting legibility.

Proofreading check list

1. Make sure every sentence begins with a capital letter and that capitals are used where otherwise necessary.

2. Make sure every sentence contains the appropriate punctuation and ends with a punctuation mark.

3. See that there are no words left out, making sentences incomplete, or words put in where they are not needed.

4. Observe words carefully to be sure the spellings are correct, that their meanings are appropriate for their usage, and that any divided words are divided correctly.

5. Note whether each paragraph is indented, each sentence belongs in that paragraph, and the sentences are arranged in a logical sequence in the paragraph.

Grammar has not been included here because grammatical rules and their exceptions are so numerous that they often confuse rather than help. For example, adults often try to follow rules that were taught to them incorrectly and many children don't write much better in the upper grades than in the lower grades even after years of grammar instruction. On the other hand, sentences that are direct and clearly written are almost always grammatical and it is much more valuable for young writers to clarify what they want to say rather than to try to remember what rules might apply.

The skills of editing and proofreading can be difficult for children to acquire since they may not understand what happened between the time they first had an idea and then later wrote it down. People who are not used to writing do not understand how their thoughts can run ahead of their writing. Even children who reread their material may not notice mistakes because they are still thinking of what they wanted to say rather than what they actually wrote. Techniques to make children more aware of what their writing actually states include: (1) reading aloud to themselves what they have written; (2) reading their material to someone else; (3) having another person read the material silently and point out errors; (4) having another person read the material aloud for the writer to listen to; (5) waiting a day or more to reread the material so they can read it as if someone else had written it.

The benefits of having children learn to edit and proofread their writing are not limited to improved writing skills and performance. They learn to organize their thoughts and pay attention to details. In essence, children learn critical thinking skills.

Writing activities

These exercises and activities are designed so that children can experience a sense of achievement while they are practicing their writing skills.

EXERCISE—Doodle descriptions

DESCRIPTION—In this activity, children draw doodles or simple line drawings and, using their imaginations, write descriptions of what the doodles represent. It is harder to recognize objects in a simple doodle since there are fewer clues, but it also gives more scope to the imagination.

To begin, show children examples of this kind of drawing and show how they can be looked at from different viewpoints.

Ex.=

Invite the participants to share their ideas for describing your examples of doodles. First have the children fill in blanks, then write a paragraph or even a story about the doodle. Then have children draw their own doodles and either find as many objects that it resembles as they can, or choose one thing it looks like to write about. This activity can be developed into a game by having children display their doodles while others try to identify it.

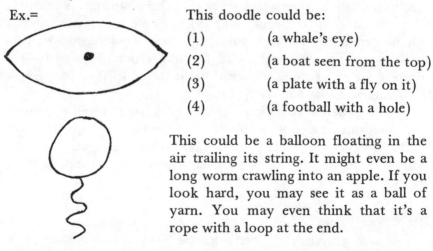

Ex.=

This doodle could be:

(1)   (a whale's eye)

(2)   (a boat seen from the top)

(3)   (a plate with a fly on it)

(4)   (a football with a hole)

This could be a balloon floating in the air trailing its string. It might even be a long worm crawling into an apple. If you look hard, you may see it as a ball of yarn. You may even think that it's a rope with a loop at the end.

EXERCISE—Word pictures

DESCRIPTION—Have children look at or imagine an object and

describe every possible characteristic of it in writing—color, shape, length, width, height, weight, texture, taste, density, usefulness, etc. This gives children practice in writing and also in noticing details.

A game can be developed by starting with the question, "What am I?" A child writes a description of an object without naming it and then reads it aloud to see if the listeners can guess the identity of the object.

Many children ehjoy expanding this exercise into describing and drawing space monsters, weird beasts or magical creatures. Descriptions can include both physical characteristics and personalities. Any illustrations should include only the traits described in writing, thus stressing to the child the importance of the written word.

EXERCISE—Personification

DESCRIPTION—Children pretend to be an animal or an object such as a tire, tree, bee, football, typewriter, sock or hat. Then they write about how they live, act and feel. This encourages children to see things from and write about different viewpoints.

Have children draw a picture of their subject, personifying it with eyes, other facial features, arms, legs, clothing, etc. Then have children write about what the animal or object does and its complaints about the things that happen to it.

The easiest way to get children started is to ask, "How would you feel if you were a _____ (ex.= sock) and people _____ (ex.= wore) you every day?" Trace the sock's complaints about feet being stuffed into it, being stretched, stuck into shoes where it's dark and scary, pounded by walking, getting hot and sweaty, being drowned in the washing machine, shrunk by a hot dryer, and finally having to do the same thing over the next day. The story can even be expanded to make the sock a rebel who fights back in funny ways. This writing exercise requires children to develop a greater awareness of other people's feelings as well as writing skills.

EXERCISE—Posters and Menus

DESCRIPTION—Writing and designing posters for imaginary

131

businesses and menus for imaginary restaurants give children writing practice that they enjoy.

Some children may wish to design posters to advertise clothing stores like Tracy's Tops and Bottoms, while others might choose to advertise a speed shop such as Racy Rick's Motors. Many children may like to design travel posters for real or imaginary places in the past, present or future. A make-believe advertising agency can have a list of clients who need advertising posters, insuring variety in designing and writing posters for the different types of businesses.

Writing and designing menus is especially appealing to children since the topic is the beloved subject of food. For example, menus can be designed for ice-cream shops or fast food outlets. Children can choose to write either serious menus representing balanced nutrition or funny ones with strange and crazy foods. Sometimes real menus can be obtained to use as examples.

EXERCISE—Newspaper ads

DESCRIPTION—Writing advertisements of the classified type is a good exercise in being both brief and clear. As subjects for advertisements, tutors can suggest funny, silly, or make-believe items or situations (ex.= child wants a magic pencil that writes its own stories, a bear wants to buy a thousand honey pots), or realistic ads (ex.= child wants to buy a goldfish, find his lost bracelet, offer services as a mower of lawns).

Show children that all essential information must be included in ads. It's a good idea to write a paragraph first and then reduce it into as few words as possible without losing any necessary facts. For "Wanted to Buy" ads, for example, children should (1) describe what they want to buy in sufficient detail, (2) state the price range they're interested in paying, and (3) list how, where and/or when to contact them. "For Sale" ads should (1) explain what is for sale and its condition, (2) quote the price wanted for the item, and (3) tell how, where, and/or when to contact the seller. Children may want to draw and color the object of their ad.

If the tutor can find a legitimate reason for it, real experience can be brought into this assignment by actually running an ad written by the children in a local newspaper. The instructor can help children edit the ad carefully to lower the cost while retaining the important facts. This can be a real writing adventure for children.

ACTIVITY—Making books or newspapers

DESCRIPTION—A good way to encourage children to practice their writing is to help them make their own books and newspapers. They can enjoy a new writing experience and end up with a treasured keepsake that can be reread or displayed and read to other people. Copies can be made on copying machines and autographed as gifts for relatives and friends.

Begin making a book by having children write, edit and proofread a short story. Check the work thoroughly and discuss any desirable changes. When both tutor and child are satisfied with the content and mechanics of the writing, decide on such details of the book as the size and number of pages, illustrations and where they should go, and the cover. If pages are separate sheets to be fastened together, there can be any number of them. If pages are made by folding larger sheets in half, the number of pages must be in multiples of four. A page size that uses standard typing paper avoids the need for cutting.

A cover is easily made by cutting out two pieces of cardboard of equal size for use as the front and back of the book. The size depends upon how big a book the child wants or what the available paper allows. Children can design the cover and then draw and/or letter it on separate sheets to be taped or pasted to the cardboard, or they can draw directly on it or even decorate it with wallpaper, gift wrapping or fabric scraps.

Sit down with children to decide which sentences and what pictures will go on each page. Then have children print each sentence as neatly as possible or the tutor can type them to look more like a printed book. Then have children draw their pictures and paint or color them. The first page should be a title page with title, name of author and illustrator, and the date of publication.

After the pages are completed, it's time to bind the book. This can be accomplished by hand-sewing together the left margins of the covers and the inside pages. Books can also be stapled or fastened with paper fasteners. Put a neat bend in the top cover to make it easy to open. Nothing is left to do but to congratulate the young authors!

A single-sheet newspaper or newsletter can provide both writing practice and enjoyment. It has the side benefit of encouraging children to be more aware of current events. It can be made into a game with the child playing reporter and the instructor as the editor. Sources of information include television, radio, other newspapers, or news about school, home and friends. While a newspaper can have more than one article by different writers, a newsletter can have more than one article by the same writer and also express an opinion after reporting the facts.

Decide on a name and an emblem for your publication and letter it at the top of your sheet. Reporters select the subjects to write about and gather information. Then they carefully write their news stories, their opinion of the news, and a title or headline. (Writing opinions will help children practice analysis and critical thinking.) The reporter then goes over the story with the editor to decide if any changes are needed. The stories are then typed and proofread a final time. Carbon or duplicator copies can be used for distribution of the paper to interested readers.

SECTION III

Arithmetic, the third R

9. Introduction

WE EXIST IN A SOCIETY OF NUMBERS as well as words! Almost every aspect of modern life involves the manipulation of numbers. A few examples are making change, taking measurements, figuring savings on sales items, balancing checkbooks, calculating interest percentages, budgeting, figuring gas mileage, and filling out tax forms. Each person must be able to perform basic computation tasks or else depend on the honesty and capability of others.

You may ask, "Why bother when calculators and computers are so common?" Calculators are not always available and it's easy to make errors which can be detected only if you already know what the approximate correct amount is. As for computers, we have all heard about or experienced computer errors, and, according to reports such as one in *Reader's Digest* for April, 1976, computer theft and fraud are very real facts. Children need to master the basic math computation skills to become self-reliant adults in a number-oriented society.

The decline of the "new math"

The goal of the "new math" was to help children understand how our system of numeration works, which was in turn supposed to help their math performance. But teachers didn't understand it well enough to teach it, parents didn't understand it well enough to help children with their math problems, and children's ability to add, subtract, multiply and divide began to decline. Survival in modern society requires people to be able to solve the number problems of daily life quickly and accurately rather than understand our number system. To cite a parallel, a person need not be an expert mechanic to be able to drive a car. The emphasis in this section, therefore, is on teaching children to become competent in performing basic computations with speed and accuracy.

Teaching patterns

Many people are hesitant about teaching arithmetic because of their unpleasant memories about the difficulties they encountered in learning math. There is no reason to be uneasy or fearful about teaching mathematical operations if you emphasize to children that there are "patterns" for solving problems. For example, the pattern for borrowing or carrying, once mastered, works for any problem regardless of length.

Two things must be stressed to children studying arithmetic: (1) they must memorize the basic math facts so well that they can recall them immediately; (2) they will have to learn the pattern for each operation. The patterns will be explained in the teaching program.

10. Teaching Arithmetic

BEFORE THE LESSONS BEGIN, the tutor needs to know the child's level of competency in order to decide at what level of the program to start.

For very young children, who have not received any formal instruction in math, it is wise to begin with the first level, identifying numbers and their values. Older children have probably learned some math in school although their ability to work problems correctly and consistently is low. In both cases, the first step is to give a diagnostic test. The results will indicate the children's weaknesses and serve as a guide to areas of difficulty on which to place special emphasis.

The physical health and emotional state of the child affect his learning of arithmetic just as they do his learning to read and write. As discussed in the first two sections, the tutor should be alert for any signs of physical problems. Note the child's general state of health and any signs of poor coordination, abnormal movement or vision difficulties like squinting, frowning or staring. If any physical problem is suspected, the child should be taken for medical advice before beginning any lessons.

There's also little chance of success in trying to teach a child who has negative feelings about math or about his ability to learn it, and whose self-confidence and self-esteem are low. The tutor must take steps to reassure the child of his worth and ability. Explain that arithmetic is a step-by-step process and that both of you will make sure he completely masters one step before going on to the next, acting as a team to overcome his problem. The instructor must do his part by scheduling lessons at acceptable times, watching for boredom or restlessness, varying the activities, and patiently explaining and demonstrating math operations as many times as necessary.

Diagnostic testing

An informal diagnostic test for the basic operations in math is neither difficult to administer nor difficult to interpret. The sample test given on pages 140-145 can be used as is to analyze children's ability levels or used as a model by substituting problems. Both the organization of the test and the number of problems are designed to show patterns of errors which reveal the areas where a child is handicapped.

Each section of the test is taught in detail in the math program. The tutor need only look at those parts of the program where the test has indicated difficulty for full instructions on teaching those skills.

The diagnostic test can be administered in two different ways, depending upon the tester's preference or the time available: (1) take one or two of the most difficult problems from each level, and if the child misses one or both have him work the rest of the problems in that level; (2) give the entire test as shown but divide the groups of levels into different testing periods. The advantage of the first method is brevity, the disadvantage being that the possibility of guessing correct answers is greater. The second method shows a pattern of errors better and reduces the chance of lucky guesses. The larger number of problems makes the test more reliable even though the length of time may be less convenient.

For one child or a small group of children, a fixed time limit for the test sections is not necessary. Just watch the child for facial or body clues indicating confusion. When the child repeatedly does problems wrong and feels that he can't do any more, stop that part of the test. If time limits are more convenient for a reason such as working with a large group, about 30 minutes should be more than enough for each section except division, for which approximately 45 minutes should be allowed. Young children will work slowly and the easier problems at the start of each section will be done faster than the harder ones, but taking too much time even when the computation is done correctly indicates the need for practice.

When giving the test, make sure children show their work since how they do the computations will often indicate problem areas. Repeated patterns of errors can reveal, for example, that the child does not understand how to borrow, carry, shift in two-place multiplication, bring down in division, place money symbols, or even which part of the fraction to manipulate.

The math program lends itself to diagnostic testing because it is organized in levels of increasingly difficult tasks. For example, it is easier to identify and name the digit 5 than to add 5 plus 19. The scale of increasing difficulty is shown by the sequence in which the operations are arranged. Being able to identify numbers and know their values is the easiest and most basic of the arithmetic tasks. Word problems are the most difficult since a child must first read and understand the problem, choose what operation to use for solving it and then compute correctly.

If a child falters at one level, it is doubtful whether he will be able to master the next level. The levels in math are like a staircase, each step building upon previous learning, and become more difficult as the learner climbs upward. The tutor will thus realize that the lessons should begin at the lowest level where a child encounters difficulty. For example, if a child shows mastery of the process of addition but falters on subtraction, then the program should begin with subtraction and work up through multiplication and division.

When analyzing the diagnostic test, tutors should watch for patterns showing three general types of error: (1) the child does not know the basic number facts (ex.= 1 + 1 = 2, 9 - 6 = 3, 3 x 2 = 6); (2) the child does not fully understand the operation itself (ex.= how to carry or how to bring down in division); (3) the child makes errors as a result of carelessness or inattention. Even an apparent lack of pattern—missing some, getting some correct—indicates carelessness or inattention. The child cannot falter on any of these three types of errors and still successfully solve math problems.

After the test has been corrected and analyzed for weaknesses and strengths, show children how it indicates where they are having trouble. Explain how overcoming these problem areas will help them perform better on more complicated math problems.

Examples of each type of problem error commonly made by children are given in the program lessons. A convenient check list for the tutor to use in deciding where to begin teaching is given at the end of the test problems. The check list, too, follows the sequence of levels from easiest to most difficult.

Arithmetic diagnostic test

Number concepts

Circle the correct number of objects

Give a number to name each group

Addition

Basic addition facts

Noncarrying addition with two or more digits

11	29	64	271	181	123	671	132	3052	6007
+12	+50	+32	+11	+17	+456	+222	+365	+4013	+1101
23	79	96	282	198	579	893	497	7065	7108

Carrying addition

16	24	17	14	38	69	253	173	4869	6576
+5	+9	+6	+37	+44	+69	+48	+268	+5850	+4982
21	33	23	51	82	138	301	441	10,719	11,558

Subtraction

Basic subtraction facts

2	9	6	4	8	7	3	5	7	9
−1	−7	−5	−4	−2	−3	−2	−1	−5	−4
1	2	1	0	6	4	1	4	2	5

Nonborrowing subtraction with two or more digits

21	66	48	99	76	88	52	395	1869	9678
−10	−21	−17	−21	−32	−48	−40	−174	−1216	−2524
11	45	31	78	44	40	12	221	653	7154

Borrowing subtraction

10	17	25	36	71	60	143	281	5247	2,802
−1	−9	−6	−28	−24	−14	−86	−93	−1874	−1,355
9	8	19	8	47	46	57	188	3373	1,447

Multiplication

Basic multiplication facts

0	1	3	4	6	8	10	5	4	7
×4	×1	×2	×7	×3	×9	×7	×9	×5	×8
0	1	6	28	18	72	70	45	20	56

Multiplication by one digit without carrying

16	22	23	41	11	220	887	4,341	1,132	2,424
×0	×4	×2	×3	×7	×4	×1	×2	×3	×2
0	88	46	123	77	880	887	8,682	3,396	4,848

Multiplication by one digit with carrying

$$\begin{array}{r} 24 \\ \times 3 \\ \hline 72 \end{array} \quad \begin{array}{r} 19 \\ \times 2 \\ \hline 38 \end{array} \quad \begin{array}{r} 35 \\ \times 3 \\ \hline 105 \end{array} \quad \begin{array}{r} 496 \\ \times 6 \\ \hline 2,976 \end{array} \quad \begin{array}{r} 780 \\ \times 5 \\ \hline 3,400 \end{array} \quad \begin{array}{r} 356 \\ \times 4 \\ \hline 1,424 \end{array} \quad \begin{array}{r} 127 \\ \times 7 \\ \hline 889 \end{array} \quad \begin{array}{r} 2,459 \\ \times 8 \\ \hline 19,672 \end{array} \quad \begin{array}{r} 3,078 \\ \times 9 \\ \hline 27,702 \end{array} \quad \begin{array}{r} 5,054 \\ \times 6 \\ \hline 30,324 \end{array}$$

Multiplication with two digits

$$\begin{array}{r} 17 \\ \times 20 \\ \hline 340 \end{array} \quad \begin{array}{r} 24 \\ \times 30 \\ \hline 720 \end{array} \quad \begin{array}{r} 65 \\ \times 52 \\ \hline 3,380 \end{array} \quad \begin{array}{r} 38 \\ \times 16 \\ \hline 608 \end{array} \quad \begin{array}{r} 567 \\ \times 28 \\ \hline 15,876 \end{array} \quad \begin{array}{r} 123 \\ \times 23 \\ \hline 2,829 \end{array} \quad \begin{array}{r} 479 \\ \times 64 \\ \hline 30,656 \end{array} \quad \begin{array}{r} 586 \\ \times 43 \\ \hline 25,198 \end{array} \quad \begin{array}{r} 8,098 \\ \times 37 \\ \hline 299,626 \end{array} \quad \begin{array}{r} 6,049 \\ \times 95 \\ \hline 574,655 \end{array}$$

Division

Basic division facts

$$1\overline{)6}^{\,6} \quad 2\overline{)4}^{\,2} \quad 3\overline{)9}^{\,3} \quad 4\overline{)8}^{\,2} \quad 7\overline{)0}^{\,0} \quad 5\overline{)5}^{\,1} \quad 8\overline{)16}^{\,2} \quad 9\overline{)27}^{\,3} \quad 4\overline{)28}^{\,7} \quad 5\overline{)20}^{\,4}$$

One-step division with remainders using one-digit divisor

$$4\overline{)5}^{\,1r1} \quad 2\overline{)9}^{\,4r1} \quad 4\overline{)7}^{\,1r3} \quad 3\overline{)8}^{\,2r2} \quad 5\overline{)7}^{\,1r2} \quad 6\overline{)23}^{\,3r5} \quad 8\overline{)26}^{\,3r2} \quad 9\overline{)82}^{\,9r1} \quad 7\overline{)58}^{\,8r2} \quad 6\overline{)19}^{\,3r1}$$

Two or more step division without remainders using one-digit divisor

$$2\overline{)38}^{\,19} \quad 7\overline{)84}^{\,12} \quad 6\overline{)96}^{\,16} \quad 5\overline{)75}^{\,15} \quad 8\overline{)96}^{\,12} \quad 4\overline{)92}^{\,23} \quad 3\overline{)75}^{\,25} \quad 4\overline{)964}^{\,241} \quad 5\overline{)1,050}^{\,210} \quad 8\overline{)1,768}^{\,221}$$

Two or more step division with remainders using one-digit divisor

$$2\overline{)51}^{\,25r1} \quad 5\overline{)73}^{\,14r3} \quad 7\overline{)96}^{\,13r5} \quad 6\overline{)82}^{\,13r4} \quad 3\overline{)73}^{\,24r1} \quad 4\overline{)99}^{\,24r3} \quad 8\overline{)957}^{\,119r5} \quad 4\overline{)713}^{\,178r1} \quad 3\overline{)5,620}^{\,1,873r1} \quad 4\overline{)6,011}^{\,1,502r3}$$

One-step division without remainders using two-digit divisor

$$10\overline{)80}^{\,8} \quad 13\overline{)78}^{\,6} \quad 36\overline{)72}^{\,2} \quad 44\overline{)88}^{\,2} \quad 25\overline{)75}^{\,3} \quad 61\overline{)427}^{\,7} \quad 75\overline{)375}^{\,5} \quad 63\overline{)126}^{\,2} \quad 82\overline{)328}^{\,4} \quad 91\overline{)728}^{\,8}$$

One-step division with remainders using two-digit divisor

$$11\overline{)23}^{\,2r1} \quad 15\overline{)46}^{\,3r1} \quad 17\overline{)87}^{\,5r2} \quad 28\overline{)60}^{\,2r4} \quad 33\overline{)98}^{\,2r32} \quad 43\overline{)190}^{\,4r18}$$

$$52\overline{)110}^{\,2r6} \quad 72\overline{)500}^{\,6r68} \quad 68\overline{)402}^{\,5r62} \quad 93\overline{)887}^{\,9r50}$$

Two or more step division without remainders using two-digit divisor

$$10\overline{)220}^{\,22} \quad 12\overline{)240}^{\,20} \quad 18\overline{)720}^{\,40} \quad 14\overline{)294}^{\,21} \quad 23\overline{)713}^{\,31} \quad 45\overline{)495}^{\,11}$$

$$15\overline{)645}^{\,43} \quad 25\overline{)1,050}^{\,42} \quad 33\overline{)20,460}^{\,620} \quad 56\overline{)40,936}^{\,731}$$

Two or more step division with remainder using two-digit divisor

$$13\overline{)278}^{\,21r5} \quad 16\overline{)591}^{\,36r15} \quad 24\overline{)502}^{\,20r22} \quad 48\overline{)1,097}^{\,22r41} \quad 65\overline{)4,023}^{\,61r58}$$

$$39\overline{)7,642}^{\,195r37} \quad 74\overline{)8,291}^{\,112r3} \quad 58\overline{)1,197}^{\,20r37} \quad 84\overline{)9,653}^{\,114r77} \quad 92\overline{)9,917}^{\,107r73}$$

Money math

Understanding money

$5¢ = \underline{5}$ pennies $28¢ = \underline{28}$ pennies

$\$1 = \underline{100}$ pennies $2\ dimes = \underline{4}$ nickels

$50¢ = \underline{5}$ dimes $\$1 = \underline{4}$ quarters

Manipulating dollar and cent signs

$$
\begin{array}{r} 12¢ \\ -2¢ \\ \hline 10¢ \end{array} \quad
\begin{array}{r} 32¢ \\ +51¢ \\ \hline 83+ \end{array} \quad
\begin{array}{r} 45¢ \\ +12¢ \\ \hline 57¢ \end{array} \quad
\begin{array}{r} 72¢ \\ +19¢ \\ \hline 91¢ \end{array} \quad
\begin{array}{r} 59¢ \\ +38¢ \\ \hline 97¢ \end{array} \quad
\begin{array}{r} 96¢ \\ -75¢ \\ \hline 21¢ \end{array} \quad
\begin{array}{r} 86¢ \\ -29¢ \\ \hline 57¢ \end{array} \quad
\begin{array}{r} 97¢ \\ -18¢ \\ \hline 79¢ \end{array}
$$

$$
\begin{array}{r} \$1.23 \\ +.11 \\ \hline \$1.34 \end{array} \quad
\begin{array}{r} \$5.13 \\ +1.65 \\ \hline \$6.78 \end{array} \quad
\begin{array}{r} \$12.13 \\ +3.89 \\ \hline \$16.02 \end{array} \quad
\begin{array}{r} \$155.67 \\ +168.32 \\ \hline \$323.99 \end{array} \quad
\begin{array}{r} \$6.49 \\ -.32 \\ \hline \$6.17 \end{array} \quad
\begin{array}{r} \$8.79 \\ -3.59 \\ \hline \$5.20 \end{array} \quad
\begin{array}{r} \$10.05 \\ -5.89 \\ \hline \$4.16 \end{array} \quad
\begin{array}{r} \$123.02 \\ -57.54 \\ \hline \$65.48 \end{array}
$$

$$
\begin{array}{r} \$1.76 \\ \times 3 \\ \hline \$5.28 \end{array} \quad
\begin{array}{r} \$18.92 \\ \times 5 \\ \hline \$94.60 \end{array} \quad
\begin{array}{r} \$3.69 \\ \times 27 \\ \hline \$99.63 \end{array} \quad
\begin{array}{r} \$41.76 \\ \times 35 \\ \hline \$1461.60 \end{array}
$$

$$4)\overline{\$7.68} = \$1.92 \qquad 25)\overline{\$100.25} = \$4.05$$

$$\$.39)\overline{\$15.99} = 41 \qquad \$.89)\overline{\$46.28} = 52$$

Fractions

Concepts—Name the colored-in parts with a fraction

$= \frac{1}{2}$ $= \frac{2}{4}$ $= \frac{2}{3}$ $= \frac{3}{8}$

$0000\ = \frac{1}{4}$ $00000\ = \frac{3}{5}$ $000000\ = \frac{5}{6}$

Manipulating fractional numbers

$$\frac{1}{2} + \frac{1}{2} = \frac{2}{2} = 1 \qquad \frac{1}{4} + \frac{2}{4} = \frac{3}{4} \qquad \frac{5}{12} + \frac{2}{12} = \frac{7}{12}$$

$$
\begin{array}{r} 1\frac{1}{3} \\ +2\frac{1}{3} \\ \hline 3\frac{2}{3} \end{array} \quad
\begin{array}{r} 6\frac{5}{11} \\ +1\frac{2}{11} \\ \hline 7\frac{7}{11} \end{array} \quad
\begin{array}{r} 3\frac{1}{9} \\ +4\frac{4}{9} \\ \hline 7\frac{5}{9} \end{array} \quad
\begin{array}{r} 1\frac{1}{9} \\ -\frac{1}{9} \\ \hline 1 \end{array} \quad
\begin{array}{r} 7\frac{5}{6} \\ -2\frac{4}{6} \\ \hline 5\frac{1}{6} \end{array} \quad
\begin{array}{r} 8\frac{6}{7} \\ -5\frac{3}{7} \\ \hline 3\frac{3}{7} \end{array}
$$

$$\frac{7}{8} \qquad \frac{6}{9} \qquad \frac{5}{7}$$
$$\frac{2}{8} \qquad -\frac{4}{9} \qquad -\frac{1}{7}$$
$$\overline{\frac{5}{8}} \qquad \overline{\frac{2}{9}} \qquad \overline{\frac{4}{7}}$$

$$\frac{4}{5} \times \frac{1}{2} = \frac{4}{10} = \frac{2}{5} \qquad \frac{3}{4} \times \frac{2}{3} = \frac{6}{12} = \frac{1}{2}$$

$$\frac{3}{6} \div \frac{1}{3} = \frac{9}{6} = 1\frac{1}{2} \qquad \frac{1}{2} \div \frac{3}{4} = \frac{4}{6} = \frac{2}{3}$$

$$\frac{1}{2} = \frac{5}{10} \qquad \frac{3}{4} = \frac{9}{12} \qquad \frac{2}{3} = \frac{4}{6} \qquad \frac{2}{5} = \frac{6}{15}$$

$$\frac{1}{4} \qquad 2\frac{5}{6} \qquad \frac{7}{8} \qquad 3\frac{6}{10} \qquad 1\frac{3}{10} \qquad 7\frac{1}{6} \qquad 10\frac{1}{10} \qquad 9\frac{4}{8}$$
$$+\frac{1}{2} \qquad +5\frac{2}{12} \qquad -\frac{1}{4} \qquad -1\frac{2}{5} \qquad +\frac{1}{5} \qquad +5\frac{2}{3} \qquad -3\frac{5}{10} \qquad -4\frac{5}{8}$$
$$\frac{3}{4} \qquad 7\frac{12}{12}=8 \qquad \frac{5}{8} \qquad 2\frac{2}{10}=2\frac{1}{5} \qquad 1\frac{5}{10}=1\frac{1}{2} \qquad 12\frac{5}{6} \qquad 6\frac{6}{10}=6\frac{3}{5} \qquad 4\frac{7}{8}$$

Fractions expressed as decimals

$$.2 \qquad .6 \qquad .18 \qquad 7.86$$
$$+.1 \qquad +.7 \qquad +.90 \qquad +3.12$$
$$.3 \qquad 1.3 \qquad 1.08 \qquad 10.98$$

$$.5 \qquad .17 \qquad 1.32 \qquad 8.22$$
$$-.2 \qquad -.08 \qquad -.42 \qquad -4.55$$
$$.3 \qquad .09 \qquad .90 \qquad 3.67$$

$$.4 \qquad .5 \qquad .15 \qquad 5.86$$
$$\times .2 \qquad \times .6 \qquad \times .3 \qquad \times .2$$
$$.08 \qquad .30 \qquad .045 \qquad 1.172$$

$$2.4 \qquad .32 \qquad 2.16 \qquad 5.1$$
$$2)\overline{4.8} \quad 3)\overline{.96} \quad .6)\overline{1.296} \quad .11)\overline{561}$$

Word problems

1. If a boy has 2 red balls and 3 green balls, what is the total number of balls? 5

2. A girl had 27 dolls and then gave 9 away. How many dolls does she have left? 18

3. If 4 candy bars cost $1.00, then what is the price for each? 25¢

4. Each cookie cost 17¢. How much does 23 cookies cost? $3.91

5. Joe gave Mark 1/4 of a pie and gave Sue 1/2 of a pie. How much of the pie did Joe give away in all? 3/4

6. Ed bought $17.34 worth of toys on sale which regularly cost $34.11. What is the difference between the sale price and the regular price? $16.77

7. Ed bought a $6.53 ball, a $.99 hammer, a $13.76 saw, and 6 nails which cost $.04 apiece. What is the total price for the things Ed bought? $21.52.
   How much would 10 nails cost?   40¢

8. Mike ran 3 miles a day for 5 days and Sue ran 2 miles a day for 6 days. What is the combined number of miles that both Mike and Sue ran?   27 miles
   Who ran the most miles?   Mike

9. Jim drove 120 miles in 5 days and Ann drove 176 miles in 4 days. Who drove the most miles each day?   Ann
   What is the total number of miles driven each day?   24 + 44 = 68 miles

10. Gary wanted to take Debbie out to dinner. He had $14.27 on Monday and would get $16.54 more on Wednesday. Each single dinner cost $15.17. Could Gary buy dinner for both himself and Debbie on Tuesday?   No
    Could he pay for both dinners on Thursday?   Yes

Planning the program

Once the tutor has diagnosed the child's math handicaps, it is time to remedy the weaknesses which hinder his performance. To find detailed teaching instructions, the tutor looks in the section of the program where the child encountered difficulty in the test.

The math lesson plans are modeled after the lesson plans for reading. As with reading, math instruction should be given at least 3 times a week at home and the same or daily in school. The periods should range from 45 minutes to 1 hour. Each lesson ought to begin with a review of basic facts, proceed to an explanation of the lesson along with some assigned problems for practice, and end with a game to reinforce and assess what has been learned. This can be followed by an informal time between child and tutor for discussing problems and even for making suggestions to improve the next lesson. Many children appreciate feeling that they are involved and participating in the program.

After instruction on a specific weakness or at a certain math level, it is a good idea to give a test to measure how much learning is retained. This posttest will indicate if the child has achieved a level of mastery or whether reteaching is needed.

Arithmetic Evaluation Sheet

Child's name _____

Date _____   Good Aver. Poor

Identifying numbers and their values

1. Has memorized the counting numbers   ____ ____ ____

2. Knows each counting number's value   ____ ____ ____

3. Knows the place value of numbers   ____ ____ ____

Addition

1. Knows basic facts   ____ ____ ____

2. Adds from right to left and vertically ____ ____ ____

3. Carries correctly   ____ ____ ____

Subtraction

1. Knows basic facts   ____ ____ ____

2. Subtracts from right to left and vertically ____ ____ ____

3. Borrows correctly   ____ ____ ____

Multiplication

1. Knows basic facts   ____ ____ ____

2. Multiplies from right to left and times
   top numbers   ____ ____ ____

3. Carries correctly   ____ ____ ____

4. Can multiply with more than one multiple ____ ____ ____

Division

1. Knows basic facts   ____ ____ ____

2. Divides with the divisor from left to right ____ ____ ____

146

3. Subtracts and brings down the next
number   _____ _____ _____

4. Can divide with more than one divisor   _____ _____ _____

Money math

1. Recognizes and understands the value of
money   _____ _____ _____

2. Manipulates the money symbols correctly   _____ _____ _____

Fractions

1. Understands the concept of fractions   _____ _____ _____

2. Can add fractions   _____ _____ _____

3. Can subtract fractions   _____ _____ _____

4. Can make equivalent fractions   _____ _____ _____

5. Can work with mixed fractions   _____ _____ _____

6. Can multiply fractions   _____ _____ _____

7. Can divide fractions   _____ _____ _____

8. Can borrow in mixed fractions   _____ _____ _____

9. Can work with fractions expressed as
decimals   _____ _____ _____

Word problems

1. Reads and understands the problem   _____ _____ _____

2. Can separate and organize the data   _____ _____ _____

3. Accurately performs the necessary
operations   _____ _____ _____

Tutors will find it best to teach lessons in the exact sequence in which the operations are presented. To maintain flexibility and prevent children from becoming discouraged, teach each step in the program until the child seems overwhelmed by a particular level. Then switch to the easiest level of the next operation, for example, from adding $\begin{array}{r} 567,899 \\ +979,868 \\ \hline \end{array}$ to the basic facts in subtraction. Teach the next level until the child again appears unable to advance further.

When children have learned most of the levels of a particular operation but stumble on the level of the highest difficulty, switching to the easiest level of the next operation is a morale booster. Children will find their confidence improved by discovering how easy the beginning steps of the next operation seem.

This program for teaching the basics in arithmetic is designed to meet the individual needs of each child, whether he needs beginning or remedial instruction in math. Since arithmetic is composed of increasingly difficult levels which require the mastery of previous steps, tutors should remind children that the key to success is to master each step on the stairs toward increasing arithmetic competency. Remember, children should learn the "patterns."

Since so many of the basic facts require memorization, the tutor may find it necessary to teach children how to memorize numbers. Things they can do to help themselves learn their basic facts are: (1) say the facts aloud over and over; (2) write the facts down again and again; (3) manipulate objects representing the facts; (4) see the basic facts in their mind with their eyes closed or open.

These techniques incorporate oral, visual, physical and mental stimuli to strengthen the learning of basic facts. Some children memorize faster using one or a combination of techniques instead of another. After trying all four, tutor and child should evaluate which way works best for him.

All memory lessons can be reinforced with games and practice exercises. Learning can also be intensified through the use of oral and written quizzes which require children to recall their basic facts under pressure and upon demand. The quizzes will also measure the amount of learning that has occurred.

Progress charts are easy to make for recording children's achievement in memorizing basic facts or in the different levels of each operation. The charts help stimulate learning by providing a visual record for children to watch their progress. See pages 17-18 for examples.

The lessons

Identifying numbers and their values

Before any child can begin to learn the four basic math operations, he must be able to identify numbers and know their values. The digits 0, 1, 2, 3, 4, 5, 6, 7, 8, 9 are used alone or in combination to form any number for a math problem. Thus children must be able to recognize the worth of the digits and their combinations.

Begin teaching the order and value of the digits by showing how they are counted and their respective worth. Choose items that the child is familiar with, such as marbles or pennies, as objects to represent the number indicated by the digit. Make a chart and arrange the objects as shown.

Ex.= 0 =

1 = O

2 = O O

3 = O O O

4 = O O O O

5 = O O O O O

6 = O O O O O O

7 = O O O O O O O

8 = O O O O O O O O

9 = O O O O O O O O O

Let the child help you sort the objects and say the numbers and then do it himself until he seems to have the idea. Make sure he knows each digit's worth by asking questions such as, "Give me 4 pennies," or showing him a group of marbles and having him write and say the number which the group represents. Questions

149

like this can easily be made into a variety of games with tutor and child asking each other.

An example of such a game is to divide a number of pennies or marbles into two equal groups. One player asks a question about digits as explained above. If the second player can't answer correctly, the first player takes that number of marbles from him. If the second player does answer correctly, he takes the specified number of marbles from the first player. It is then the second player's turn to ask the digit question.

Another game is to make flash cards with one set marked with digits and the other set with objects drawn to represent a number.

Ex.=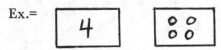

The cards are then mixed and laid down in orderly rows face up. Players take turns reading the number from a number card, picking up that card and a matching object card. If the cards match, the player keeps the cards for 2 points. Otherwise the cards are put back. The winner is the player with the most points when all the cards have been picked up.

When the child has mastered the use of these single digits, it's time to begin teaching him to manipulate numbers and digits. Reviewing the chart, point out that each digit represents a value of one more than the preceding digit. Review the digits with their values.

Get children used to the idea of combining numbers by playing games in which some digits are placed together to produce a new counting number on the chart (ex. 1 and 4 become 5). Use flash cards or objects and allow the child to use the chart until he becomes comfortable and accurate in performing this task. Such exercises teach both the concept of beginning addition and the concept of an equation. Learning the digits and their order can be further reinforced by asking the child to name the digits in sequence or by asking him to name the digit that comes either before or after another digit.

Then explain that often there are more things to count than represented by 9, so you're going to show how to combine these digits to make bigger numbers and how to know what they represent.

The next step is to expand the chart to represent the number 10 by showing the child how to combine the 1 with the 0 to make 10. Then teach the child how to continue counting while showing each increase in number value.

Ex.= 9 = oooooooo

10 = ooooooooo

11 = ooooooooooo or [10] + 1

12 = oooooooooooo or [10] + 2

13 = ooooooooo o ooo or [10] + 3

20 = oooooooooooooooooooo or [10] + [10]

Explain that to show more than 9, two digits must be combined and so you are going to combine the two smallest digits. Point out that 0 (zero) means an empty group or "set" and that the digit 1 in front of it means a group of 10 objects, one more than 9. Show that the number 11 means a group of 10 plus 1 more. Continue by displaying the rest of the pattern of one group of 10 plus 2, then 3, etc. When 20 is reached, demonstrate how the 2 represents two groups of 10 and repeat the procedure for explaining how to combine the digits in order. Keep the progression of numbers going up to at least 100. Have children learn the words twenty, thirty, etc., and point out that after 100 these are repeated. A chart like the following will help explain the place values of digits and introduce children to the idea of ever larger numbers. The first four place values are the most important for children to learn because most of the math problems they encounter in school use 1 to 4 digits.

151

Etc.	1,000,000's Millions	100,000's Hundred thou	10,000's Ten thousands	1,000's Thousands	100's Hundreds	10's Tens	1's Ones	
							9	= 9 ones
						1	9	= 1 ten + 9 ones
					2	1	9	= 2 hundreds + 1 ten + 9 ones
				3	2	1	9	= 3 thousands + 2 hundreds + 1 ten + 9 ones

This chart can help children learn both the total value of a number and the value of each of its digits. Have them memorize each place value so well that they can point to each column and identify its place value without error.

Then ask children to name each digit place value and the total number (ex. 219 = 2 hundreds, 1 ten, 9 ones). The next step is to write numbers down without the columns and have children name each digit's place value and the total value. Finally, say numbers orally and have the child write the numbers down to see if he understands the spoken names for numbers.

With older children, you may wish to write numbers with words and have the child express them in digits (ex.= thirty-nine = 39). Generally children will not have too much difficulty understanding place value if they have learned to count up to 100 and memorized the numbers in their order (ex.= 20's, 30's, 40's, etc.). Continue both visual and oral practice on place values until the student demonstrates that he understands.

Tell children that long numbers—more than 3 digits—are marked off by commas spaced 3 digits apart moving from right to left. Practice reading numbers in thousands, ten thousands, hundred thousands, and millions.

Ex.=   2,164   42,164   942,164   1,942,164

Although some children are helped by the charts, children must realize how important it is to memorize these counting numbers and their order.

A numbering activity that young children often enjoy is connecting numbered dots to make a picture which they can color. These number pictures are easily made: (1) take a picture from a magazine or newspaper; (2) place it on top of a piece of drawing paper; (3) press dots on the outline of the picture hard enough to appear on the drawing paper; (4) remove the picture and fill in the dot impressions with pencil or pen; (5) number the dots in sequence by the counting numbers of 1, 2, 3, 4, etc. Such pictures can be used later for practicing the times tables by numbering the dots with a progression of multiples (ex.= 3, 6, 9, 12, etc.).

Making calendars can not only be a fun activity, but it also gives children practice in writing their numbers in order along with providing practice in both reading and spelling the days of the week and the months of the year. As for the illustrations, encourage children to make a series of related pictures with titles. When finished, allow the children to hang their calendars up or give them away as gifts.

To further reinforce learning the counting numbers, games can be played with different colored digit flash cards. The digits 0 to 9 are put on white cards for the 1's value, on blue cards for the 10's value, and on red cards for the 100's value. (This color code is merely an aid to learning and should be discontinued once children have learned place values.) Learning the counting numbers will be further reinforced by having children help make the cards.

One game played with multicolored flash cards begins by having players group the cards according to their colors. One player challenges the other to make a specific three-digit number. If the other makes the number correctly, he keeps the cards. If his answer is wrong, the cards are put back and the second player challenges. When all the cards have been picked up, each player counts his cards to see who has won the game, thereby getting more counting practice!

An easy variation of the flash card game is to have the first player make a three-digit number for the other player to name. If the second player can name the number, he keeps the cards. If the second player can't name the number correctly, the flash cards are put back. The game continues with the second player making a number and asking the first player to name it. The winner is the player with the most cards, again adding to counting practice.

Addition

Basic addition facts—The basic facts of addition must be mastered before children can compute more complex addition problems. These facts are nothing more than the addition or combination of numbers from 0 to 9 (ex.= 4 + 1 = 5, 6 + 5 = 11). Children must study and memorize them so that any sum can be quickly named. Mastery of these basic facts is so important for accurate and quick computation that the need for their memorization can't be over-emphasized. If the child does not memorize them, he will later have to struggle with the basic facts when he should be concentrating on the process of carrying in difficult addition problems.

One type of basic fact chart for addition is provided below as an aid for helping children memorize these facts. To use the chart, tell the child to place one finger on a number at the top and place a finger from the other hand on a number in the first (left) column. He should bring his fingers straight across and straight down until they meet on a number. This is the sum of the two numbers added together. Once children learn to use this chart, they will probably not need to use their fingers but merely use their eyes to locate a sum.

Addition chart

+	0	1	2	3	4	5	6	7	8	9	10	11	12
0	0	1	2	3	4	5	6	7	8	9	10	11	12
1	1	2	3	4	5	6	7	8	9	10	11	12	13
2	2	3	4	5	6	7	8	9	10	11	12	13	14
3	3	4	5	6	7	8	9	10	11	12	13	14	15
4	4	5	6	7	8	9	10	11	12	13	14	15	16
5	5	6	7	8	9	10	11	12	13	14	15	16	17
6	6	7	8	9	10	11	12	13	14	15	16	17	18
7	7	8	9	10	11	12	13	14	15	16	17	18	19
8	8	9	10	11	12	13	14	15	16	17	18	19	20
9	9	10	11	12	13	14	15	16	17	18	19	20	21
10	10	11	12	13	14	15	16	17	18	19	20	21	22
11	11	12	13	14	15	16	17	18	19	20	21	22	23
12	12	13	14	15	16	17	18	19	20	21	22	23	24

To combine fun with practice, any of the basic math fact charts can easily be made into number jigsaw puzzles. Substitute the charts for paragraphs and follow the steps for making paragraph jigsaw puzzles described on page 88 in the reading activities.

Another type of study aid involves making either individual flash cards or strips for each combination of numbers. Explain that the plus sign means to combine or put together. It may help to use objects as examples to clarify the meaning of the plus sign by joining groups.

Ex.=

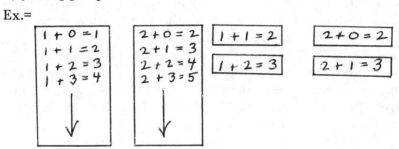

It is a good idea to practice by showing the child the flash cards and having him orally name the sum. Such practice easily lends itself to many types of game. Don't overlook written exercises using sheets of problems like those in Appendix B, page 235, or timed quizzes. Both speed and accuracy are the desired goals.

Addition without carrying—When children have thoroughly memorized the basic addition facts, it is time to teach them to apply their knowledge. Begin by reviewing the facts, then tell children that they are ready to do harder addition problems.

Place a group of flash cards on the basic addition facts spread out evenly from each other.

Ex.=

$$\frac{\begin{array}{r}1\\+2\end{array}}{3} \qquad \frac{\begin{array}{r}3\\+4\end{array}}{7} \qquad \frac{\begin{array}{r}2\\+6\end{array}}{8} \qquad \frac{\begin{array}{r}1\\+8\end{array}}{9} \quad \leftarrow Begin\ here$$

Then have the child start doing each problem in order, from right to left, to get him used to working in that direction. When this is

155

accomplished, tell the child that instead of four problems you're going to make one problem out of all the numbers by moving the cards together.

Ex.=

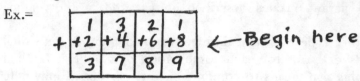

Make sure he compares the problem with the earlier basic fact arrangement, and tell him that only one plus sign is needed in this kind of grouping. Reinforce the idea of still working straight up and down and from right to left when adding.

Work several problems together, checking to make sure children follow the addition pattern of straight up and down and right to left. Sometimes children try to add sideways, diagonally, or from the middle or left side if they see an easier basic fact that they know.

When the child seems to understand the pattern for adding in noncarrying problems, allow him to work more problems independently while you check his answers and show him any mistakes. Continue with practice exercises of mixed problems up to five digits and skill games to reinforce learning.

Addition with carrying—It is time to introduce addition problems involving the process of carrying. Explain to children that they have done so well they are now going to learn how to do the hardest kind of addition problems. Write down several examples of problems that require the carrying of only one number for the easiest form of computation.

Ex.=
$$17 \qquad 18 \qquad 14 \qquad 19$$
$$+9 \qquad +6 \qquad +7 \qquad +4 \qquad \leftarrow Begin\ here$$

Starting with the right-hand problem, ask children if they remember their basic addition facts, and what 9 plus 4 equals? When they say 13, tell them there is a pattern for carrying that they must always follow when the sum is more than 9. The rule is: Write down the last part of the number to the right underneath the line (ex.= the 3 from 9 + 4 = 13) and carry or put the first part of the number (ex.= the 1 from 13) to the left and above the next

156

number to be added. Then the carried number is added to the number directly below it.

Ex.=

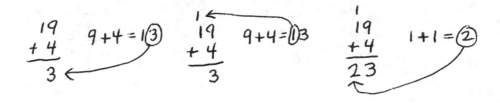

Once children grasp the rule for carrying, increase the difficulty of the problems. Continue with this type of problem until the children are proficient.

Ex.=

$$\overset{1}{3}7 \quad \overset{1}{4}7$$
$$\underline{+\ 6} \quad \underline{+\ 5}$$
$$43 \quad 52$$

Now include another number on the bottom part of the problem. Show that the carried number is added the same way. This also provides a good opportunity to reemphasize the importance of orderly columns when writing down problems. Continue with this type of problem until the child demonstrates mastery.

Ex.=

$$\overset{1}{3}7 \quad \overset{1}{4}7$$
$$\underline{+16} \quad \underline{+25}$$
$$53 \quad 72$$

The next step requires that all the previously learned levels of addition be applied. Explain that even though these are the hardest types of addition problems, the student already knows everything he needs to solve them. Write down problems which involve both column addition and a great deal of addition. Help children with such problems until they demonstrate a high degree of accuracy. Further reinforce learning with practice sheets.

Ex.=

$$
\begin{array}{r}
7 \\
9 \\
6 \\
+4 \\
\hline
26
\end{array}
\qquad
\begin{array}{r}
\overset{1}{6}5 \\
72 \\
+38 \\
\hline
175
\end{array}
\qquad
\begin{array}{r}
5,671 \\
3,689 \\
+1,253 \\
\hline
10,613
\end{array}
\qquad
\begin{array}{r}
\overset{1}{6},\overset{1}{4}32 \\
+9,788 \\
\hline
16,220
\end{array}
\qquad
\begin{array}{r}
62,\overset{1}{1}\overset{1}{9}5 \\
+58,207 \\
\hline
129,402
\end{array}
$$

With complex addition, three types of carrying errors are common: (1) placing the carried number above the wrong part of the problem; (2) not carrying when necessary in either the middle or the end of the problem; (3) forgetting to add the carried numbers or adding them to the wrong numbers. All of these errors can be remedied by thoroughly reviewing the pattern for carrying, then helping apply that pattern to problems until children demonstrate their understanding.

Subtraction

Basic subtraction facts—Subtraction is the "undoing" of addition through removing numbers. As with addition, children must memorize the basic facts of subtraction. These are generally easy to learn for children who already know the addition facts because subtraction is the opposite or inverse of addition. Thus in the problem $\begin{array}{r}7 \\ -2 \\ \hline\end{array}$, all a child has to do is remember what number + 2 = 7, or 5.

The process of subtraction can be clearly illustrated by taking a group of pennies or other objects and separating or subtracting out a smaller group as a set to show what is left.

Ex.=

00000   000   00   00   000   00000
  5   −   3   =   2   because   2 + 3   =   5

A subtraction chart on the basic facts follows. To stimulate children's interest, point out the patterns of numbers on the chart and then have them try to figure out why or how the pattern was developed. For example, note that the diagonal squares running from top left to bottom right are the same number, and the diagonal squares running from top right to bottom left are alternating lines of even and odd numbers.

Subtraction Chart

−	0	1	2	3	4	5	6	7	8	9	10	11	12
0	0												
1	1	0											
2	2	1	0										
3	3	2	1	0									
4	4	3	2	1	0								
5	5	4	3	2	1	0							
6	6	5	4	3	2	1	0						
7	7	6	5	4	3	2	1	0					
8	8	7	6	5	4	3	2	1	0				
9	9	8	7	6	5	4	3	2	1	0			
10	10	9	8	7	6	5	4	3	2	1	0		
11	11	10	9	8	7	6	5	4	3	2	1	0	
12	12	11	10	9	8	7	6	5	4	3	2	1	0

Note: Subtract the numbers in the top column to the right of the minus sign from numbers on the left side column below the minus sign.

Further reinforcement of the subtraction facts can be achieved through the use of subtraction flash cards, practice sheets (see Appendix B) and games. Sometimes children learn faster by using flash cards with three numbers in a subtraction equation on the front and the same three numbers in an addition equation on the back. This is a beginning for teaching "families" of facts.

Ex.=

Front

$$5 - 3 = 2$$

Back

$$2 + 3 = 5$$

Subtraction without borrowing—Once children can answer questions on the subtraction facts accurately and quickly, the tutor can introduce more complex problems involving more numbers. Write several sample problems and review the principle of working each problem straight up and down and from right to left. Then guide children through solving the problems until they have mastered this type of subtraction. Watch carefully to make sure that the child subtracts each number in a problem properly and accurately. Gradually introduce more numbers into the problems.

Ex.=

$$\begin{array}{r} 9 \\ -7 \\ \hline 2 \end{array} \qquad \begin{array}{r} 75 \\ -21 \\ \hline 54 \end{array} \qquad \begin{array}{r} 17 \\ -10 \\ \hline 7 \end{array} \qquad \begin{array}{r} 946 \\ -121 \\ \hline 825 \end{array} \qquad \begin{array}{r} 7{,}493 \\ -5{,}261 \\ \hline 2{,}232 \end{array} \qquad \begin{array}{r} 85{,}367 \\ -14{,}151 \\ \hline 71{,}216 \end{array}$$

Subtraction with borrowing—Borrowing problems present the highest level of difficulty in subtraction. Be sure children are listening carefully to your instructions and stress how important it is to memorize the borrowing pattern. Start by writing down a problem in which the number in the ones' place is larger on the bottom than on the top (ex.= $\begin{array}{r} 52 \\ -7 \\ \hline \end{array}$). Demonstrate with your pennies or other objects that you can't take 7 of them away from a group having only 2. In order to subtract, therefore, you must borrow from the larger number to make the top number bigger. Show that the borrowing pattern always takes away 1 from the nearest top number to the left, which is in the tens' place. The number is crossed out and the reduced number written above it to take its place. Then show how the 1 is placed with the 2 to make the large number 12 (one 10 + 2 = 12) from which 7 can be subtracted. If there is no number below the reduced number, it is the same as subtracting 0 from it because zero represents an empty set.

Ex.=

$$\begin{array}{r} 52 \\ -7 \\ \hline \end{array} \qquad \begin{array}{r} {}^{4}\!\!\not{5}{,}2 \\ -7 \\ \hline 5 \end{array} \qquad \begin{array}{r} {}^{4}\!\!\not{5}{,}2 \\ -7 \\ \hline 45 \end{array}$$

Repeat this pattern of borrowing with math problems having two numbers on top and one on the bottom until children have the pattern memorized. Then supervise the work with practice problems.

When this type of problem has been mastered, introduce larger problem of progressive difficulty. Do not proceed from one level of difficulty to another until children are proficient.

Ex.= Borrowing only once

$$\begin{array}{r} \overset{6}{\cancel{7}}{}^{1}4 \\ -\ 28 \\ \hline 46 \end{array} \qquad \begin{array}{r} {}^{4}\overset{}{\cancel{5}}{}^{1}3 \\ -\ 26 \\ \hline 27 \end{array} \qquad \begin{array}{r} {}^{5}\overset{}{\cancel{6}}{}^{1}4 \\ -\ 19 \\ \hline 45 \end{array}$$

$$\begin{array}{r} 7\,\overset{6}{\cancel{7}}{}^{1}4 \\ -\ 28 \\ \hline 746 \end{array} \qquad \begin{array}{r} 3\,{}^{4}\overset{}{\cancel{5}}{}^{1}3 \\ -\ 26 \\ \hline 327 \end{array} \qquad \begin{array}{r} 4\,{}^{5}\overset{}{\cancel{6}}{}^{1}4 \\ -\ 19 \\ \hline 445 \end{array}$$

$$\begin{array}{r} 7\,\overset{6}{\cancel{7}}{}^{1}4 \\ -428 \\ \hline 346 \end{array} \qquad \begin{array}{r} 3\,{}^{4}\overset{}{\cancel{5}}{}^{1}3 \\ -126 \\ \hline 227 \end{array} \qquad \begin{array}{r} 4\,{}^{5}\overset{}{\cancel{6}}{}^{1}4 \\ -219 \\ \hline 245 \end{array}$$

Now introduce successive borrowing. Stress that the borrowing pattern remains the same in that 1 is always borrowed from the nearest top number to the left.

Ex.=

$$\begin{array}{r} {}^{4}\cancel{5}{}^{11}\cancel{2}{}^{1}4 \\ -\ \ 68 \\ \hline 456 \end{array} \qquad \begin{array}{r} {}^{6}\cancel{7}{}^{11}\cancel{2}\,13 \\ -\ \ 54 \\ \hline 669 \end{array}$$

$$\begin{array}{r} \cancel{6}{}^{5}\cancel{4}{}^{13}{}^{1}5 \\ -178 \\ \hline 467 \end{array} \qquad \begin{array}{r} \cancel{7}{}^{6}\cancel{3}{}^{12}{}^{1}3 \\ -687 \\ \hline 46 \end{array}$$

Continue supervising the working of problems until you are sure that successive borrowing does not confuse the children. The next step is to introduce staggered borrowing. Various games and practice sheets will help reinforce the borrowing pattern for use on both successive and staggered borrowing problems.

Ex.=

$$
\begin{array}{r}
\overset{4}{\cancel{5}}\ \overset{3}{\cancel{1}}\ \overset{}{\cancel{4}}{}^{1}2 \\
-\ 1\ \ 4\ \ 2\ \ 5 \\
\hline
3\ \ 7\ \ 1\ \ 7
\end{array}
\qquad
\begin{array}{r}
\overset{7}{\cancel{8}}\ \overset{}{1}2\ \overset{8}{\cancel{9}}{}^{1}5 \\
-\ 2\ \ 6\ \ 7\ \ 6 \\
\hline
5\ \ 6\ \ 1\ \ 9
\end{array}
$$

An area where many children encounter difficulty in borrowing is where one or more zeros are present in the top number. Generally they have little trouble when the zero is the first number on the right but more if it is in the middle. The reason is they can't see how they can borrow from a zero. Explain that since 0 is an empty set it must have another number before it to make a larger number. Therefore, the 1 is borrowed from the 30, which is crossed out and 29 written above it. The 2 is then subtracted from the 9 of 29.

Ex.=

$$
\begin{array}{r}
\overset{2\ 9}{\cancel{3\ 0}}1 \\
-\ \ 2\ 9 \\
\hline
2\ 7\ 2
\end{array}
$$

Give children practice with this type of problem until they have mastered it, then give problems with more digits.

Ex.=

$$
\begin{array}{r}
\overset{6}{\cancel{7}}\ \overset{13}{\cancel{4}}\ \overset{9}{\cancel{0}}{}^{1}0 \\
-\ 5\ \ 5\ \ 4\ \ 2 \\
\hline
1\ \ 8\ \ 5\ \ 8
\end{array}
$$

Errors with borrowing in subtraction are largely caused by children not memorizing the pattern for borrowing and thereby failing to apply the borrowing pattern correctly. Once a child thoroughly understands the pattern and is accurate in his computations, he may not need to cross out and write down the carried number but may be able to do it in his head. If accuracy fails, however, go back to the physical action since it serves as a visual stimulus to reinforce the learning process.

Checking subtraction—Checking subtraction is a valuable tool for helping children to increase accuracy and confidence even though it takes time and thereby reduces the speed of computation. Its principal value lies in the fact that a child who is unsure of his answer to a problem can check it for accuracy.

In teaching the pattern for checking, begin with easy problems. Explain that an answer is correct if it can be added to the bottom number of the problem to equal the top number.

Ex.=
$$\begin{array}{r} 17 \\ -9 \\ \hline 8 \end{array}$$
$$\left(\begin{array}{r} 17 \\ -9 \\ \hline +8 \\ \hline 17 \end{array}\right)$$
or
$$\begin{array}{r} 17 \\ -9 \\ \hline 8 \end{array} \qquad \begin{array}{r} 9 \\ +8 \\ \hline 17 \end{array}$$

Repeat until the pattern for checking has been learned and then have children check problems of increasing difficulty.

Ex.=
$$\begin{array}{r} 86 \\ -24 \\ \hline \end{array} \qquad \begin{array}{r} 103 \\ -29 \\ \hline \end{array} \qquad \begin{array}{r} 412 \\ -176 \\ \hline \end{array} \qquad \begin{array}{r} 5,211 \\ -2,788 \\ \hline \end{array}$$

Multiplication

Basic multiplication facts—It is an absolute necessity that children learn their times tables! Of course it's true that multiplication is simply repeated addition (ex.= 4 x 3 = 3 + 3 + 3 + 3), and that children can add repetitively to figure out a times table. But such repeated addition interferes with quick and accurate computation because of both the time lost and the distraction from other steps in solving problems.

Three types of teaching aids should be provided to help children study their multiplication facts. Depending upon the preference of the tutor or the child, these aids can be used for quiet study, oral practice drills or games. They include individual flash cards with the answers on front or back, strips with the answers on front or back, and a 0-to-12 multiplication chart.

Ex.= Individual flash cards   Strips

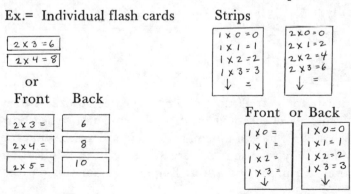

163

Multiplication chart

X	0	1	2	3	4	5	6	7	8	9	10	11	12
0	0	0	0	0	0	0	0	0	0	0	0	0	0
1	0	1	2	3	4	5	6	7	8	9	10	11	12
2	0	2	4	6	8	10	12	14	16	18	20	22	24
3	0	3	6	9	12	15	18	21	24	27	30	33	36
4	0	4	8	12	16	20	24	28	32	36	40	44	48
5	0	5	10	15	20	25	30	35	40	45	50	55	60
6	0	6	12	18	24	30	36	42	48	54	60	66	72
7	0	7	14	21	28	35	42	49	56	63	70	77	84
8	0	8	16	24	32	40	48	56	64	72	80	88	96
9	0	9	18	27	36	45	54	63	72	81	90	99	108
10	0	10	20	30	40	50	60	70	80	90	100	110	120
11	0	11	22	33	44	55	66	77	88	99	110	121	132
12	0	12	24	36	48	60	72	84	96	108	120	132	144

Multiplication by one digit without/with carrying— After the basic facts are mastered, introduce multiplication of larger numbers by one digit. Write down a few problems which do not require any carrying. Explain that multiplication is worked from right to left like addition and subtraction, except that the single digit by which the top number is multiplied is moved to the left mentally rather than physically.

Ex.=

$$\begin{array}{r} 1,213 \\ \times\ 3 \\ \hline 3,639 \end{array}$$

Point out that so far all the products have been 9 or less than 9 and have children check their multiplication charts to see how relatively few squares have numbers of 9 or less. Explain that for numbers over 9 they're going to learn to carry in multiplication much like they learned in addition. Emphasize that this pattern for carrying must be memorized since it will always remain the same for solving any multiplication problems.

Write down a problem such as 16 times 5. Ask what 5 times 6 equals. When told 30, show where to write the 0 and how to place the 3 above the next top number to the left. Then ask what 5 times 1 equals. When they say 5, tell children to add in their heads the 5 to the number they carried, which equals 8. Write down the 8 to the left of the 0.

Ex.=

$$
\begin{array}{r} 16 \\ \times\,5 \\ \hline \end{array}
\qquad
\begin{array}{r} {}^{3}16 \\ \times\,5 \\ \hline 0 \end{array}
\qquad
\begin{array}{r} {}^{3}16 \\ \times\,5 \\ \hline 80 \end{array}
$$

$5 \times 6 = 30$ Write 0, carry 3
$5 \times 1 = 5 +$ carried $3 = 8$

Continue with problems of this type requiring only one carried number until the children are proficient.

Ex.=

$$
\begin{array}{r} {}^{4}26 \\ \times\,7 \\ \hline 182 \end{array}
\qquad
\begin{array}{r} 52 \\ \times\,8 \\ \hline 416 \end{array}
\qquad
\begin{array}{r} {}^{2}36 \\ \times\,4 \\ \hline 144 \end{array}
$$

Then introduce problems requiring two or more numbers to be carried.

Ex.=

$$
\begin{array}{r} {}^{1\,3}425 \\ \times\,6 \\ \hline 2{,}550 \end{array}
\qquad
\begin{array}{r} {}^{2}728 \\ \times\,3 \\ \hline 2{,}184 \end{array}
\qquad
\begin{array}{r} {}^{8\,1}392 \\ \times\,9 \\ \hline 3{,}528 \end{array}
$$

$$
\begin{array}{r} {}^{3\,4\,1}5{,}682 \\ \times\,5 \\ \hline 28{,}410 \end{array}
\qquad
\begin{array}{r} {}^{5\,1\,4}1{,}716 \\ \times\,8 \\ \hline 13{,}728 \end{array}
\qquad
\begin{array}{r} {}^{5\,5\,2}8{,}783 \\ \times\,7 \\ \hline 61{,}481 \end{array}
$$

Be sure to watch for such common errors as misplacing carried numbers, forgetting to add the carried number or attempting to multiply the carried number.

Multiplication by two or more digits without/with carrying— Multipliers with two or more digits present the greatest level of difficulty in multiplication. Each multiplier greatly increases the number of steps, thereby increasing the chances of error.

Before attempting this type of problem, children need to have mastered all the other levels of multiplication so they can concentrate on the required shifting pattern.

Begin by writing down a simple problem with only one multiplier in order to review the right-to-left sequence of multiplying. Then add another digit to the multiplier, again one that will not require any carrying so the emphasis will be on the shifting pattern.

Ex.=
$$\begin{array}{r} 134 \\ \times\ 2 \\ \hline 268 \end{array} \qquad \begin{array}{r} 134 \\ \times\ 12 \\ \hline \end{array}$$

Now tell children that adding another multiplier causes the answer to shift so the right side number of the answer will be under the digit by which you are multiplying. Explain that to begin shifting, a filled-in zero is placed under the 8, and then begin multiplying with the 1. The filled-in zero can be dropped when the child has the shifting pattern firmly in mind.

Ex.=
$$\begin{array}{r} 134 \\ \times\ 12 \\ \hline 268 \\ 134\bullet \end{array}$$
First multiplier used
Filled-in zero and second multiplier used

Remind children they still multiply from right to left and that they must keep their numbers in line because they must add them later. If a child keeps trying to reuse the first multiplier, it may be a good idea to have him cross out each multiplier after he has used it.

Ex.=
$$\begin{array}{r} 134 \\ \times\ 1\!\!\!/2 \\ \hline 268 \end{array} \qquad \begin{array}{r} 134 \\ \times\ \!\!\!/1\!\!\!/2 \\ \hline 268 \\ 134\bullet \end{array}$$

After all the multipliers have been used, tell children the next step is to draw a line and begin to add. Point out that this is just like any addition problem, and remind them how to carry in the addition if necessary.

Ex.=
$$
\begin{array}{r}
134 \\
\times\ 12 \\
\hline
{}^1268 \\
+134\bullet \\
\hline
1{,}608
\end{array}
$$

Go over several problems until the shifting pattern has been learned, then introduce problems with one multiplier that requires carrying.

Ex.=
$$
\begin{array}{r}
{}^1\ {}^2 \\
123 \\
\times\ 27 \\
\hline
{}^1861 \\
+246\bullet \\
\hline
3{,}321
\end{array}
$$

After that, introduce problems with both multipliers requiring carrying. Children often become confused with all the carried numbers resulting from two or more multipliers. One technique for eliminating confusion is to have them cross out the carried numbers after they have been used.

Ex.=
$$
\begin{array}{r}
{}^1\ {}^2 \\
157 \\
\times\ 23 \\
\hline
471
\end{array}
\qquad
\begin{array}{r}
{}^{\not1}\ {}^{\not2} \\
157 \\
\times\ 23 \\
\hline
471 \\
+314\bullet \\
\hline
3{,}611
\end{array}
$$

From this point, introduce multiplication problems with three or more multipliers. Do several of these complex problems with the child, reviewing each step, before he goes ahead on his own.

Ex.=

$$\begin{array}{r} \overset{2}{\cancel{2}}\ \overset{2}{\cancel{2}} \\ \cancel{4}\ \cancel{4} \\ 567 \\ \times\ 3\cancel{4}\cancel{2} \\ \hline 1\,134 \\ 2268\ \bullet \\ +1701\ \bullet\ \bullet \\ \hline 193,914 \end{array}$$

While evaluating the children's work on these problems, keep in mind the high level of difficulty and expect errors until they have the whole operation clear in their minds. Remember this kind of problem causes children difficulty as late as high school.

When using zero in the multiplier, don't teach shortcuts until the child knows the pattern for shifting thoroughly, and will not become confused or dependent upon the shortcut method.

Ex.=   Shortcut

$$\begin{array}{r} \overset{1}{} \\ 15 \\ \times\ 20 \\ \hline 00 \\ +30\ \bullet \\ \hline 300 \end{array} \qquad \begin{array}{r} 15 \\ \times 20 \\ \hline 300 \end{array} \qquad 0 \times 15 = \textcircled{0}$$

Then multiply by 2

It should be especially clear now why children must memorize the basic multiplication facts so they can recall them immediately and correctly, thereby allowing them to concentrate on manipulating numbers and learning the patterns for operations. The more difficult the problem, the greater the handicap that a child who does not know his times tables must bear.

Division

Basic division facts—Division is the opposite or inverse of multiplication. Just as multiplication may be considered repeated addition, division may be considered repeated subtraction. Even though division is a different operation with numbers in contrast to multiplication, it requires the use of times tables. Children therefore should have mastered their times tables before attempting division, but learning the division basic facts will also help reinforce memorization of the times tables.

Introduce the division signs of ÷ and ⌐. Point out that ÷ means "divided by" and the other sign, when numbers are read left to right, means "divided into." This means in the same problem stated the two different ways, the numbers are exchanged (ex.= **6 ÷ 3 = 2** is the same as **3⌐6̄**).

Explain that division is solved through the use of multiplication. When they see a problem like 6 ÷ 2 or 2 ⌐ 6 , they must

ask themselves what number times 2 gives 6. When the children answer "three," say, "Right! Two divided into six equals three because two times three equals six." This reinforces understanding of the relationship between multiplication and division, extends their knowledge of families of number facts, and introduces the basic form for checking division. Give many of these problems until the children can answer correctly and quickly.

Flash cards for division can be made by taking the products of the times tables and dividing them by one of the two smaller numbers to get the other number.

Ex.=

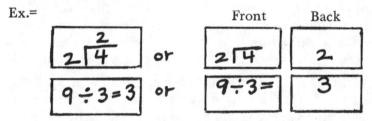

Like the multiplication flash cards, the answer can be either on the front of the card or on the back. You may also want to make division strips to match the multiplication strips. Having children help you make the cards and strips will help reinforce learning and give them the feeling of participation.

Ex.=

Multiplication   Division Strips
Strip

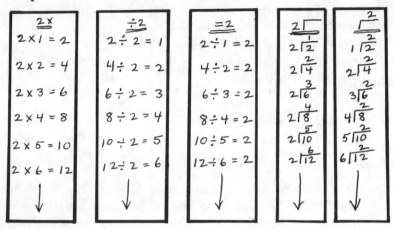

The multiplication chart can also be used for division. Show children that any number in the body of the chart divided by the number in the same row at the far left equals the number at the top of the column, and vice versa. It is easy to make an informal game of finding division facts on the chart. Be sure to tie in the multiplication facts often (ex.= $42 \div 6 = 7$ because $7 \times 6 = 42$).

One-step division without remainder using one-digit divisor—Once children are familiar with both the division signs and facts, introduce the working form for one-step division by writing down a sample problem (ex.= $3\overline{)9}$). Ask the children what multiple of 3 is equal to 9 in the times table. When they answer $3 \times 3 = 9$, show them how to write the answer 3 above the 9. Then show children that the answer 3 is multiplied by the divisor 3 with the result written below the 9, which is then subtracted. Since $3 \times 3 = 9, 9 - 9 = 0$.

Ex.=

$$\begin{array}{r} 3 \\ 3\overline{)9} \end{array} \qquad \begin{array}{r} 3 \\ 3\overline{)9} \\ -9 \\ \hline 0 \end{array}$$

Explain that this is part of the pattern for division—to divide, multiply, subtract, draw a line and write the answer. Also point out that you realize this is a division fact they already know and can do in their heads, but that it's important to know this pattern for use in longer problems.

Continue with the working form of division until children have mastered this level.

One-step division with remainder using one-digit divisor—Tell children that not all numbers can be divided as easily as the previous problems and that some problems have numbers left over or remaining. Give a demonstration problem (ex.= $3\overline{)7}$). Now ask what multiple of 3 or what number times 3 equals 7. They should say "none." Agree and tell them that they must look for the multiple of 3 that comes closest to 7 without going over 7. Since 3 x 2 = 6, show children how to write the 2 above the 7, multiply and write the 6 below the 7. Now have them subtract 6 from 7 leaving 1. The 1 can be either left as is or written in the answer following a printed " r," the symbol for "remainder."

Ex.=

$$\begin{array}{r} 2 \\ 3\overline{)7} \\ -6 \\ \hline 1 \end{array} \qquad \begin{array}{r} 2\ r\ 1 \\ 3\overline{)7} \\ -6 \\ \hline 1 \end{array}$$

Demonstrate that if the remainder is larger than the divisor, they haven't used a big enough multiple and the answer will be wrong. When the remainder is smaller than the divisor as it is in the example, it shows that the answer is correct—that is, if they multiplied and subtracted correctly! Continue to work with the children on division problems with remainders until they have mastered them.

Two or more step division without remainder using one-digit divisor—Announce to children that they're going to learn how to divide larger numbers involving two steps. Write down the pattern of "divide, multiply, subtract, and bring down the next number," pointing out that bringing down the next number is new. Give a sample problem that starts out like one they have already worked

171

on in the previous level and show them how to continue by
bringing down the next number.

Ex.=

$$3\overline{)75} \qquad 3\overline{)75} \atop \begin{array}{r} 2 \\ -6 \\ \hline 1 \end{array} \qquad \begin{array}{r} 2 \\ 3\overline{)75} \\ 6 \\ \hline 15 \end{array} \longleftarrow$$ Bring down the next
number in the problem.

Tell children that the pattern of "divide, multiply, subtract
and bring down" may have to be repeated several times before a
problem is solved. Now ask what multiple of 3 equals 15. When
the response is 3 x 5 = 15, show them how to write the 5 above
the 5 in the problem, then multiply 5 x 3 and write down 15
below. Then subtract. Point out that the problem is over only
when there are no more numbers to bring down.

Ex.=

$$3\overline{)75} \qquad \begin{array}{r} 2 \\ 3\overline{)75} \\ -6 \\ \hline 15 \end{array} \qquad \begin{array}{r} 25 \\ 3\overline{)75} \\ -6 \\ \hline 15 \\ -15 \\ \hline 0 \end{array}$$

Next have children work problems like the following:

Ex.=

$$\begin{array}{r} 44 \\ 4\overline{)176} \\ -16 \\ \hline 16 \\ -16 \\ \hline 0 \end{array}$$

Show that 4 can't divide into 1 since it's too small a number
but it can divide into 17 because 17 is larger than 4. Continue
working this kind of problem until children feel comfortable in
grouping digits together to make a large enough number for
division by that divisor.

When children become successful and confident in working
these small problems, challenge them with longer problems that
involve more steps.

Ex.= $5\overline{)7,655}$ $2\overline{)13,582}$

Two or more step division with remainder using one-digit divisor—Review the two-step division procedure. Remind children that division problems can end with remainders, and that the remainder is written after the letter r in the answer. Give examples of doing two-step division with remainders, reviewing each step.

Ex.=

$$
\begin{array}{r}
24\ r\ 1 \\
4\overline{)97} \\
-8 \\
\hline
17 \\
-16 \\
\hline
1
\end{array}
\qquad
\begin{array}{r}
39\ r\ 6 \\
7\overline{)279} \\
-21 \\
\hline
69 \\
-63 \\
\hline
6
\end{array}
$$

Supervise children's work on practice problems and then give them more challenging ones.

Ex.= $5\overline{)9,763}$ $8\overline{)3,765}$

If children know their times tables and have learned to follow the division pattern, they shouldn't have too much trouble with problems like the examples given. However, they sometimes have difficulty with problems having a zero in the answer. Some will not falter at the 01 step, but others will require direction. Tell these that the closest multiple of 5 to 1 is 0, since 1 is too small for 5 to divide into evenly. Then show how to continue the problem.

Ex.=

$$
\begin{array}{r}
102\ r\ 3 \\
5\overline{)513} \\
-5 \\
\hline
01 \\
-0 \\
\hline
13 \\
-10 \\
\hline
3
\end{array}
$$

For the child who handles these problems easily, you may wish to show a shortcut. This involves putting 0 in the answer and bringing down the next digit until the number brought down is large enough to be divided by the divisor.

Ex.=

$$5\overline{)513} \quad \begin{array}{r} 102\,r3 \\ \hline \end{array}$$

$$\begin{array}{r} 102\,r3 \\ 5\overline{)513} \\ -5 \\ \hline 013 \\ -10 \\ \hline 3 \end{array}$$

One-step division without remainder using two-digit divisor—The use of two-digit divisors forces children to work with larger numbers, thereby increasing the difficulty of the task. Begin this level of division by explaining to children that they are now ready for harder division problems. Do *not* go on to this level until children have mastered the easier ones.

Give a sample problem using 10, 11 or 12 as the divisor because they should know their times tables up to 12. Work the problems with the children, pointing out that the larger divisor can not be divided into the number represented by the first digit so they have to use the number created by combining the first and second digits.

Ex.=

$$\begin{array}{r} 2 \\ 10\overline{)20} \\ -20 \\ \hline 0 \end{array} \qquad \begin{array}{r} 5 \\ 11\overline{)55} \\ -55 \\ \hline 0 \end{array} \qquad \begin{array}{r} 4 \\ 12\overline{)48} \\ -48 \\ \hline 0 \end{array}$$

After children have worked a series of problems with 10, 11 and 12, introduce larger two-digit divisors. Tell children that they may have to try several numbers to find the closest multiple. They can do this methodically by multiplying on paper or in their head first by 1, by 2, by 3, etc., until they get too large an answer. Another way is to see how many times the first digit of the divisor could go into the first two digits of the number being divided.

Ex.=

$$\begin{array}{r} 2 \\ 24\overline{)48} \\ -48 \\ \hline 0 \end{array} \qquad \begin{array}{r} 24 \\ \times 1 \\ \hline 24 \end{array}\text{(Too sm)} \qquad \begin{array}{r} 24 \\ \times 2 \\ \hline 48 \end{array}\text{(O.K.)} \qquad \begin{array}{r} 24 \\ \times 3 \\ \hline 72 \end{array}$$

                         (Too small)   (O.K.)   (Too large)

Reassure children that such estimating and trial and error is how everyone does these problems, and that all they need is practice.

Next try problems in which the divisor is too large for the first two digits so the third digit must be used. Estimate with children until the correct multiple is found and proceed with the problem.

Ex.=   2 divides into 12 6 times

$$\begin{array}{r} 5 \\ 24\overline{)120} \\ -120 \\ \hline 0 \end{array}\qquad \begin{array}{r} 24 \\ \times 6 \\ \hline 144 \end{array}\text{(Too large)}\qquad \begin{array}{r} 24 \\ \times 5 \\ \hline 120 \end{array}\text{(O.K.)}$$

One-step division with remainder using two-digit divisor—Review what has been learned in the use of two-digit divisors. Tell children that once again remainders can and do occur. Proceed to explain sample problems.

Ex.=

$$\begin{array}{r} 2 \ r\ 4 \\ 13\overline{)30} \\ -26 \\ \hline 4 \end{array}\qquad \begin{array}{r} 13 \\ \times 3 \\ \hline 39 \end{array}\qquad \begin{array}{r} 13 \\ \times 2 \\ \hline 26 \end{array}$$

When children become alarmed at the size of large remainders, remind them that it's only when the remainder is larger than the divisor that the problem is wrong. Also tell them that when the remainder is too large, first check the subtraction. If the subtraction is correct, then try the next larger multiple.

Ex. of correct answer=

$$\begin{array}{r} 4 \ r\ 28 \\ 33\overline{)160} \\ -132 \\ \hline 28 \end{array}$$

Ex. of two common errors=

$$\begin{array}{r} 4 \\ 33\overline{)160} \\ -132 \\ \hline 38 \end{array}$$

(Subtraction error)

$$\begin{array}{r} 3 \\ 33\overline{)160} \\ -99 \\ \hline 61 \end{array}$$

(Multiple too small)

Continue working until children can compute these problems accurately.

Two or more step division without remainder using two-digit divisor—Tell children that they're going to learn how to work problems involving two or more steps. Remind them that they must keep dividing as long as there is a number remaining to bring down in the problem. Begin with two steps, then go on to three and four steps. Remember that these are quite difficult problems, but point out to children that each step is done exactly the same way so they only need patience and care to work the longest problems correctly.

Ex.=

$$
\begin{array}{r}
11 \\
12\,\overline{)132} \\
-12 \\
\hline
12 \\
-12 \\
\hline
0
\end{array}
\qquad
\begin{array}{r}
231 \\
22\,\overline{)5{,}082} \\
-44 \\
\hline
68 \\
-66 \\
\hline
22 \\
-22 \\
\hline
0
\end{array}
\qquad
\begin{array}{r}
5{,}324 \\
31\,\overline{)165{,}044} \\
-155 \\
\hline
100 \\
-93 \\
\hline
74 \\
-62 \\
\hline
124 \\
-124 \\
\hline
0
\end{array}
$$

Two or more step division with remainder using two-digit divisor—If children are competent at the previous levels of division, problems ending with a remainder should not present too much difficulty. Show sample problems which end with a remainder, reviewing each step in the procedure. Here again the size of the remainder may bother some children. Remind them again that an answer is wrong only when the remainder is larger than the divisor.

Ex.=

$$
\begin{array}{r}
22\ \text{r}\ 23 \\
25\,\overline{)573} \\
-50 \\
\hline
73 \\
-50 \\
\hline
23
\end{array}
$$

When the children can compute two-step problems accurately, you may wish to challenge them with three- and four-step problems. Be patient—these kinds of problems can be difficult for even some high-school students! Each step increases the chance for error due to the greater number of digits and operations.

Ex.=

$$
\begin{array}{r}
322 \text{ r } 1 \\
59\overline{)18999} \\
-177 \\
\hline
129 \\
-118 \\
\hline
119 \\
118 \\
\hline
1
\end{array}
\qquad
\begin{array}{r}
9{,}028 \text{ r } 53 \\
61\overline{)550{,}761} \\
-549 \\
\hline
17 \\
-0 \\
\hline
176 \\
-122 \\
\hline
541 \\
-488 \\
\hline
53
\end{array}
$$

When children are working division problems with several steps, show them they can save time in estimating the multiple of a divisor by looking back at previous multiples. For example, in the problem below the child already knows what the multiples of 2, 6 and 1 are. He can see that 6 x 38 = 228 is too small, so he tries 7 x 38 = 266 to find the closest number to 296.

Ex.=

$$
\begin{array}{r}
2{,}61 \text{ ?} \\
38\overline{)99{,}476} \\
-76 \\
\hline
234 \\
-228 \\
\hline
67 \\
38 \\
\hline
296
\end{array}
$$

To analyze children's work in division, the tutor should look for: (1) neat and orderly rows of numbers because many errors are caused directly by lack of these; (2) correct multiplication; (3) correct subtraction; (4) proper following of the pattern of "divide, multiply, subtract and bring down." It is a good idea to compare problems where similar errors have been made to show children how and why they are repeating their mistakes. Be sure to do this in such a way that children realize the analysis is meant to help them improve and not to embarrass or punish them.

One technique to help children keep their numbers neat and in the correct column is to have them work their problems on graph paper, putting one number in each box. (Use larger-spaced graph paper for young children.) Switch back to regular paper as soon as you can, pointing out to children that legible numbers and orderly columns are not meant merely to look nice but rather to enable them to work the problems accurately.

Checking Division—Division answers can of course be checked by multiplying the answer times the divisor and adding any remainder. It can't take the place of children learning and applying the pattern for division, and in fact it slows down the speed of computation for a group of problems. On the other hand, checking reinforces all of the division operations.

Show children how to check an easy problem without a remainder, then with.

Ex.=

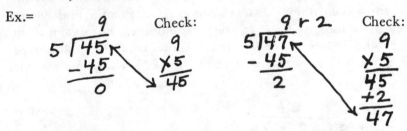

If a child has done the division correctly but makes mistakes in the checking process, it indicates that he needs more practice in multiplication. This kind of error occurs most frequently in long division with two-digit divisors which require shifting in the multiplication check.

Ex.= $37\overline{\smash{\big)}674{,}893}$

You can play a "Detective Game" by writing down a division problem with mistakes in it and show children that the check indicates that the answer is wrong. Have children detect what mistakes were made in "The Case of the Wrong Answer."

Another version of the detective game is to have a series of problems written on separate pieces of paper, each having on the back a clue for naming an object in the room (ex.= this object hangs on the wall (one clue), is black (second clue), is written on with chalk (third clue). As each problem is solved, the tutor reads aloud the clue. The first child who can name the object is "the detective who solves the case."

Money math

Understanding money—Money math refers to the practical use of basic operations with money signs and the understanding of the values of money symbols. In our society individuals must know the value of money and how to express it. It is important for children to be able to make purchases and count their change correctly, or they are at the mercy of whoever wishes to take advantage of them.

For children who do not recognize the names or the values of coins and bills, begin by displaying each commonly used coin and bill while explaining that the money system is based on the cent and its combinations. Introduce the cent and dollar signs (¢ and $). Teach the facts shown in the chart below, though you may wish to teach only part of it depending upon how much money the children have to spend.

Money Conversion Chart

		Cents	Pennies	Nickels	Dimes	Half Dollars	Dollars
Coins	Penny	1¢	1				
	Nickel	5¢	5	1			
	Dime	10¢	10	2	1		
	Quarter	25¢	25	5			
	Half dollar	50¢	50	10	5	1	
	Silver dollar	100¢	100	20	10	2	$1
Bills	Dollar bill	100¢	100	20	10	2	$1
	2-dollar bill	200¢	200	40	20	4	$2
	5-dollar bill	500¢	500	100	50	10	$5
	10-dollar bill	1000¢	1000	200	100	20	$10
	20-dollar bill	2000¢	2000	400	200	40	$20

When children have learned the values of the coins and bills, begin teaching them to make combinations. For example, ask a child to show you two cents. Then increase the difficulty of the task by asking him to make 7 cents in two different ways—7 pennies or 1 nickel and 2 pennies. Continue having children make various amounts of money in different combinations of coins until they can convert money easily.

One of the best ways to reinforce the importance of making change accurately is to play a "Store Game." The children are given a certain amount of money which they are to use to buy store goods such as toys or food. If they pay the wrong amount of money or accept the wrong change, they lose both their money and the things they wanted to buy. Real shopping experiences are especially valuable. This field trip can include having children figure out whether they have enough money to buy certain items and how much more money they would need to make the purchase.

Manipulating ¢ and $ signs in operations—Another important aspect of money math is the addition and subtraction of numbers involving money signs. Begin instruction with the cent and dollar signs used separately in problems. Emphasize how important it is to bring down each sign into the answer.

Ex.=

$$\begin{array}{r} 65¢ \\ +24¢ \\ \hline 89¢ \end{array} \qquad \begin{array}{r} 31¢ \\ -\ 7¢ \\ \hline 24¢ \end{array} \qquad \begin{array}{r} \$5 \\ +\$6 \\ \hline \$11 \end{array} \qquad \begin{array}{r} \$10 \\ \$6 \\ \hline \$16 \end{array}$$

After children have worked problems using the cent and dollar signs separately, demonstrate that dollars and cents can be written together. Show that the number of cents can be shown by a dot or decimal point after the number of dollars, followed by two digits. All the digits before the decimal point—that is, to the left of it—are dollars, while the two-digit number to the right of the point indicates the number of cents.

Tell children the money signs do not change the operations, and repeat the importance of bringing the dollar sign and decimal point straight down. Then show them how to do addition and subtraction problems.

180

Ex.=

$1.65	$13.42	$7.55	$29.86
+$ .33	+$25.51	-$ .21	-$15.23
$1.98	$38.93	$7.34	$14.63

When children are able to do such problems quickly and accurately, introduce problems involving carrying and borrowing. Remind pupils that they carry and borrow just as they learned with previous problems.

Ex.=

$1.65	$45.76	$8.37	$78.125
+$ .28	+$27.84	-$ .19	-$ 39.45
$1.93	$73.60	$8.18	$38.80

Although multiplication and division are not used as commonly as addition and subtraction in money math, tutors may wish to teach these operations. Start instruction by explaining that the multiplication and division in money problems are done the way they have already learned. The only thing they have to remember is how to move the decimal point. If neither the multiplier nor the divisor has a decimal, the decimal is brought straight down in multiplying and straight up in division.

Ex.=

$3.25 each
X 3 items
$9.75 total price

$3.25 price for each
3)$9.75 total price
items

It is not often that an amount of money is multiplied by another amount of money so don't get into that subject—it will be taken up later in Multiplying Decimals. As for dividing an amount of money by another amount to find out, for example, how many boxes of popcorn at $.12 each you could buy if you had $3.72, demonstrate these patterns and have children learn them: (1) when dividing the number of times into dollars and cents, the answer will always be in dollars and cents; (2) when dividing dollars and cents into dollars and cents, the answer will always be the number of times.

Ex.=

$$\begin{array}{r} \$\ .21 \\ 6\overline{\smash{)}\$1.26} \end{array}$$

$$\begin{array}{r} 31 \\ \$.12\overline{\smash{)}\$3.72} \\ -36 \\ \hline 12 \\ 12 \\ \hline 0 \end{array}$$

number of times $\overline{\smash{)}\ \$ \text{ and } ¢}$ $\$$ and $¢$

$\$$ and $¢$ $\overline{\smash{)}\ \$ \text{ and } ¢}$ number of times

Fractions

Concept of fractions—Since the fractions are sometimes used in tasks requiring measurement, children should learn both the concept and the manipulation of fractions.

Begin teaching the concept by writing the word "fraction" so children can see it. Define fraction as "part of a whole." Show them an apple or any other familiar object that can easily be cut. State that this is one complete, whole apple which can be represented by the number 1. Tell children that one whole can also be written $\frac{1}{1}$.

Go on to say that any part of this whole apple is a fraction, which has to be written in a certain way. Cut the apple into two equal pieces and write the fractional number $\frac{1}{2}$. Explain that the number above the line represents the number of parts separated from the others and is called the numerator. The number below the line represents the total pieces forming one whole object and is the denominator. Label the numerator and denominator and draw arrows to your example.

Ex.= $\frac{1}{2}$ Numerator = number of parts separated
Denominator = total number of pieces

Rejoin the two halves of the apple to show that the two pieces can be put back together to form a whole object, and that this fact can be represented by $\frac{2}{2}$. Any time the top and bottom numbers of a fraction are the same, that fraction represents a whole object (ex.= $\frac{4}{4}$, $\frac{6}{6}$, $\frac{9}{9}$, $\frac{15}{15}$).

Draw pie shapes to compare and contrast fractions. At first you can actually cut the pies into equal pieces and have children handle the fractional part or parts. Then just color the wanted parts.

Ex.=

1 = = $\frac{3 \text{ parts}}{3 \text{ total pieces}}$ = $\frac{1 \text{ part}}{3 \text{ total pieces}}$

1 = = $\frac{2 \text{ parts}}{2 \text{ total pieces}}$ = $\frac{1 \text{ part}}{2 \text{ total pieces}}$

1 = = $\frac{4 \text{ parts}}{4 \text{ total pieces}}$ = $\frac{3 \text{ parts}}{4 \text{ total pieces}}$

Continue with such exercises until children can easily recognize and name fractional numbers. The major mistake children make in naming fractions is to confuse the numbers for the numerators and denominators. It is only through practice that they learn the pattern of separated parts over total pieces.

Now introduce the idea of equivalent fractions. Demonstrate with the pie shapes such facts as $\frac{1}{2}$ equals $\frac{2}{4}$, $\frac{1}{3}$ equals $\frac{2}{6}$, $\frac{2}{3}$ is equal to $\frac{4}{6}$, and $\frac{3}{6}$ is the same as $\frac{1}{2}$. Let children play with the pie diagrams to reinforce these facts and perhaps discover other equivalencies.

Ex.=

$$\frac{3}{4} = \frac{6}{8} \qquad \frac{4}{12} = \frac{1}{3}$$

Point out that what they have done with the pies can be done with numbers by multiplying or dividing both the numerator and the denominator by the same number. Give examples, emphasizing the need for a common multiplier or a common divisor.

Ex.=
$$\frac{1}{4} = \frac{1 \times 2}{4 \times 2} = \frac{2}{8} \qquad \frac{5}{10} = \frac{5 \div 5}{10 \div 5} = \frac{1}{2}$$

$$\frac{2}{3} = \frac{2 \times 5}{3 \times 5} = \frac{10}{15} \qquad \frac{12}{16} = \frac{12 \div 4}{16 \div 4} = \frac{3}{4}$$

Manipulation of fractional numbers—Once children have learned the concept of fractions, announce that they are now ready to learn how to add, subtract, multiply and divide with fractions. Start by saying that only fractions with the same denominator can be added, and that only the numerators are added. Have them repeat the rule, "Add only the numerators," until they have it memorized. Give them some sample problems.

Ex.=
$$\frac{1}{4} + \frac{1}{4} = \frac{2}{4} \qquad \frac{1}{6} + \frac{4}{6} = \frac{5}{6} \qquad \frac{2}{3} + \frac{1}{3} = \frac{3}{3} \text{ or } 1$$

At this point, teach children to reduce fractions to their lowest terms. This means to see if the fraction can be made into an equivalent one with the lowest possible numerator and denominator. It is done by looking at each answer to see if both the numerator and denominator can be divided by the same divisor. Work examples while explaining each part of the process. Emphasize that both the numerator and denominator must be divisible by the same divisor, not two different ones. They know they have found the lowest term for a fraction when it cannot be further divided by any common divisor.

Ex.=
$$\frac{2}{4} = \frac{2 \div 2}{4 \div 2} = \frac{1}{2} \qquad \frac{6}{9} = \frac{6 \div 3}{9 \div 3} = \frac{2}{3} \qquad \frac{10}{15} = \frac{10 \div 5}{15 \div 5} = \frac{2}{3}$$

Next have children work addition problems in vertical form. Remind them the denominators must be the same and that numerators only are added.

Ex.=

$$\frac{2}{3}$$
$$+\frac{1}{3}$$
$$\frac{3}{3}=1$$

$$\frac{4}{9}$$
$$+\frac{1}{9}$$
$$\frac{5}{9}$$

$$\frac{2}{8}$$
$$+\frac{4}{8}$$
$$\frac{6}{8}=\frac{6\div2}{8\div2}=\frac{3}{4}$$

Now introduce mixed fractions—that is, whole numbers followed by a fraction. Show children on a ruler that any whole number can be followed by fractions up to a fraction that represents another whole number (ex.= $\frac{8}{8}$). Tell students to work the fractions first and the whole numbers second. Even though they're working with both fractions and whole numbers, the operation of addition remains the same.

Ex.=

$$1\frac{1}{4}$$
$$+2\frac{2}{4}$$
$$3\frac{3}{4}$$

$$4\frac{5}{10}$$
$$+1\frac{3}{10}$$
$$5\frac{8}{10}=5\frac{8\div2}{10\div2}=5\frac{4}{5}$$

For subtraction of fractions, children are to subtract only numerators and continue to use the common denominator as they did in addition. Reinforce this rule with sample problems, first in horizontal form, then vertical form, and with mixed fractions.

Ex.=

$$\frac{7}{8}-\frac{1}{8}=\frac{6}{8}=\frac{3}{4}$$

$$\frac{5}{6}$$
$$-\frac{1}{6}$$
$$\frac{4}{6}=\frac{2}{3}$$

$$4\frac{9}{12}$$
$$-1\frac{2}{12}$$
$$3\frac{7}{12}$$

In multiplication of fractional numbers, the two numerators are multiplied together and the two denominators are multiplied together. A common denominator is not necessary as it is in

185

addition and subtraction. Demonstrate the procedure to children.

Ex.=

$$\frac{2}{3} \times \frac{1}{5} = \frac{2}{15} \qquad \frac{3}{4} \times \frac{2}{3} = \frac{6}{12} = \frac{1}{2} \qquad \frac{4}{6} \times \frac{2}{3} = \frac{8}{18} = \frac{4}{9}$$

In multiplying a whole number by a fraction, the whole number is considered a numerator. Do some of these problems until that is clear.

Ex.=

$$3 \times \frac{1}{3} = \frac{3}{3} = 1 \qquad 5 \times \frac{1}{8} = \frac{5}{8} \qquad 2 \times \frac{3}{7} = \frac{6}{7}$$

In the case of mixed fractions, multiply the whole number times both the other whole number and the numerator of the fraction.

Ex.=

$$3 \times 1\frac{1}{5} = 3\frac{3}{5} \qquad 5 \times 2\frac{2}{12} = 10\frac{10}{12} = 10\frac{5}{6}$$

$$2 \times 2\frac{1}{9} = 4\frac{2}{9}$$

In division of fractions, there is one very important rule that must be memorized: Invert the divisor and multiply. Explain that to invert a fraction means to turn it upside down. Show how to change the division problem into a multiplication problem by inverting the divisor and changing the ÷ sign to an x. Then proceed as in any multiplication of fractions, multiplying both the numerators and the denominators.

Ex.=

$$\frac{2}{5} \div \frac{3}{5} = \frac{2}{5} \times \frac{5}{3} = \frac{10}{15} = \frac{2}{3}$$

A whole number will have to be changed into a fraction in order to be able to invert it. Since $\frac{1}{1}$ equals 1 whole, any number can be used as the numerator over a denominator of 1 (ex.= $\frac{4}{1}$ = 4 wholes). Inverted, $\frac{4}{1}$ becomes $\frac{1}{4}$. Thus a fraction that is divided by 4 or any number will be multiplied by $\frac{1}{4}$ or 1 over the number.

Ex.= $$\frac{1}{4} \div 4 = \frac{1}{4} \div \frac{4}{1} = \frac{1}{4} \times \frac{1}{4} = \frac{1}{16}$$

Next, point out that the children have become experts in adding and subtracting fractions with common denominators but now they need to know how to work with unlike denominators. This is done by changing one or both of the fractions into equivalent fractions that do have a common denominator. Review the process of making equivalent fractions by multiplying or dividing both the numerator and denominator by the same number. Reinforce their skills by leaving digits out of equations for children to identify and fill in.

Ex.= $\frac{1}{2} = \frac{1 \times 3}{2 \times ?} = \frac{3}{6}$ $\frac{3}{4} = \frac{? \times 5}{? \times 5} = \frac{15}{20}$ $\frac{?}{?} = \frac{2 \times 2}{4 \times 2} = \frac{4}{8}$

$\frac{9}{12} = \frac{9 \div 3}{12 \div 3} = \frac{?}{4}$ $\frac{2}{6} = \frac{2 \div 2}{6 \div 2} = \frac{1}{?}$ $\frac{6}{15} = \frac{6 \div 3}{15 \div 3} = \frac{?}{?}$

Then see if they can compute the equivalent fractions without using the long working form.

Ex.= $\frac{1}{2} = \frac{?}{4}$ $\frac{2}{6} = \frac{?}{3}$ $\frac{1}{3} = \frac{2}{?}$

If children are confused as to whether to multiply or divide, show them that they need only look at the relationship between the numbers that are given. In the first example above, the denominator 2 is multiplied by 2 to equal 4, so the numerator 1 should be also multiplied by 2 to get 2 for an answer of $\frac{2}{4}$. In the second problem, 6 has to be divided by 2 to make 3, so the numerator 2 is also divided by 2 to make 1. Go through these problems step by step to make them clearer.

Learning to find missing numerators or denominators is a difficult but necessary task. It is better to teach children how to approach these problems than to expect them to develop an intuitive grasp for solving them.

187

The next step is to apply the ability to make equivalent fractions to the task of finding common denominators for working with unlike fractions. The common denominator, it should be explained, is a number that can be divided by both of the present denominators. There are three ways of finding such a number. (1) If the smaller denominator divides evenly into the larger, use the larger denominator as the common denominator. Proceed to make equivalent fractions and solve the problem.

Ex.=

$$\frac{1}{4} = \frac{1}{4}$$
$$+\frac{1\times2}{2\times2} = \frac{2}{4}$$
$$\overline{\quad\quad\frac{3}{4}}$$

$$\frac{2\times2}{5\times2} = \frac{4}{10}$$
$$-\frac{3}{10} = \frac{3}{10}$$
$$\overline{\quad\quad\frac{1}{10}}$$

(2) If the first step fails, take the larger denominator and find the lowest multiple which the smaller denominator will divide into evenly. Make equivalent fractions and solve the problem.

Ex.=

$$\frac{1\times2}{5\times2} = \frac{2}{10}$$
$$+\frac{1\times5}{2\times5} = \frac{5}{10}$$
$$\overline{\quad\quad\frac{7}{10}}$$

(3) A last resort is to multiply the denominators together and use the product as a common denominator. The drawback to this is that the answer will probably be a larger fraction than necessary and require a reduction to its lowest terms.

Ex.=

$$\frac{1\times4}{6\times4} = \frac{4}{24}$$
$$+\frac{2\times6}{4\times6} = \frac{12}{24}$$
$$\overline{\quad\quad\frac{16}{24} = \frac{2}{3}}$$

188

After the children master the addition and subtraction of unlike fractions, challenge them with mixed fractions. The common denominator is found the same way.

Ex.=

$$1\frac{1}{4} = \frac{2}{8}$$
$$+2\frac{3}{8} = \frac{3}{8}$$
$$\overline{3\quad\frac{5}{8}}$$

$$4\frac{5}{6} = \frac{10}{12}$$
$$-3\frac{1}{4} = \frac{3}{12}$$
$$\overline{1\quad\frac{7}{12}}$$

When they demonstrate proficiency, teach children how to do problems involving borrowing. To subtract $2\frac{3}{8}$ from $5\frac{1}{8}$, for example, point out that the $\frac{3}{8}$ can't be subtracted from $\frac{1}{8}$ because $\frac{1}{8}$ is too small. Therefore 1 or $\frac{8}{8}$ is borrowed from the 5 and added to the $\frac{1}{8}$ to become $\frac{9}{8}$. Then the problem can be worked.

Ex.=

$$5\frac{1}{8} = \overset{4}{\cancel{5}}\frac{9}{8} \quad \left(\frac{8}{8}+\frac{1}{8}=\frac{9}{8}\right)$$
$$-2\frac{3}{8} = 2\frac{3}{8}$$
$$\overline{\quad 2\frac{6}{8} = 2\frac{3}{4}}$$

$$8\frac{1}{5} = \overset{7}{\cancel{8}}\frac{6}{5} \quad \left(\frac{5}{5}+\frac{1}{5}=\frac{6}{5}\right)$$
$$-3\frac{2}{5} = 3\frac{2}{5}$$
$$\overline{\quad 4\frac{4}{5}}$$

Children sometimes become confused not on how to borrow but how to convert the 1 into an equivalent fraction with the desired denominator. Review the concept of 1 whole having many different fractional equivalents (ex.= 1 = $\frac{1}{1}$, $\frac{2}{2}$, $\frac{5}{5}$, $\frac{8}{8}$, etc.). Point out that when borrowing they only have to match these equivalents to 1 with the common denominator in the problem.

Ex.=

$$3\frac{1}{8} = 2\frac{9}{8} \qquad 4\frac{2}{5} = 3\frac{7}{5}$$

Fractions greater than 1 are used when borrowing or carrying with fractions so it is useful for children to know what these fractions mean. Write down a fraction such as $\frac{10}{8}$. Since $\frac{8}{8}$ equals 1 whole, then $\frac{10}{8}$ is $\frac{2}{8}$ more than 1, and is equal to the mixed fraction of $1\frac{2}{8}$. To find out how much more than 1 a fraction is, the denominator is divided into the numerator (8 ⌐ 10) which gives you 1 with a remainder of 2 representing $\frac{2}{8}$. Another way to remember this is to think of the line in the fraction as meaning "divided by." In this case, then, $\frac{10}{8}$ means $10 \div 8$, which again results in $1\frac{2}{8}$. Work several problems until the children can convert fractions with ease.

Ex.=

$$\frac{3}{4} + \frac{2}{4} = \frac{5}{4} = 1\frac{1}{4} \qquad \frac{5}{6} + \frac{4}{6} = \frac{9}{6} = 1\frac{3}{6} = 1\frac{1}{2} \qquad \frac{12}{5} + \frac{2}{5} = \frac{14}{5} = 2\frac{4}{5}$$

It is also useful to show children how to convert a mixed fraction into a fraction greater than 1. The denominator is multiplied by the whole number and the numerator is added to the result. This operation is often useful when multiplying or dividing fractions.

Ex.=

$$2\frac{1}{8} = \frac{17}{8} \qquad 1\frac{15}{16} = \frac{31}{16} \qquad 6\frac{1}{7} = \frac{43}{7}$$

Fractions expressed as decimals—Fractions can also be expressed as decimals, which represent fractions with a denominator of 10 or a multiple of 10. A decimal point is used, and the first digit to the right of the decimal point stands for that number of tenths, a second digit added to the first digit stands for that number of hundredths. We generally use two digits after the decimal point, indicating how many hundredths there are in the decimal fraction.

Ex.=

$$\frac{39}{100} = .39 \qquad \frac{65}{100} = .65 \qquad \frac{7}{10} = .7 \text{ or } .70 \text{ or } .700$$

As can be seen, any number of zeros can be added to the right of the decimal point without changing the number.

Tell children that any fraction can be expressed as a decimal fraction. To convert it, take the numerator, add a decimal after it followed by two zeros and then divide *by* the numerator. Just as in money math, the decimal point is brought straight up in the answer.

Ex.= Fraction Conversion Decimal   Fraction Conversion Decimal

$$\frac{1}{2} = 2\overline{)1.00}^{.50} = .50 \qquad \frac{3}{4} = 4\overline{)3.00}^{.75} = .75$$

You may also wish to give children practice in converting fractions greater than 1 into a decimal statement.

Ex.=   Fraction   Conversion   Decimal

$$\frac{5}{2} = 2\overline{)5.00}^{2.50} = 2.50$$

Once children become proficient in converting fractions into decimals, instruction on the operations with decimals can begin. Explain each pattern while showing several examples to reinforce learning. Point out that in adding or subtracting decimals, the problem is set up with the decimal points aligned vertically.

The pattern for adding decimal fractions is to add the digits and bring the decimal point straight down.

Ex.=
$$\begin{array}{r} .4 \\ +.4 \\ \hline .8 \end{array} \qquad \begin{array}{r} .12 \\ +.3 \\ \hline .42 \end{array} \qquad \begin{array}{r} .13 \\ +.16 \\ \hline .29 \end{array} \qquad \begin{array}{r} 1.45 \\ +.93 \\ \hline 2.38 \end{array}$$

The pattern for subtracting decimal fractions is to subtract the digits and bring the decimal point straight down.

Ex.=
$$\begin{array}{r} .7 \\ -.1 \\ \hline .6 \end{array} \qquad \begin{array}{r} .29 \\ -.13 \\ \hline .16 \end{array} \qquad \begin{array}{r} .62 \\ -.4 \\ \hline .22 \end{array} \qquad \begin{array}{r} 7.34 \\ -1.21 \\ \hline 6.13 \end{array}$$

The pattern for multiplication is to multiply the digits to get the product in the usual way, then add the total number of decimal places in the problem and transfer them to the answer. When counting decimal places for the answer, count from right to left.

$$\text{Ex.} = \left.\begin{array}{r} .4 \\ \times\ .6 \\ \hline .24 \end{array}\right\} \begin{array}{l} \text{2 decimal places} \\[4pt] \text{2 decimal places} \end{array}$$

$$\left.\begin{array}{r} .311 \\ \times\ 5 \\ \hline 1.555 \end{array}\right\} \begin{array}{l} \text{3 decimal places} \\[4pt] \text{3 decimal places} \end{array}$$

Sometimes there are more decimal places in the problem than there are digits in the answer. Show children that zeros must be added to the left of the product in order to occupy the correct number of decimal places. To multiply .12 x .5, for example, the product is 60 but there are three decimal places in the problem so a zero is added and the answer is .060.

$$\text{Ex.} = \begin{array}{r} .12 \\ \times\ .5 \\ \hline .060 \end{array} \qquad \begin{array}{r} .567 \\ .11 \\ \hline 567 \\ 567 \\ \hline .06237 \end{array}$$

For division with decimals, have children memorize the following rules.

(1) If the divisor has no decimal point, divide and bring the decimal point straight up into the answer.

$$\text{Ex.} = \quad 4\overline{\smash{\big)}\,1.6}^{\ .4} \qquad 2\overline{\smash{\big)}\,6.4}^{\ 3.2}$$

(2) If the divisor has decimal points, move the decimal point to the right until it becomes a whole number. Then move the decimal point in the problem the same number of places. Divide and raise the new decimal point straight up.

$$\text{Ex.} =$$

$$.5\overline{\smash{\big)}\,.655} = 5\overline{\smash{\big)}\,6.55}^{\ 1.31} \qquad .10\overline{\smash{\big)}\,.6070} = 10\overline{\smash{\big)}\,60.70}^{\ 6.07}$$

Almost always it is the movement of the decimal point in both the divisor and the problem which causes some children difficulty. Therefore, much practice may be needed for children to learn this pattern.

Percentage—Any discussion of teaching decimals should include percentage. Remind children that 1.00 equals 1 whole and numbers after the decimal point are fractional parts of a whole. All digits to the left of the decimal point represent whole numbers (ex.= 65.00) and all digits to the right of the decimal point represent fractions or parts of numbers (ex.= .43). Explain that decimal fractions are converted into percentages by moving the decimal to the right two places and adding a percent sign (%) at the end.

Ex.=

$$1.00 = 100\% \quad .75 = 75\% \quad .03 = 3\% \quad .30 = 30\%$$

If there are more than two digits after the decimal point, the decimal point is moved to the right two places and the percent sign added, but the decimal point is kept in the new position.

Ex.=

$$.7563 = 75.63\% \quad .0456 = 4.56\%$$

Now show children that to convert a percentage into a decimal fraction, the decimal point is moved to the left two places and the percent sign dropped. To find a percentage of any number, it is changed into a decimal fraction and multiplied like any decimal fraction. For example, if you want to know what 25% of 12 is, you multiply 12 by .25 for an answer of 3. Percentages of amounts of money are calculated the same way.

Ex.=

25% of 12 = 12 × .25 = 3

$$\begin{array}{r} 12 \\ .25 \\ \hline 60 \\ 24 \\ \hline 3.00 = 3 \end{array}$$

$1.98 + 4\%$ $4\% = .04$

$$\begin{array}{r} \$1.98 \\ \times .04 \\ \hline \$.0792 \end{array} \qquad \begin{array}{r} \$1.98 \\ + .0792 \\ \hline \$2.0592 = \$2.06 \end{array}$$

Word problems

Word problems are considered the most demanding tasks in arithmetic. To solve a problem, children must: (1) read and understand it; (2) decide what question is being asked or what task is required; (3) identify and organize the given information necessary for solving the problem; (4) choose the correct operation or series of operations for working the problem; and (5) perform all the computations correctly. An error at any point in this sequence can lead to an incorrect answer.

The major cause of children's difficulties lies not in the computations but in understanding the problem and choosing the proper way to solve it. Children who can compute accurately when given numbers and signs may flounder helplessly when confronted by a word problem asking for the same computation.

Interpreting word problems can be made easier if children learn to follow the five steps for approaching problems given above. Learning certain clue words is also helpful to indicate which operation to use.

Find the sum
What is the total or total number
What is the combined amount   means ADD
How many in all
How many were used

How much less than
How many more
How much more than   means SUBTRACT
What is the difference
Who has the least

Find the product
How many times   means MULTIPLY
What is the quotient
How many for each   means DIVIDE

It is important for children to learn to solve word problems because many of the real problems they will face in life that need

194

arithmetic for solving will be in that form. It is a good idea for the tutor to include practice problems using names and incidents from the child's own life or from current circumstances (ex.= If you had 32¢ and had to pay 24¢ for your school lunch, would you have enough left to buy a 15¢ popsicle?). Using such problems makes working them more interesting and shows the reason for needing to know how to do arithmetic. Children should also be encouraged to write their own word problems, either made up or real.

It is only through practice that children will develop a better grasp for handling word problems. The more such problems are worked, the broader the experience and greater the background knowledge they can apply. Remember that even adults sometimes encounter difficulty when they attempt to solve some word problems!

Math games

The use of games helps generate enthusiasm in children and reinforce their computation skills. The basic facts for the operations of addition, subtraction, multiplication, and division are easy to put on flash cards. These serve as valuable learning tools which can be used for individual study or game activities.

Flash cards can be made in different ways for different uses. Both time and paper will be saved by using both sides of the cards. Ex.=

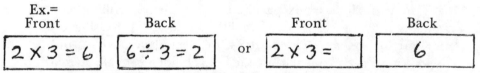

Front	Back		Front	Back
$2 \times 3 = 6$	$6 \div 3 = 2$	or	$2 \times 3 =$	6

As with reading flash cards, allowing children to help make them encourages learning of the basic facts.

The number of math games which can be used for teaching are limited only by the tutor's imagination. Children also can be encouraged to create their own games as long as they understand that they must know the arithmetic needed to explain the game. This encourages children to be both creative and responsible.

Most of the games described on pages 63 to 80 for developing reading ability can easily be adapted for improving arithmetic skills by substituting math flash cards for reading flash cards. For example, only a few minor adjustments are needed to change the game of "Vocabulary Baseball" into "Multiplication Baseball" or to change "Phonic Relay" into "Addition Fact Relay." Here are steps to follow when changing reading games to math:

(1) Choose a game from the phonic games and vocabulary games in "Reading Games and Activities," pages 63 to 80.

(2) Read the instructions for playing the game. The purpose will change from teaching reading to teaching arithmetic. The procedures, materials, and players will remain basically the same.

(3) Decide what basic facts (ex.= times tables) or operation (ex.= addition with carrying) the game is to teach.

(4) Make the appropriate math flash cards if they are needed.

(5) Explain to children how to play the game, giving enough examples so they understand the procedure and rules.

(6) Go ahead and play!

A few additional math games and activities are suggested:

[Note: Games can reinforce both math and reading skills]

GAME—Find the Fox

PURPOSE—To help children memorize basic math facts.

MATERIALS—Charts on basic facts of addition, subtraction, or multiplication and pencils for each player.

PLAYERS—Tutor and child, or group of children.

PROCEDURE—Each player is given a copy of a basic fact chart and told to "hide a fox" in the chart by secretly filling in three squares anywhere they choose with the letters f-o-x. The search for the opponent's fox starts with one player calling out an equation to see if one part of the fox is hidden in that square. For example, if the multiplication fact chart is being used, $2 \times 1 = 2$ can be called out. If a fox is not hidden on that square, the first player crosses it out so he won't try it again. If a hit is made on one of the three squares, the hit player must acknowledge it by calling out the letter that was found. Each player takes turns searching for the fox with equations until one player has found all three letters of the other player's hidden fox. The first player to find all three letters is the winner of that game.

Any word or words can be used for variations of this game including troublesome spelling or vocabulary words.

GAME—Multiples

PURPOSE—To speed the recall of multiplication facts.

MATERIALS—None (players must have memorized the times tables).

PLAYERS—Tutor and child, or group of children.

PROCEDURE—One player chooses a number from the times tables. Each player takes turns calling out a counting number in order until a multiple of the chosen number comes up. That player then must call out an equation to equal that multiple. (Ex.= 3's are chosen; players in turn say 1, 2, 3 x 1 = 3, 4, 5, 3 x 2,= 6, 7, 8, 3 x 3 = 9, etc.) The emphasis must be placed on speed since how rapidly the answers come will often determine the amount of fun and learning.

GAME—Math message

PURPOSE—To provide practice in manipulating the basic facts with simple operations.

MATERIALS—Pencils and paper.

PLAYERS—Tutor and child, or group of children.

PROCEDURE—Secret messages are given and decoded according to number formulas requiring one of the operations. Assign a number to every letter in the alphabet (ex.= a = 1, b = 2, c = 3, etc.). The code is made by applying an operation (ex.= x 4 or - 6) to each letter to camouflage the message which is decoded by the opposite operation (ex.= ÷ 4 or + 6). Complete sentences and even paragraphs can be made into secret messages. This activity serves to reinforce math lessons along with providing practice in reading and spelling.

Ex.= Code: x 6 (Each letter's number is multiplied by 6)

Word: Be   B=2 x 6 = 12   e=5 x 6 = 30

Encoded word: 12, 30

Decode: ÷ 6 (Each code number is divided by 6)

12 ÷ 6 = 2=B   30 ÷ 6 = 5=e   Decoded word: Be

ACTIVITY—Math number puzzles

DESCRIPTION—Number puzzles are made like vocabulary word puzzles (p. 88): (1) Draw a box divided into squares or use graph paper; (2) in a column close to the box, list the answers you want the players to find; (3) transfer those numbers from the list into the squares in left-to-right horizontal lines, left-to-right diagonals, or vertical lines; (4) fill in the remaining empty squares with other numbers. The numbers you want children to find can be counting numbers, numbers expressed as two or more digits, numbers expressed in words or names of numbers written as digits. Other answers might be addition facts, times tables, etc. Explain to the players that the numbers listed are to be found and circled in the squares of the box. It often helps to give children an example as a starter. This activity combines an exercise in recognizing numbers with an enjoyable game. Children benefit from the practice of identifying numbers and improve the speed and accuracy of recognition.

Ex.=

⓪	⑧	26	③	89
35	39	①	52	91
②	41	⑥	⑦	⑤
21	⑨	④	68	55

Find these counting numbers and circle:
0 1 2 3 4 5 6 7 8 9

8	⑨	②	7	1
①	1	3	4	②
7	0	2	3	⑤
6	5	6	4	6

Find and circle the following numbers:
25   106   92

Note: The examples below provide practice in spelling.

t	w	ⓞ	i	a
i	m	h	n	b
t	h	r	e	e
c	e	d	r	s

Find and circle these numbers expressed in words:
1 2 3

6	①	3	7	9
2	4	⑤	4	8
3	②	ⓞ	6	4
8	8	1	9	6

Find and circle the numbers expressed in digits:
one   five   twenty

ACTIVITY—Dice games

DESCRIPTION—Dice in sets of one or two or in combined sets of four or six tossed from a container are valuable for inventing games using math. Here are some ideas around which games can be developed:

(1) Dice addition: adding the dice total, high score wins.

(2) Dice subtraction: subtracting the lower die from the higher, low score wins.

(3) Dice multiplication: multiplying the dice, high score wins.

(4) Dice division: numbers on dice must be made into an equation.

(5) Elimination: Numbers (ex.= 1 to 12) are written on each sheet of paper and two dice are thrown. They can be added, subtracted, multiplied or divided, and if the sum, difference, product or quotient is one of the numbers, it can be crossed off. The player who eliminates all the numbers first wins.

(6) Obstacle course: Write down problems along with squares for the answers in a straight line of six boxes from "Start" to "Finish." A player throws a die and tries to solve the problem or obstacle indicated by the die number. If he can solve it, he moves his marker to that square. The second player throws the die and solves that problem if he can. The first player either to solve the most problems or to finish the course wins. As a variation, more than six boxes can be used and arranged in long curved lines for exciting races.

Ex.=   Finish

$$12\overline{)146} =$$

$$8 \times 32 =$$

$$7\overline{)95} =$$

$$8 \times 2 =$$

$$4 + 1 =$$

$$12 - 9 =$$

Start

Each of these ideas can easily be made into numerous games with a variety of rules by keeping number scores for each player. Try experimenting with different rules to find which ones you and the children prefer.

Using newspapers for practice in math

Since numbers are used in news contexts, newspapers can also be used to provide practice in arithmetic for children. Each newspaper serves as an inexpensive source of material which can be either left intact or cut up for use in forming a variety of math problems.

The sections dealing with advertisements are the most useful for developing math materials. By using ads in the paper which have both words to describe items and numbers to indicate costs, both basic skills in reading and competencies in solving word problems can be reinforced. But remember, it's your choice as to whether you wish to just use the numbers to make a problem (ex. $5 + $7.50 =) or whether you wish to include the words or labels (ex. cat=$5.00 and dog=$7.50—The total for both pets equals ____).

In general, the "miscellaneous" ads provide smaller numbers for easier problems while the "house for sale" ads provide the largest numbers for more complex problems. Because prices include $ and ¢ signs, not only the basic operations of +, -, x, and ÷ will be reinforced but also valuable instruction on money math is provided. However, if practice with money math is not desired at this time, simply drop the $ and ¢ signs to provide regular math problems in computation.

For practicing skills in addition, subtraction, multiplication and division with newspapers, you may choose to have children: (1) copy numbers directly from the paper to practice writing their numbers, (2) cut out or copy a group of numbers and then have them arranged in order from the lowest to the highest, (3) write the problem and only have the children match the correct answers from a group of cut out or copied numbers, (4) cut out and paste or tape the numbers for problems on paper for children to work—it may help to generate even greater enthusiasm in children if you allow them to help in the choosing, cutting and pasting process, (5) cut out a bunch of ads either with or without the numbers and spread them out for children to create their own games and activities, (6) spread out numbers cut from the newspaper for children to make games where the children challenge each other to make and solve problems with each correct answer counting as 1 point.

CONCLUSION

Additional help

This book was designed to be the complete classroom-tested instructional manual for teaching reading, writing, and arithmetic either in the classroom or in the home. Yet it would be unrealistic to assume that "all behavior or emotionally based educational problems" can be solved for "every single child" with this handbook. For parents who are overwhelmed by their child's problems and feel the need for extra help, many options are available. Those who demonstrate their interest in their child's learning and describe how they have been trying to help will be enthusiastically received by dedicated teachers who can often make specific recommendations. Finally doctors, school psychologists, counselors, and special reading or math teachers in the school districts are other close and available sources for further advice. Even if a teacher proves uncooperative, parents generally need only to make their concerns emphatically known to have the school principal, district officials and school boards offer to help. In all respects, professional educators want parental support in helping children to succeed. In fact, you may be reading this book as the result of a referral from one or more of these persons and agencies.

Although step-by-step instruction and a good attitude on the part of the tutor can be effective even in difficult cases, there may be times when a particular parent or teacher cannot help a special child. It may be something as simple as a lack of time or, on the other hand, the child may have a disturbing emotional problem, a perceptual handicap or an unusual learning disability that needs professional help. If a child seems too immature or his problem seems temporary, you may wish to try teaching the more complex and advanced learning skill levels again at a later date. If the trouble seems deeper or more extensive, seek the best outside help you can obtain. Because if this book is used as explained, there are few children who with the right instruction and adult support cannot gain enough of the basic skills of reading, writing, and arithmetic to become at least self-sufficient!

Family vs. school

In the past, the family was the main source of guidance on such matters as religion, citizenship, health and sex, while the school provided basic instruction in reading, writing, and arithmetic. Yet in our present society we see a reversal in the role of the school and the home. An obvious antagonism is growing between the school and the family about who is responsible—and to blame—for the actions of our youth.

While there are many scapegoats for problems with youth, there is no doubt that the family is the foundation upon which young people build their lives. Deterioration of the family cannot help but contribute to the problems which hinder both development and learning in schools. One means of opening the lines of communication is for parents to become involved in learning activities with their children. When such experiences are shared, not only are the children's educational skills improved but the institution of the family is strengthened.

Failure of the schools?

"Schools are failing!" is often heard. In terms of discipline and standardized test scores, there is cause for public concern. Schools have been criticized for lowering their educational standards and watering down their curriculum. Even the high school diploma has come under question in regard to both its present meaning and value. As a result, there is a growing movement towards accountability for schools and towards requiring students to display at least a minimum competency in the basics.

Yet the issue also arises as to whether it is the schools that are failing or whether the problems in education could be a symptom of society's illness. Violence and other disciplinary problems are on the increase throughout all grade levels—including elementary grades—in the school systems of America. Physical attacks, verbal abuse and vandalism are directed at both teachers and other students trying to get an education. Children who attend classes with fear cannot focus their full concentration on learning. Also, children who aren't concentrating often do more poorly than they otherwise would on standardized tests.

Discipline problems in schools work a hardship on all students, but such distraction has a particularly damaging effect on slow learners, poor readers, and highly strung or sensitive children. When teachers have to be more concerned about discipline than teaching, children suffer because the teacher has less time to meet the individual needs of the children.

It is generally accepted that poverty and troubled or broken homes can contribute to juvenile problems. It is not so well recognized that there are other causes: (1) a decline in religious training and beliefs; (2) loss of respect for the rights of others; (3) failure of authority figures to hold children responsible for their attitudes, actions and citizenship; (4) the misuse of television in allowing it to reduce both conversation and studying in the home along with its possible effect of desensitizing children to violence; (5) an insensitive and callous society in which individuals feel small and overwhelmed; and (6) the tremendous changes taking place in both the economy and technology.

To prevent interference in the learning process which we call education, a change in thinking may be needed. Education may have to be considered a privilege open to all persons who wish to learn and not a right for those who only wish to hinder or disturb the learning of others. Until this change occurs, more tutoring with a greater emphasis on both teaching the basics and meeting each child's special needs is essential in preparing our society's youth for their roles as literate citizens.

APPENDIX A

Table 1 Vowel sounds

This list gives word examples of different vowel sounds along with notes on spelling patterns for making flash cards to use with reading lessons. These words show the individual vowel letter/ sounds and help expand a child's sight vocabulary.

Short or simple a sound

sat	fat	hat
fad	lad	had
tab	bad	and
cab	sad	cat
mad	dad	an

Long or complex a sound
Note: **a, ai, ay,** and **a**-consonant-**e** spellings give the **ā** sound.

bait	mate	maid
say	bay	make
able	aid	late
cake	day	ate
made	play	laid

Short or simple e sound
Note: **ea** spellings cannot be used to distinguish **ĕ** from **ē** sounds.

well	sell	debt
end	fell	elk
pet	let	fret
set	wear	wet
dead	met	tell

Long or complex e sound
Note: **ee, e**-consonant-**e** and sometimes **ea** spellings give the **ē** sound.

reed	free	bee
bead	tea	see
deed	seed	key

eat	flea	these
meat	reason	be

Short or simple i sound

pit	dish	fish
hit	lit	fit
sit	bit	it
kick	with	is
trick	sick	wish

Long or complex i sound

Note: **y, ie, igh, ight,** and **i-consonant-e** spellings give the ī sound.

lie	by	sight
might	bite	I
tie	die	ride
fly	my	ice
right	tight	sigh

Short or simple o sound

rot	odd	cot
sod	bottom	plop
lot	got	knock
not	stop	rock
dot	sock	doll

Long or complex o sound

Note: **oe, ow, oa** and **o-consonant-e** spellings give the ō sound.

oh	no	low
go	blow	open
below	grow	toe
so	soap	road
own	rope	rode

Short or simple u sound

rug	bun	lug
tug	bug	under
dug	luck	hug

rut	run	gun
until	shrug	mutt

Long or complex u sound

Note: ew, ue and u-consonant-e spellings often give the ū sound.

cute	fuse	usage
mule	abuse	huge
few	human	use
cue	usual	mew
beauty	union	fuel

Note: The vowel sounds of ū and o͞o are so close in their letter sounds that identification is often difficult and may even vary in pronunciation due to regional dialects or differences in an individual's speech reproduction. In fact, even some dictionaries with earlier copyright dates differ from later dictionaries in their diacritical markings of the same word. However, it should be remembered that slight differences in sound will neither make the word unrecognizable nor cause any loss of meaning.

Vowel sounds of o͞o, o͝o, ou, oi and au with different spellings

o͞o = soon, cruel, blue, rule, jewel, glue, food, new

o͝o = book, look, nook, poor, shook, hook, cushion

ou = pout, sow, trout, foul, pow, cow, how, meow, about

oi = boil, soil, coil, foil, toy, boy, coy, royal, broil

au = ball, call, fall, haul, saw, claw, hog, wrong, long, maul, brought, caught, fought, sought

Note: There is an obscure, vague, unstressed, almost gone vowel sound which children will sometimes encounter in multiple syllable words. Called the schwa (represented in dictionaries by the symbol ə), it ranges in sound from uh to almost eh as in a-about, ago, e-spoken, problem, i-engine, pencil, o-atom, lemon, u-minus, circus. Since the schwa sound doesn't follow a uniform spelling or sound pattern, children must simply memorize the schwa sounds in such words as they are met during reading.

Table 2 Consonant sounds

This list contains easy word examples along with notes on spelling patterns to be used to teach the consonant letter/sounds and to improve children's sight vocabularies. Examples show letter sounds in various positions within words.

b sound

boy	bark	bake
bend	about	rob
tub	cab	lab
robe	tube	cube

Note: The letter c gives the k and s sounds.

d sound

dog	door	during
did	do	rod
rode	raid	made
trade	said	laid

f sound

Note: **ph** spelling gives f sound.

for	farm	foul
fence	phrase	half
loaf	phone	safe
life	knife	stiff

g sound

great	gone	get
game	got	fog
tag	log	smog
goal	give	gun

h sound

him	heat	hear
his	here	hello

how	hate	hold
hi	has	hot

j sound

Note: **ge** and **dge** spellings give the **j** sound.

jug	jar	jello
jam	gentle	gem
cage	sage	age
ridge	bridge	lodge

k sound

Note: **c** and **ck** spellings give the **k** sound.

kiss	kin	kill
neck	corral	close
lick	sick	nick
pike	shake	poke

l sound

leg	lump	lend
mail	kill	hill
will	tale	hail
mile	rule	hole

m sound

miss	met	man
mask	plum	bomb
sum	limb	lamb
time	make	some

n sound

Note: **kn** spellings give the **n** sound.

now	near	new
knife	knot	knit
fin	pin	tin
mine	bone	fine

212

p sound

pin	pal	pain
pat	poor	map
trap	sap	lap
shape	hope	ripe

q sound

Note: **qu** spellings give the q sound.

quiet	quick	quit
question	queer	quite
quarrel	quill	squirt

r sound

rake	ran	rob
turn	burn	rest
diver	silver	never
store	more	here

s sound

Note: **ss, ce, se, ci,** and **x** spellings give the s sound.

see	send	saw
glass	kiss	circle
twice	cent	race
gas	fox	tax

t sound

tell	tear	tall
take	sat	rat
bat	fat	feet
write	hate	note

v sound

very	van	invade
vital	rave	save
invite	cave	calves

w sound

win	witch	we

wear	will	weak
went	way	wore
water	winter	well

x sound (see s sound)

y sound (as an initial consonant sound in words)

yes	yet	yellow
you	yard	yonder
your	year	yell

z sound

Note: **ze**, **se** and **s** spellings give the z sound.

zero	zip	squeeze
sneeze	freeze	breeze
days	hose	toes
ease	rose	those

Table 3 Sounds of consonant blends

This list contains easy words to be used to teach the sounds of the consonant blends and to expand children's vocabularies. Examples show blends in various positions within words.

bl sound

bleed	black	blame
bless	blend	able
blow	blew	table
bleak	bland	fable

br sound

bridge	bring	breeze
brew	bright	broke
break	brown	brief
brought	broke	brave

ch sound

chair	chin	witch
chug	choice	stitch
choose	which	hitch
choke	switch	chase

ck sound

check	thick	jacket
neck	sick	pocket
lick	track	locket
chick	pick	track

cl sound

close	cliff	clean
clear	clan	clip
climb	class	clam
clap	cling	include

cr sound

crate	cry	crawl
crow	crept	creep
crack	cringe	cream
cradle	crop	cross

dl sound

saddle	cradle	meddle
ladle	waddle	fiddle
muddle	cuddle	huddle

dr sound

drop	drill	draw
drive	drink	drape
drank	dress	droop
drip	drift	drew

fl sound

flee	floor	flop
flavor	float	flip
flap	flake	flow
flag	flat	flea

fr sound

free	fresh	frame
frown	fright	frog
fry	friend	front
from	froze	fruit

gl sound

glad	glass	glen
glow	glade	glide
glee	glance	gland
globe	glare	gloom

gr sound

grill	grand	grass

216

grade	great	group
grin	grow	growl
green	grew	grip

pl sound

please	plank	plug
place	plate	plum
play	plenty	plan
plain	plane	plant

pr sound

press	pray	print
pride	prick	prop
prime	praise	prize
price	proof	prim

sc sound

scare	scoot	scram
screw	escape	scan
scream	scat	scamper
score	scoop	scale

sh sound

show	shake	fish
shell	shame	dish
shrug	wish	sheep
shall	shine	leash

sk sound

skin	skip	skid
skill	sky	skim
task	ski	skirt
skunk	skull	skit

sl sound

| slip | sleek | slow |
| slide | slender | slave |

| sleep | slim | slam |
| slot | slick | slope |

sm sound

small	smart	smile
smell	smash	smear
smog	smooth	smoke
smug	smack	smooch

sn sound

snap	snip	sneak
snow	sneeze	snore
snake	snack	snoop
snug	sniff	snail

sp sound

spin	sport	spoke
spell	speak	spread
spring	spot	spare
spoil	spoon	spark

st sound

steep	stand	stood
still	store	stay
sting	stamp	stop
fist	list	mist

sw sound

swing	sweep	swell
sway	swim	swipe
switch	swat	swore
sweat	swift	sweet

th sound

thin	there	this
death	their	then
wealth	those	these
breath	that	than

tl sound

kettle	little	settle
bottle	battle	rattle
tattle	cattle	prattle
brittle	mettle	turtle

tr sound

trip	treat	troup
try	train	trash
trend	trade	true
tree	trim	trail

tw sound

twin	twice	twist
twine	twitch	twirl
twelve	twig	twenty
tweet	tweed	twinkle

wh sound

where	whip	which
when	while	what
why	white	wheel
whim	whine	wheat

Table 4 Sounds of letter families and word groups

This list contains word examples which help teach combinations of letter/sounds and also help enrich the vocabularies of children.

ab sound

cab	dab	tab
jab	lab	gab

ace sound

face	grace	lace
place	race	trace

ack sound

flack	sack	rack
black	back	lack

ad sound

mad	sad	fad
glad	bad	dad

ade sound

fade	grade	shade
made	wade	trade

ag sound

tag	rag	sag
lag	bag	drag

age sound

cage	page	rage
sage	stage	wage

ain sound

slain	lain	main
gain	strain	rain

ake sound

| make | bake | lake |
| fake | rake | flake |

all sound

| tall | fall | stall |
| wall | ball | hall |

am sound

| jam | cram | dam |
| ram | clam | ham |

ame sound

| same | came | flame |
| blame | tame | game |

an sound

| tan | ran | can |
| man | pan | fan |

and sound

| sand | bland | hand |
| stand | grand | band |

ane sound

| mane | crane | plane |
| sane | lane | pane |

ank sound

| blank | sank | rank |
| plank | tank | bank |

ap sound

| tap | map | rap |
| lap | gap | flap |

ar sound

bar	far	star
car	jar	par

are sound

snare	hare	flare
care	bare	rare

ash sound

flash	mash	clash
dash	rash	cash

ast sound

fast	mast	cast
last	past	blast

at sound

sat	fat	hat
bat	rat	cat

ate sound

date	late	matc
rate	hate	fate

ave sound

cave	save	rave
shave	crave	gave

aw sound

saw	jaw	law
paw	claw	draw

ed sound

red	bed	fled
fed	bled	led

eat sound

treat	seat	meat
feat	beat	neat

ead sound

head	bread	spread
dead	thread	tread

eed sound

feed	seed	bleed
weed	deed	reed

eek sound

seek	week	reek
meek	peek	sleek

eep sound

deep	sleep	sweep
keep	weep	creep

en sound

pen	ten	men
hen	den	wren

end sound

blend	bend	send
tend	mend	lend

ent sound

sent	bent	rent
dent	lent	went

et sound

get	let	set
met	pet	wet

ick sound

chick	flick	click
sick	pick	trick

id sound

did	hid	bid
rid	lid	middle

ide sound

side	ride	glide
hide	tide	wide

ig sound

dig	pig	fig
rig	big	wig

ight sound

sight	might	light
fight	flight	night

ill sound

drill	pill	bill
dill	fill	will

im sound

dim	him	whim
slim	rim	import

ime sound

time	chime	crime
slime	dime	lime

in sound

tin	win	fin
sin	chin	bin

ine sound

fine	mine	nine
dine	pine	line

ing sound

ring	sing	fling
sting	wing	king

ink sound

sink	drink	wink
blink	think	pink

ip sound

dip	slip	lip
sip	hip	whip

iss sound

kiss	miss	bliss
Swiss	hiss	prissy

it sound

sit	mit	fit
hit	bit	pit

ob sound

sob	mob	rob
slob	job	cob

ock sound

lock	sock	clock
block	knock	pocket

od sound

sod	rod	nod
cod	pod	god

one sound

cone	bone	phone
stone	tone	zone

ong sound

song	wrong	strong
long	bong	prong

ook sound

took	look	book
hook	crook	brook

op sound

top	drop	mop
cop	hop	chop

ope sound

slope	cope	mope
rope	lope	dope

ore sound

chore	sore	more
core	bore	tore

ot sound

hot	lot	dot
pot	rot	shot

ound sound

sound	round	mound
bound	pound	hound

ow sound

how	sow	now
brow	cow	chow

226

own sound

frown	down	brown
town	crown	clown

ub sound

rub	sub	club
tub	cub	shrub

ug sound

lug	rug	bug
dug	hug	tug

um sound

sum	slum	lump
bum	dumb	crumb

un sound

sun	run	fun
gun	shun	pun

ung sound

hung	sung	swung
rung	lung	slung

ur sound (with ur, ir and er spellings)

burn	shirt	serve
curt	dirt	person

Note: Dictionaries often refer to the sound of **ur** in **fur** and **hurt**, **ir** in **fir** and **bird**, and **er** in **better** and **mercy** as the u-vowel-r sound. However, children will most often recognize and associate this sound with the letters "er" simply because they see "er" in so many words in their reading materials—both as part of root words and used as a suffix (ex. root= her, nerve; suffix= singer, trucker).

Table 5 Affixes

A great deal of debate surrounds the question of whether learning the Latin derivations, prefixes, root words and suffixes will help children to grasp a word's meaning. Generally it is felt that the effort spent in learning these clues could be better used. Criticism focuses on the following arguments: (1) Words have evolved to the point that they bear little resemblance to their Latin derivations. (2) Decoding one part of the word's meaning often does not help unless the meaning of the rest of the word is known. (3) Since the prefix and suffix meanings do not always hold true, they can be misleading. On the other hand, there is support for teaching affixes and root words as clues to the sounds and meanings of words, especially the most common prefixes and suffixes whose meanings almost always remain constant. The following list of common affixes and their meanings will allow tutors to use them if they wish.

Prefixes

re-	to do again or over	replay = to play again
non-	not or no	nonsense = no sense
un-	not	unhappy = not happy
dis-	not or opposite	disagree = not agree
pre-	before or already	premixed = already mixed
de-	undo or remove	defrost = to remove frost
anti-	against	antiwar = against war
mid-	middle or mid point of	midstream = middle of the stream
in-	into or on	inland = into the land
be-	come by or make	beside = come by the side
ex-	out or outside of	expand = grow out

Suffixes

-ed	did in the past or have done	walked = did walk

-s or -es	more than one	girls = more than one girl
		dresses = more than one dress
-er or -or (added to verbs to make nouns)	one who does	trainer = one who trains
		actor = one who acts
-ing	act of doing	jumping = act of jumping
-able	fit to be, do, or use	eatable = fit to eat
-less	without	moneyless = without money
-like	resembling or appearing like	childlike = resembling or like a child
-y	full of or like	creamy = full of cream or like cream
-ous	full of or having	joyous = full of joy or having joy
-ly	done in the way named in the first part of the word	thoroughly = done with thoroughness
-ful	full of	thoughtful = full of thought
-ish	like or resembling	reddish = like or resembling red
-er (added to adjectives or adverbs)	more or better than something else in comparison	faster = having more speed than another
-est (added to adjectives or adverbs)	most or best of all in comparison	faster = having the most speed

Table 6 Contractions

Contractions are encountered often enough in reading material that children can benefit from recognizing them on sight and knowing their meanings. An additional value of studying contractions is that they are formed from small common words, serving to reinforce children's basic sight vocabulary. Point out to students that the apostrophe marks the place where letters are omitted.

I'm = I am

you're = you are

we're = we are

he's = he is, he has

she's = she is, she has

it's = it is

here's = here is

there's = there is

I'd = I had, I would,
    or I should

I'll = I will

you'll = you will

he'll = he will

she'll = she will

we'll = we will

they'll = they will

aren't = are not

can't = can not

couldn't = could not

doesn't = does not

don't = do not (base word changes
    pronunciation)

hadn't = had not

hasn't = has not

haven't = have not

isn't = is not

shouldn't = should not

wasn't = was not

weren't = were not

won't = will not (base word changes
    spelling and pronunciation)

wouldn't = would not

let's = let us

Table 7 High-frequency and easy words

These words are part of a group so common in reading material that children need to be able to recognize and pronounce each word on sight. This sample list, for use in teaching both reading and spelling, is a result of my teaching experience and an informal survey of literature. Depending upon the grade level and the nature of the material, some words occur more often than others. However, such short and common words along with their various forms of usage in contractions, compound words and in combinations with affixes generally account for between 50 to 75 percent of all words excepting proper nouns used in sentences.

a= a, at, as, am, also, across, able, and, answer, age, already, air, all, an, arm, always, above, about, are, any, ask, action, ate, add, act, away, after, along, ate, afraid, alone, apart, ache, another, again, answer, around, anger, aim, approach, appear, attack, ant, animal, angry, art, aware, awake

b= be, buy, boy, big, better, best, build, blow, begin, brave, broke, blast, blame, blood, bleed, boil, bake, bank, body, belt, began, box, bow, bark, bake, bird, bee, bit, bet, ball, boot, brought, bat, been, brown, black, blue, bite, bell, bad, bag, bill, bull, bug, baby, beach, bottom, back, bang, blew, because, became, both, boat, believe, bring, before, between, by, book, bowl, below, bread, bright, butter, bust, break, but, beside, bear, broom, brother, bare, birth, bush, bend, bent, base, bore, bar, band

c= came, could, can, cross, crawl, cap, case, car, call, cake, carry, close, clean, cut, cup, cry, color, cook, crowd, cold, center, clothes, care, catch, caught, chair, child, cloud, come, chicken, cook, city, coat, count, climb, cat, careful, cow, cent, crew, children, cast, cool, class, clear, creep, crept, clip, crazy, cave, card, choice, chose, choose, chance, coarse, crayon, cream, crash, chew, circle

d= do, did, done, does, dig, door, die, died, drip, drop, draw, dug, deep, doll, dish, drive, dry, day, due, damp, dear, den, dog, dance, dark, deer, duck, down, dress, dip, deal, death,

231

dim, dump, dot, dare, dam, deed, date, danger, dumb, dust, drank, drunk, dash, deal, dirt, dime, dollar, drew, drain, drag

e= end, eat, easy, easier, enter, eight, every, each, east, egg, else, even, ever, enough, else, evil, empty, early, eye, ear, enemy, event, edge

f= for, fast, farm, from, free, follow, found, fall, fought, fuel, food, fence, four, five, few, full, flower, fire, freeze, froze, fill, fast, fan, fat, father, feel, feed, fake, far, finger, forgot, fish, fit, fun, fresh, forget, face, family, feet, foot, fight, fell, felt, funny, field, fade, first, fourth, fifth, forest, flock, force, find, farther, feature, fly, fine, fail, finish, fool, flip, fault, future, fold, fact, false, fear, friend, flow, fox, fin, flew, flown

g= go, gone, great, grass, ground, gave, ghost, green, gold, good, grow, game, garden, get, glad, got, guess, goose, gulf, give, gave, gun, girl, geese, good-by, gray, grand, glass, gain, glue, guard, gate, goes, group, grew, gas, grip, grab, goal, growl, grin, gentle

h= he, him, house, have, had, hate, has, how, hard, hear, hero, habit, high, hunt, hurry, hurt, hour, hot, hop, home, hide, hi, half, hit, hid, hair, hole, hold, hill, hat, hand, head, held, herd, hello, help, heavy, her, here, his, happen, happy, heard, heap, hang, hope, horse, ham, hen, horn, him, hate, handle, hip, hood, heart, husband, hung, hammer, hoe, health

i= it, I, its, instead, inside, in, ice, is, into, if, Indian, island, ill

j= jar, jug, jam, joke, jump, just, jelly, jewel, jet

k= key, know, knee, keep, kind, knew, kiss, kill, king, kept, knock, kitten, knot, knew, knife, kick

l= line, lady, laid, lay, learn, leg, laugh, lie, long, lip, limp, look, loud, lot, lunch, left, last, little, large, letter, light, less, love, life, live, let, lost, like, listen, low, lamp, like, lose, loose, leap, lake, lump, lift, leave, limb, leak, late, lend, lean, lack, lent, leaf, lead, luck, laugh

m= me, made, my, most, must, men, might, make, man, Mr., Miss, month, Mrs., miss, money, mud, milk, minute, meat, meet, may, main, male, much, more, mail, many, mice, mile, mess, mouse, met, mother, mouth, move, music, muscle, mark, mention, magic, mat, motion, mule, mound, mass, mean, motor, mad, mind

n= no, not, nothing, note, nail, noise, new, need, nut, near, never, now, nine, name, nest, night, next, north, nose, neck, need, noise, nice, nap, nick, neat, net, none, nickel

o= of, off, over, often, on, one, out, our, once, own, only, oh, old, okay, or, open, orange, other, outside, order, ounce, oil, ocean

p= past, poor, pin, pen, pie, pill, pan, part, paper, paw, pay, pony, party, people, pig, place, pad, pail, problem, pet, piece, present, plan, place, please, plant, promise, plow, prove, past, point, pant, pale, print, prince, play, pot, put, push, pull, pick, princess, pig, pink, paint, protect, pond, press, pretty, pack, puppy, pitch, prepare, plot, plastic, pain, pure, pencil, paid, pour, person, pepper, penny

q= quick, quiet, quit, queen, question, quart, quarter, quiz

r= ran, read, run, raise, roll, red, real, rain, race, rabbit, rake, raid, roast, rip, resent, rib, release, root, reduce, right, river, roar, rode, roof, rope, round, rub, receive, rack, rut, rob, remember, return, repeat, rat, rang, rule, rock, rest, ring, road, ready, ride, room, row, result, rude, rim, rust, right, roam, rack, rescue, rise, rose, reply, rung, rug, ray, rush, raw, rate, ram, rough, ruin, rail, rot, rage

s= sit, sat, so, soft, set, store, save, slow, safe, sand, sea, sing, sent, sang, sung, star, shake, sheep, shop, should, side, sled, slender, sell, sold, send, slide, see, say, shut, south, shell, shine, satisfy, sister, smoke, salt, sugar, sad, strike, smart, struck, seat, seem, seed, she, said, seen, saw, shore, six, strip, soil, such, slid, skin, story, snow, smile, seven, stripe, sign, sure, sent, sick, slow, short, scrap, spring, summer, steep, sting, stuff, stall, scream, stake, stamp, surprise, sleep, show, shoe, swung, swam, sway, string, slap, sweep, swept, stood, stuck, slave, stack, slip, slam, seal, slim, slept, sack, sore, sale, search, start, swing, swim, star, stay, some, step, stick, sail, snail, stew, super, stick, stuck, stare, steady, shake, ship, snap, spot, still, stone, strong, son, sun, straight, space, speak, spoke, stay, shook, student, state, sled, smash, street, stand, soon, sound, song, smell, small, sky

233

t=   tell, told, ten, two, three, test, take, tan, to, touch, tire. tail, talk, teacher, tie, took, taken, thin, team, train, true, twice, track, too, time, table, those, there, their, these, the, trash, tin, trample, trade, them, think, tip, tame, threat, trip, thing, throw, threw, this, that, they, toy, try, tried, turn, them, thrown, today, toe, tomorrow, town, teach, treat, tough, together, tool, tree, trap, turtle, then, thought, thank, teach, top, tap, tear, tore, trick, tape, tack, taught, tease

u=   us, up, upon, use, until, under, upper, urge, usual

v=   very, visit, voice, vegetable, value, vacation, van

w=   who, why, what, wet, with, wood, wing, warm, were, war, was, waste, water, weed, wife, wide, winter, world, week, wild, warn, worn, worm, wind, win, would, wait, way, went, where, which, wake, wrap, wish, wipe, whip, well, window, wade, wolf, woman, write, will, witch, while, when, write, wade, west, wrong, whale, welcome, wrote, wall, worse, wake, white, work, wheel, we, wreck, weak, word, want, walk, wash, watch, wear, wore, wave

y=   yes, yellow, yell, you, your, year, yet, yard, yield

z=   zoo, zipper, zero

Note: Many forms of words (using such endings as ing, y, ly, ed, es, er, est, and s for example) have been left out both to conserve space and because most children will easily learn to recognize such forms during lessons on affixes and contractions with root words.

APPENDIX B

Arithmetic practice pages

Table 8

Identifying numbers and their values

Name the number of objects:

O	= 1	✩✩✩ ✩ ✩✩✩	= 7
| | |	= 3	▭ ▭ ▭	= 3
△ △ △△	= 5	ⅅ ⅅ ⅅ	= 3
▢ ▢	= 2	o o o o o	= 5
▯▯▯▯	= 4	△ △ △ △	= 4
ⅅⅅ	= 2	▯▯▯▯▯▯▯▯	= 8
oooooooo	= 9	|	= 1
△△△ △△△	= 6	OO	= 2

Draw as many circles as named by the number:

4 = O O O O
1 = O
9 = O O O O O O O O O
3 = O O O
5 = O O O O O
7 = O O O O O O O
2 = O O
8 = O O O O O O O O
4 = O O O O
6 = O O O O O O

Table 9 Addition

Basic Addition facts

1 +1 — 2	2 +2 — 4	5 +6 — 11	4 +3 — 7	7 +8 — 15	9 +1 — 10	7 +5 — 12	4 +9 — 13
1 +8 — 9	3 +1 — 4	2 +3 — 5	2 +4 — 6	7 +7 — 14	5 +2 — 7	6 +3 — 9	10 +1 — 11
8 +8 — 16	9 +6 — 15	5 +9 — 14	7 +6 — 13	2 +7 — 9	6 +8 — 14	9 +9 — 18	12 +2 — 14
11 +6 — 17	4 +7 — 11	9 +8 — 17	6 +8 — 14	5 +9 — 14	12 +5 — 17	8 +11 — 19	12 +7 — 19
9 +5 — 14	5 +6 — 11	8 +3 — 11	4 +6 — 10	7 +4 — 11	12 +8 — 20	2 +12 — 14	3 +1 — 4
4 +2 — 6	4 +1 — 5	2 +9 — 11	12 +9 — 21	11 +0 — 11	0 +8 — 8	11 +1 — 12	2 +3 — 5
8 +9 — 17	3 +0 — 3	7 +6 — 13	3 +1 — 4	12 +5 — 17	10 +5 — 15	6 +1 — 7	12 +1 — 13
3 +4 — 7	8 +2 — 10	6 +4 — 10	6 +9 — 15	11 +6 — 17	12 +0 — 12	7 +7 — 14	5 +5 — 10
3 +6 — 9	12 +12 — 24	11 +0 — 11	10 +10 — 20	3 +2 — 5	0 +1 — 1	8 +9 — 17	8 +8 — 16

Addition without carrying

```
 12        17        18        26
+ 3       + 0       + 1       + 2
 15        17        19        28


 99        25        75        34
+00       +71       +24       +13
 99        76        99        47


 136       546       710       836
+ 21      + 42      + 69      + 43
 157       588       779       879


 506       782       837       365
+241      +107      +112      +521
 747       889       949       886


 8,826     4,562     2,538     3,717
+  102    +  317    +  410    +  262
 8,928     4879      2,948     3,979


 7,256     6,512     7,516     3,901
+1,423    +3,043    +2,182    +1,096
 8,679     9,555     9,698     4,997
```

238

Addition with carrying

18	49	57	83
+9	+7	+6	+8
27	56	63	91

26	46	72	65
+17	+35	+19	+27
43	81	91	92

478	542	683	423
+ 18	+ 29	+ 39	+ 98
496	571	722	521

647	238	579	794
+269	+578	+566	+866
916	816	1,145	1,660

1,457	6,828	3,976	6,783
+384	+ 131	+494	+ 539
1,841	6,959	4,470	7,322

8,436	7,622	6,476	8,695
+ 1,351	+ 2,589	+ 5,985	+7,829
9,787	10,211	12,461	16,524

239

Table 10 Subtraction

Basic subtraction facts

7 −2 ― 5	1 −1 ― 0	2 −0 ― 2	4 −4 ― 0	6 −1 ― 5	9 −2 ― 7
3 −3 ― 0	6 −0 ― 6	5 −1 ― 4	9 −2 ― 7	7 −1 ― 6	8 −5 ― 3
12 −6 ― 6	10 −2 ― 8	8 −0 ― 8	9 −3 ― 6	11 −1 ― 10	6 −5 ― 1
8 −7 ― 1	10 −3 ― 7	7 −2 ― 5	2 −1 ― 1	8 −6 ― 2	4 −3 ― 1
12 −2 ― 10	11 −6 ― 5	9 −7 ― 2	9 −1 ― 8	8 −3 ― 5	5 −2 ― 3
7 −3 ― 4	8 −4 ― 4	9 −9 ― 0	2 −2 ― 0	7 −5 ― 2	11 −7 ― 4
12 −11 ― 1	10 −7 ― 3	3 −1 ― 2	5 −4 ― 1	4 −1 ― 3	7 −0 ― 7
17 −5 ― 12	18 −1 ― 17	19 −7 ― 12	14 −0 ― 14	13 −2 ― 11	16 −6 ― 10
16 −8 ― 8	17 −9 ― 8	14 −6 ― 8	18 −2 ― 16	17 −7 ― 10	15 −7 ― 8

Subtraction without borrowing

25 −11 ___ 14	76 −24 ___ 52	89 −72 ___ 17	56 −45 ___ 11	94 −64 ___ 30
137 −21 ___ 116	456 −42 ___ 414	789 −16 ___ 773	642 −12 ___ 630	578 −52 ___ 526
628 −417 ___ 211	573 −461 ___ 112	843 −621 ___ 222	937 −726 ___ 211	321 −310 ___ 11
1,439 −418 ___ 1,021	7,521 −401 ___ 7,120	6,896 −762 ___ 6,134	9,367 −254 ___ 9,113	8,732 −501 ___ 8,231
2,879 −1,063 ___ 1,816	5,849 −5,638 ___ 211	7,297 −6,295 ___ 1,002	8,983 −6,341 ___ 2,642	4,652 −3511 ___ 1,141

Subtraction with borrowing

23 −16 ___ 7	45 −26 ___ 19	78 −49 ___ 29	65 −39 ___ 26	98 −69 ___ 29	451 −29 ___ 422
635 −27 ___ 608	848 −19 ___ 829	347 −58 ___ 289	576 −88 ___ 488	976 −347 ___ 629	841 −332 ___ 509
1,532 −348 ___ 1,184	2,782 −694 ___ 2,088	5,643 −279 ___ 5,364	8,721 −578 ___ 8,143	9,655 −679 ___ 8,976	
6,549 −2,869 ___ 3,680	7,842 −1,953 ___ 5,889	3,961 −1,972 ___ 1,989	4,722 −3,865 ___ 857	9,311 −7,526 ___ 1,785	

Table 11 Multiplication

Basic multiplication facts

0	1	2	8	5	4	5	6
×0	×0	×1	×3	×6	×3	×2	×6
0	0	2	24	30	12	10	36

8	11	10	7	6	3	5	8	9
×9	×3	×0	×5	×8	×4	×4	×2	×9
72	33	0	35	48	12	20	16	81

12	6	8	9	4	3	4	1
×7	×4	×7	×5	×4	×2	×2	×9
84	24	56	45	16	6	8	9

3	7	5	12	10	9	8
×8	×1	×8	×9	×7	×7	×8
24	7	40	108	70	63	64

7	1	2	8	6	7	5	1
×7	×6	×9	×4	×9	×9	×3	×3
49	6	18	32	54	63	15	3

4	1	6	11	12	9	7	7
×4	×5	×6	×5	×6	×3	×4	×3
16	5	36	55	72	27	28	21

4	6	6	11	12	10	7	5
×8	×5	×9	×2	×5	×6	×0	×5
32	30	54	22	60	60	0	25

6	9	9	1	6	7	5	10
×4	×3	×2	×1	×2	×6	×7	×9
24	27	18	1	12	42	35	90

Multiplication by one digit without/with carrying

Without carrying

```
   16      12      11      12
   x1      x4      x9      x3
   16      48      99      36

  123     479     891     121
   x2      x1      x0      x3
  246     479       0     363

  323     101     100     434
   x3      x5      x6      x2
  969     505     600     868

 1,101   1,231   3,134   1,201
   x8      x3      x2      x4
 8,808   3,691   6,268   4,804

 12,310    21,001   97,986   44,312
   x3        x4       x1       x2
 36,930   84,004   97,986   88,614
```

With carrying

```
   17      18      29      36      85      45
   x6      x3      x5      x2      x3      x7
  102      54     145      72     255     315

  346     789     435     963     764     572
   x4      x8      x2      x4      x3      x9
 1,384   6,317     870   3,852   2,292   5,148

 1,427   3,625   7,829   4,549
   x8      x5      x7      x6
 11,416  18,125  54,803  27,294

 3,457   8,563
   x4      x9
 13,828  77,067
```

```
 72,536      14,536      78,026      40,497
    ×6         ×·2          ×5          ×4
435,216      29,072     390,130     161,988

 29,863      39,547
    ×7          ×3
209,041     118,641
```

Multiplication by two digits without/with carrying

Without carrying

```
   87         96         43         42         32         23
  ×11        ×10        ×12        ×22        ×23        31
  957        960        516        924        736        713

  121        341        402        231        789        214
  ×34        ×12        ×23        ×30        ×11       ×21
4,114      4,092      9,246       6930      8,679     4,494

1,210      1,330      3,231      4,044      3,103       101
 ×24        ×32        ×21        ×12        ×31      ×50
29,040     42,560     67,851     48,528    96,193    50,550

3,032      4,310
 ×23        ×20
69,736     86,200
```

244

With carrying

56	78	96	78	43	39
X 15	X 23	X 44	X 36	X 75	X 28
840	1,794	4,224	2,808	3,225	1,092

185	356	594	636	754	829
X 24	X 47	X 78	X 48	X 66	X 73
4,440	16,732	46,332	30,528	49,764	60,517

4,567	8,965	7,638	6,748
X 37	X 45	X 69	X 78
168,979	403,425	527,022	526,344

578	674	479	863
X 125	X 493	X 356	X 579
72,250	332,282	170,524	499,677

Table 12 Division

Basic division facts

$9 \div 3 = 3$ $7 \div 1 = 7$ $12 \div 6 = 2$ $10 \div 2 = 5$ $28 \div 4 = 7$

$49 \div 7 = 7$ $63 \div 9 = 7$ $3 \div 0 = 0$ $8 \div 8 = 1$ $30 \div 5 = 6$

$60 \div 10 = 6$ $54 \div 6 = 9$ $48 \div 4 = 12$ $18 \div 3 = 6$ $8 \div 2 = 4$

$40 \div 5 = 8$ $72 \div 8 = 9$ $36 \div 6 = 6$ $56 \div 7 = 8$ $36 \div 9 = 4$

$24 \div 4 = 6$ $77 \div 11 = 7$ $56 \div 7 = 8$ $18 \div 2 = 9$ $27 \div 3 = 9$

$15 \div 5 = 3$ $48 \div 6 = 8$ $81 \div 9 = 9$ $24 \div 8 = 3$ $9 \div 1 = 9$

$42 \div 6 = 7$ $14 \div 2 = 7$ $21 \div 3 = 7$ $4 \div 2 = 2$ $25 \div 5 = 5$

$2 \div 2 = 1$ $42 \div 6 = 7$ $64 \div 8 = 8$ $50 \div 10 = 5$ $44 \div 11 = 4$

$24 \div 12 = 2$ $25 \div 5 = 5$ $21 \div 7 = 3$ $12 \div 3 = 4$ $30 \div 6 = 5$

One-step division without remainder using one-digit divisor

$$2\overline{)6}^{\,3} \qquad 3\overline{)9}^{\,3} \qquad 4\overline{)8}^{\,2} \qquad 6\overline{)6}^{\,1}$$

$$6\overline{)18}^{\,3} \qquad 7\overline{)49}^{\,7} \qquad 5\overline{)25}^{\,5} \qquad 4\overline{)16}^{\,4}$$

$$9\overline{)81}^{\,9} \qquad 8\overline{)64}^{\,8} \qquad 2\overline{)14}^{\,7} \qquad 3\overline{)24}^{\,8}$$

$$1\overline{)9}^{\,9} \qquad 4\overline{)32}^{\,8} \qquad 7\overline{)28}^{\,4} \qquad 9\overline{)54}^{\,6}$$

$$5\overline{)45}^{\,9} \qquad 6\overline{)48}^{\,8} \qquad 3\overline{)15}^{\,5} \qquad 8\overline{)72}^{\,9}$$

One-step division with remainder using one-digit divisor

$$6\overline{)19}^{\,3r1} \qquad 2\overline{)11}^{\,5r1} \qquad 3\overline{)17}^{\,5r2} \qquad 5\overline{)27}^{\,5r2}$$

$$8\overline{)53}^{\,6r5} \qquad 4\overline{)38}^{\,9r2} \qquad 9\overline{)86}^{\,9r5} \qquad 7\overline{)52}^{\,7r3}$$

$$3\overline{)26}^{\,8r2} \qquad 6\overline{)50}^{\,8r2} \qquad 5\overline{)42}^{\,8r2} \qquad 8\overline{)17}^{\,2r1}$$

$$2\overline{)19}^{\,9r1} \qquad 7\overline{)25}^{\,3r4} \qquad 9\overline{)40}^{\,4r4} \qquad 6\overline{)58}^{\,9r4}$$

$$5\overline{)22}^{\,4r2} \qquad 4\overline{)13}^{\,3r1} \qquad 2\overline{)11}^{\,5r1} \qquad 7\overline{)37}^{\,5r2}$$

Two or more step division without remainder using one-digit divisor

$$5 \overline{) 75} = 15 \qquad 3 \overline{) 96} = 32 \qquad 2 \overline{) 76} = 38 \qquad 4 \overline{) 92} = 23$$

$$6 \overline{) 84} = 14 \qquad 8 \overline{) 96} = 12 \qquad 7 \overline{) 84} = 12 \qquad 3 \overline{) 45} = 15$$

$$5 \overline{) 80} = 16 \qquad 4 \overline{) 52} = 13 \qquad 6 \overline{) 96} = 16 \qquad 2 \overline{) 78} = 39$$

$$9 \overline{) 135} = 15 \qquad 8 \overline{) 264} = 33 \qquad 3 \overline{) 171} = 57 \qquad 7 \overline{) 574} = 82$$

$$2 \overline{) 9,562} = 4,781 \qquad 6 \overline{) 8,052} = 1,342 \qquad 5 \overline{) 2,335} = 467 \qquad 9 \overline{) 7,308} = 812$$

Two or more step division with remainder using one-digit divisor

$$4 \overline{) 73} = 18r1 \qquad 6 \overline{) 95} = 15r5 \qquad 2 \overline{) 53} = 26r1 \qquad 3 \overline{) 89} = 29r2$$

$$5 \overline{) 61} = 12r1 \qquad 7 \overline{) 83} = 11r6 \qquad 4 \overline{) 65} = 16r1 \qquad 2 \overline{) 37} = 18r1$$

$$3 \overline{) 79} = 26r1 \qquad 5 \overline{) 96} = 19r1 \qquad 6 \overline{) 77} = 12r5 \qquad 7 \overline{) 93} = 13r2$$

$$9 \overline{) 127} = 14r1 \qquad 8 \overline{) 115} = 14r3 \qquad 2 \overline{) 173} = 86r1 \qquad 5 \overline{) 431} = 86r1$$

$$4 \overline{) 8,531} = 2,132r3 \qquad 6 \overline{) 7,947} = 1,324r3 \qquad 7 \overline{) 6,527} = 932r3 \qquad 9 \overline{) 5,870} = 652r2$$

One-step division without remainder using two-digit divisor

$$10\overline{)40} = 4 \qquad 11\overline{)77} = 7 \qquad 12\overline{)84} = 7 \qquad 15\overline{)75} = 5$$

$$20\overline{)60} = 3 \qquad 25\overline{)50} = 2 \qquad 36\overline{)72} = 2 \qquad 13\overline{)78} = 6$$

$$89\overline{)89} = 1 \qquad 17\overline{)85} = 5 \qquad 42\overline{)84} = 2 \qquad 21\overline{)42} = 2$$

$$16\overline{)112} = 7 \qquad 30\overline{)240} = 8 \qquad 23\overline{)207} = 9 \qquad 11\overline{)88} = 8$$

$$45\overline{)270} = 6 \qquad 67\overline{)469} = 7 \qquad 91\overline{)364} = 4 \qquad 53\overline{)424} = 8$$

One-step division with remainder using two-digit divisor

$$10\overline{)17} = 1\,r\,7 \qquad 11\overline{)79} = 7\,r\,2 \qquad 12\overline{)80} = 6\,r\,8 \qquad 18\overline{)97} = 5\,r\,7$$

$$30\overline{)93} = 3\,r\,3 \qquad 23\overline{)75} = 3\,r\,6 \qquad 16\overline{)86} = 5\,r\,6 \qquad 27\overline{)94} = 3\,r\,13$$

$$56\overline{)73} = 1\,r\,17 \qquad 42\overline{)86} = 2\,r\,2 \qquad 15\overline{)79} = 5\,r\,4 \qquad 31\overline{)57} = 1\,r\,26$$

$$21\overline{)128} = 6\,r\,2 \qquad 33\overline{)261} = 7\,r\,30 \qquad 85\overline{)147} = 1\,r\,62 \qquad 46\overline{)411} = 8\,r\,43$$

$$52\overline{)401} = 7\,r\,37 \qquad 97\overline{)333} = 3\,r\,42 \qquad 68\overline{)372} = 5\,r\,32 \qquad 26\overline{)200} = 7\,r\,18$$

249

Two or more step division without remainder using two-digit divisor

$$\overset{25}{10\overline{)250}} \qquad \overset{71}{11\overline{)781}} \qquad \overset{42}{12\overline{)504}} \qquad \overset{21}{40\overline{)840}}$$

$$\overset{62}{15\overline{)930}} \qquad \overset{31}{25\overline{)775}} \qquad \overset{54}{18\overline{)972}} \qquad \overset{22}{34\overline{)748}}$$

$$\overset{71}{13\overline{)923}} \qquad \overset{17}{31\overline{)527}} \qquad \overset{21}{28\overline{)588}} \qquad \overset{53}{17\overline{)901}}$$

$$\overset{34}{53\overline{)1,802}} \qquad \overset{13}{76\overline{)988}} \qquad \overset{55}{18\overline{)990}} \qquad \overset{31}{26\overline{)806}}$$

$$\overset{81}{95\overline{)7,695}} \qquad \overset{83}{44\overline{)3,652}} \qquad \overset{620}{39\overline{)24,180}} \qquad \overset{751}{68\overline{)51,068}}$$

Two or more step division with remainder using two-digit divisor

$$\overset{56r3}{10\overline{)563}} \qquad \overset{33r5}{11\overline{)368}} \qquad \overset{41r5}{12\overline{)497}} \qquad \overset{43r11}{20\overline{)871}}$$

$$\overset{26r20}{35\overline{)930}} \qquad \overset{55r11}{16\overline{)891}} \qquad \overset{12r5}{47\overline{)569}} \qquad \overset{31r20}{31\overline{)981}}$$

$$\overset{47r9}{18\overline{)855}} \qquad \overset{24r}{40\overline{)970}} \qquad \overset{5r23}{27\overline{)158}} \qquad \overset{32r13}{25\overline{)813}}$$

$$\overset{5r11}{23\overline{)126}} \qquad \overset{8r18}{59\overline{)490}} \qquad \overset{42r9}{19\overline{)807}} \qquad \overset{12r25}{74\overline{)913}}$$

$$\overset{20r27}{65\overline{)1,327}} \qquad \overset{63r19}{28\overline{)1,783}} \qquad \overset{235r24}{41\overline{)9,659}} \qquad \overset{769r3}{37\overline{)28,456}}$$

Table 13 Money Math

Understanding money

5¢	= 5 pennies	50¢	= 2 quarters
37¢	= 37 pennies	15¢	= 3 nickels
$2	= 200 pennies	$1	= 2 half dollars
$1	= 10 dimes	$5	= 5 silver dollars

Name the following amounts in coins:

(Note: Other answers are possible.)

13¢	= 1 dime + 3 pennies
29¢	= 2 dimes + 1 nickel + 4 pennies
46¢	= 4 dimes + 6 pennies
72¢	= 2 quarters + 2 dimes + 2 cents
53¢	= 1 half dollar + 3 pennies
68¢	= 1 half dollar + 1 dime + 1 nickel + 3 pennies

Name the following amounts in bills and coins:

(Note: Other answers are possible.)

$1.13	= 1 dollar bill + 1 dime + 3 pennies
$3.46	= 3 dollar bills + 4 dimes + 1 nickel + 1 penny
$2.72	= 1 two-dollar bill + 1 half dollar + 2 dimes + 2 pennies
$5.65	= 1 five-dollar bill + 1 half dollar + 1 dime + 1 nickel
$1.89	= 1 dollar bill + 3 quarters + 1 dime + 4 pennies
$10.03	= 1 ten-dollar bill + 3 pennies

Manipulating dollar and cents signs ($ and ¢)

15¢	27¢	76¢	25¢
+03¢	+41¢	+18¢	+38¢
18¢	68¢	94¢	63¢

79¢	85¢	76¢	37¢
−23¢	−21¢	−59¢	−18¢
56¢	64¢	17¢	19¢

$1.23	$7.80	$12.56	$60.42
+$2.46	+$2.19	+$23.18	+$12.39
$3.69	$9.99	$35.74	$72.81

$7.89	$4.65	$36.48	$57.84
−$5.27	−$1.42	−$10.39	−$26.95
$2.62	$3.23	$26.09	$30.89

$4.75	$16.21	$ 5.21	$11.25
×3	× 8	4)$20.84	5)$55.75
$14.25	$129.68		

$121.37	$602.49	21	43
×25	× 68	$.38)$7.98	$.16)$6.88
$3,034.25	$40,969.32		

252

Table 14 Fractions and decimals

Concept of fractions

Name the colored parts of the circles in fractional numbers:

$$= \frac{1}{2} \qquad = \frac{3}{4}$$

$$= \frac{2}{3} \qquad = \frac{4}{5}$$

$$= \frac{5}{6} \qquad = \frac{5}{8}$$

$$= \frac{1}{6} \qquad = \frac{1}{4}$$

$$= \frac{2}{5} \qquad = \frac{7}{9}$$

$$= \frac{7}{10} \qquad = \frac{4}{7}$$

Manipulation of fractional numbers

Addition

Common denominators

$$\frac{1}{3} + \frac{1}{3} = \frac{2}{6} = \frac{1}{3} \qquad \frac{1}{4} + \frac{2}{4} = \frac{3}{4} \qquad \frac{2}{5} + \frac{1}{5} = \frac{3}{5} \qquad \frac{1}{6} + \frac{1}{6} = \frac{2}{6} = \frac{1}{3} \qquad \frac{7}{9} + \frac{1}{9} = \frac{8}{9}$$

$$\frac{8}{10} + \frac{1}{10} = \frac{9}{10} \qquad \frac{2}{7} + \frac{3}{7} = \frac{5}{7} \qquad \frac{4}{12} + \frac{3}{12} = \frac{7}{12} \qquad \frac{6}{11} + \frac{2}{11} = \frac{8}{11} \qquad \frac{2}{8} + \frac{3}{8} = \frac{5}{8}$$

Different denominators

$$\frac{1}{3} + \frac{1}{6} = \frac{3}{6} = \frac{1}{2} \qquad \frac{1}{2} + \frac{1}{4} = \frac{3}{4} \qquad \frac{1}{3} + \frac{3}{6} = \frac{5}{6} \qquad \frac{4}{8} + \frac{1}{4} = \frac{6}{8} = \frac{3}{4} \qquad \frac{2}{5} + \frac{5}{10} = \frac{9}{10}$$

$$\frac{3}{4} + \frac{2}{8} = \frac{8}{8} = 1 \qquad \frac{1}{6} + \frac{4}{12} = \frac{6}{12} = \frac{1}{2} \qquad \frac{2}{4} + \frac{3}{16} = \frac{11}{16} \qquad \frac{1}{2} + \frac{4}{10} = \frac{9}{10} \qquad \frac{2}{5} + \frac{1}{15} = \frac{7}{15}$$

Subtraction

Common denominators

$$\frac{2}{3} - \frac{1}{3} = \frac{1}{3} \qquad \frac{4}{6} - \frac{2}{6} = \frac{2}{6} = \frac{1}{3} \qquad \frac{7}{10} - \frac{3}{10} = \frac{4}{10} = \frac{2}{5} \qquad \frac{4}{5} - \frac{1}{5} = \frac{3}{5} \qquad \frac{9}{11} - \frac{3}{11} = \frac{6}{11}$$

$$\frac{3}{4} - \frac{1}{4} = \frac{2}{4} = \frac{1}{2} \qquad \frac{6}{7} - \frac{2}{7} = \frac{4}{7} \qquad \frac{5}{8} - \frac{3}{8} = \frac{2}{8} = \frac{1}{4} \qquad \frac{12}{15} - \frac{11}{15} = \frac{1}{15} \qquad \frac{10}{12} - \frac{9}{12} = \frac{1}{12}$$

Different denominators

$$\frac{1}{2} - \frac{1}{4} = \frac{1}{4} \qquad \frac{2}{3} - \frac{2}{6} = \frac{2}{6} = \frac{1}{3} \qquad \frac{4}{8} - \frac{1}{4} = \frac{2}{8} = \frac{1}{4} \qquad \frac{8}{12} - \frac{2}{6} = \frac{4}{12} = \frac{1}{3} \qquad \frac{1}{2} - \frac{3}{8} = \frac{1}{8}$$

$$\frac{4}{5} - \frac{2}{10} = \frac{6}{10} = \frac{3}{5} \qquad \frac{3}{4} - \frac{1}{12} = \frac{8}{12} = \frac{2}{3} \qquad \frac{2}{3} - \frac{3}{9} = \frac{3}{9} = \frac{1}{3} \qquad \frac{1}{2} - \frac{4}{10} = \frac{1}{10} \qquad \frac{4}{6} - \frac{2}{9} = \frac{8}{18} = \frac{4}{9}$$

Multiplication

$$\frac{3}{4} \times \frac{1}{2} = \frac{3}{8} \qquad \frac{4}{5} \times \frac{1}{3} = \frac{4}{15} \qquad \frac{2}{3} \times \frac{3}{6} = \frac{6}{18} = \frac{1}{3}$$

$$\frac{1}{2} \times \frac{4}{5} = \frac{4}{10} = \frac{2}{5} \qquad \frac{3}{4} \times \frac{2}{3} = \frac{6}{12} = \frac{1}{2} \qquad \frac{5}{7} \times \frac{2}{3} = \frac{10}{21}$$

$$5 \times \frac{1}{6} = \frac{5}{6} \qquad 7 \times \frac{1}{9} = \frac{7}{9} \qquad 3 \times \frac{2}{12} = \frac{6}{12} = \frac{1}{2}$$

$$4 \times \frac{2}{10} = \frac{8}{10} = \frac{4}{5} \qquad 6 \times \frac{3}{20} = \frac{18}{20} = \frac{9}{10} \qquad 2 \times \frac{4}{9} = \frac{8}{9}$$

$$7 \times 1\frac{1}{8} = 7\frac{7}{8} \qquad 3 \times 4\frac{2}{9} = 12\frac{6}{9} = \frac{2}{3} \qquad 1 \times 6\frac{3}{8} = 6\frac{3}{8}$$

$$2 \times 5\frac{3}{9} = 10\frac{6}{9} = \frac{2}{3} \qquad 4 \times 3\frac{4}{20} = 12\frac{16}{20} = \frac{4}{5} \qquad 6 \times 2\frac{2}{15} = 12\frac{12}{15} = \frac{4}{5}$$

Division

$$\frac{1}{3} \div \frac{2}{3} = \frac{3}{6} = \frac{1}{2} \qquad \frac{1}{5} \div \frac{3}{5} = \frac{5}{15} = \frac{1}{3} \qquad \frac{2}{6} \div \frac{3}{6} = \frac{12}{18} = \frac{2}{3} \qquad \frac{1}{4} \div \frac{2}{4} = \frac{4}{8} = \frac{1}{2}$$

$$\frac{1}{2} \div \frac{3}{4} = \frac{4}{6} = \frac{2}{3} \qquad \frac{2}{6} \div \frac{3}{5} = \frac{10}{18} = \frac{5}{9} \qquad \frac{3}{8} \div \frac{2}{4} = \frac{12}{16} = \frac{3}{4} \qquad \frac{1}{3} \div \frac{3}{6} = \frac{6}{9} = \frac{2}{3}$$

$$\frac{1}{7} \div \frac{2}{3} = \frac{3}{14} \qquad \frac{1}{6} \div \frac{1}{2} = \frac{2}{6} = \frac{1}{3} \qquad \frac{5}{10} \div \frac{2}{3} = \frac{15}{20} = \frac{3}{4} \qquad \frac{2}{9} \div \frac{1}{2} = \frac{4}{9}$$

$$\frac{1}{2} \div 4 = \frac{1}{8} \qquad \frac{2}{3} \div 6 = \frac{2}{18} = \frac{1}{9} \qquad \frac{3}{4} \div 9 = \frac{3}{36} = \frac{1}{12} \qquad \frac{1}{5} \div 3 = \frac{1}{15}$$

$$10 \div \frac{2}{5} = 25 \qquad 15 \div \frac{3}{5} = 25 \qquad 3 \div \frac{1}{4} = 12 \qquad 2 \div \frac{2}{6} = 6$$

Fractions expressed as decimals

```
   .1        .7      .73     1.96      6.82       35.28
  +.2       +.8     +.65    +.45      +7.19      +17.16
  ────      ────    ─────   ─────     ──────     ──────
   .3       1.5     1.38     2.41      14.01      52.44


   .6       1.1      .58     3.26       5.76      12.12      48.04
  -.2       -.4     -.39     -.35      -1.23      -9.56     -29.26
  ────      ────    ─────   ─────     ──────     ──────     ──────
   .4        .7      .19     2.91       4.53       2.56      18.78


   .2        .3       2      3.5
  X.4       X7      X.8      X5
  ────      ────    ─────    ────
  .08       2.1      1.6     17.5


   7.6       89     1.34      67.4
  X.3       X.8      X5      X.8
  ─────     ────    ─────    ─────
  2.28      71.2    6.70      53.92


   .28      16       .35       6.6
  X12      X1.4     X.26      X11
  ─────    ─────    ─────     ─────
  3.36      22.4    .0910      72.6
```

```
      .2          .2          3.1
   4)‾.8       5)‾1.0      6)‾18.6


     31         3.19          8.2
  .2)6.2     .3).957      .8)6.56


     .8          .7           .2
  10)8.0      11)7.7       13)2.6


      2           5.1          303
  .20).40     .15).765    3.3)9,999
```

256

Table 15 Word problems

1. If a girl has 5 flowers in one hand and 7 flowers in her other hand, how many flowers does she have in all?   12 flowers.

2. A boy had 17 marbles until he gave 6 away.
   How many did he have left?   11 marbles.

3. If each can of soda pop cost 13¢, how much would 6 cans cost?   78¢.

4. If 7 ice-cream bars cost 77¢, then how much does each ice cream cost?   11¢.

5. A baker sold 1/3 of a cake in the morning and 2/6 of the cake in the afternoon.
   What was the total amount of cake sold?   4/6 = 2/3.

6. The zoo had 7 lions and a circus had 11 lions.
   How many fewer lions did the zoo have than the circus?   4.

7. A store sold 13 pounds of apples for $26.39.
   How much did each pound cost? $2.03.

8. If one puppy costs $5.50, how much would 3 puppies cost? $16.50.

9. Debbie bought a coat for $37.29, a dress for $21.75 and a sweater for $9.46.
   How much money did Debbie spend in all? $68.50.

10. Gary had 5/10 of a pie and gave away 1/10.
    How much pie did he have left?   4/10 = 2/5 of a pie.

11. One airplane flew 160 miles in 4 hours and a second airplane flew 240 miles in 8 hours.
    What was the total number of miles flown by both airplanes?   400 miles.
    How many miles did each airplane fly per hour?   #1 - 40 miles per hr., #2 - 30 miles per hr.

12. One car used 2 quarts of oil for every 500 miles.
    A second used car used 3 quarts of oil every 600 miles.
    Which car uses the most oil per mile?   #2.
    How many quarts of oil would the second car need to go 1800 miles?   9 quarts.

13. A dog was chasing a cat.
    The dog could run 13 miles per hour and the cat could run 17 miles per hour.
    Which animal is the fastest?   The cat.
    If both animals ran for 3 hours, then how many miles would each animal run?   Dog=39 miles, cat=51 miles.

14. Irma bought 2 record albums for $10.66 and Vernon bought 5 record albums for $25.75.
    How much did Irma pay per record? $5.33.
    How much did Vernon pay per record? $5.15.
    Who paid the most per record?   Irma.

APPENDIX C

Use of Television
to Supplement the
Regular 3R's
Instructional
Program

Optional phonic, vocabulary, spelling
and writing activities

This special appendix has been included for those parents and teachers who may wish to "supplement" the regular 3R's program by sometimes using television to reinforce the basic skills. Such activities as I have listed below will help counter three major criticisms of T.V.'s effect on education, which are: (1) children watch T.V. instead of doing their homework; (2) television may involve a student in watching the set but it doesn't require children to be both involved and participating as is required in reading a book; and (3) T.V. distracts students from learning and/or communicating with other members of the family.

Yet if such optional activities as described below are utilized, then children will no longer be just passively sitting in front of the T.V. but will be actively engaged in a learning process to reinforce their basic skills. In addition, conversation skills can be developed to raise the level of communication within the family through discussion of these learning exercises. But remember, such television activities are only meant to be used "in addition to" and not "in replacement of" the 3R's program described in this book.

> The T.V. programs used for these exercises can include movies, cartoons, soap operas, variety shows, nature shows, news reports, etc.—depending upon the tutor's and child's preferences.

Phonics

Note: These lists are to be examined by the parent or teacher and/or compared to the tutor's own list after listening to the T.V. programs.

Listen to the dialogue of characters in a T.V. program and list those words you hear with the beginning consonant sound of *(exs.-See Appendix A in this book).*

Listen to the dialogue of characters in a T.V. program and list those words you hear with the ending consonant sound of *(exs.-See Appendix A in this book).*

Listen to the dialogue of characters in a T.V. program and list those words you hear with the short or simple vowel sound of *(exs.-See Appendix A in this book).*

Listen to the dialogue of characters in a T.V. program and list those words you hear with the long or complex vowel sound of *(exs.-See Appendix A in this book).*

Listen to the dialogue of characters in a T.V. program and list those words you hear with the sound of the consonant blend of *(exs.-See Appendix A in this book).*

Listen to the dialogue of characters in a T.V. program and list those words you hear containing the letter group or word family of *(exs.-See Appendix A in this book).*

Listen to the dialogue of characters in a T.V. program and list those words you hear containing affixes *(exs.-See Appendix A in this book).*

Listen to the dialogue of characters in a T.V. program and list those words you hear which are contractions *(exs.-See Appendix A in this book).*

Note: These activities strengthen phonic skills and spelling ability while also providing an exercise in listening.

Vocabulary & Spelling

Note: These vocabulary and spelling lists can be used as individual assignments or exchanged between students and tutors after the T.V. program.

Listen to the program and write down (any number) words to define their meanings.

Listen to the program and write down (any number) words to use in sentences to demonstrate their meanings.

Listen to the program and write down (any number) words to later use in a poem.

Listen to the program and write down (any number) words to use in a spelling quiz.

Listen to the program and write down (any number) words to use in either reading or spelling games chosen from this book.

Listen to the program and write down (any number) words that are synonyms (see pg. 115).

Listen to the program and write down (any number) words that are antonyms (see pg. 116).

Listen to the program and write down (any number) words that are homonyms (see pg. 116).

Listen to the program and write down (any number) words with (any number) of syllables (see pg. 117).

Listen to the program and write down (any number) words that are compound words (see pg. 117).

Note: While these exercises reinforce vocabulary, spelling, and writing skills, oral reading performance can be strengthened by having children read their answers outloud to the tutor.

Writing

Note: These writing activities can be read to and read by parents or teachers. If desired by either the child or tutor, pictures can be drawn to accompany certain exercises.

Listen to the News Reports on T.V. and write your feelings about certain items which can be later read to and shared with other members of the family.

Tell how certain News items can affect you or your family.

Tell why certain News items might be important to the world.

After listening to a story or weekly program, write a new ending that you prefer.

Describe in words a character that you saw on T.V.

Explain in writing why you liked or disliked a particular character.

Compare, or tell similarities in, programs and characters that you either like or dislike.

Contrast, or tell differences in, programs and characters that you either like or dislike.

Tell which character was the most unlike you and explain the differences.

Describe what you have learned from watching a program.

Explain what could be done to improve a program.

Pretend to be a critic and evaluate the commercials or programs of your choice.

Take a survey of the most popular or unpopular programs and arrange a ratings scale or chart.

Explain why you think a certain program has become better or worse during the season.

Explain why you think a certain program is more popular with either children or adults.

Tell what makes a certain part of a program funny or sad.

Note: These learning activities not only provide practice in writing, spelling, oral reading, vocabulary choice and usage, but they also stimulate critical thinking skills.

INDEX